Zane Goebel (Ed.)
Rapport and the Discursive Co-Construction of Social Relations in Fieldwork Encounters

Language and Social Life

Editors
David Britain
Crispin Thurlow

Volume 19

Rapport and the Discursive Co-Construction of Social Relations in Fieldwork Encounters

Edited by
Zane Goebel

DE GRUYTER
MOUTON

ISBN 978-1-5015-2535-3
e-ISBN (PDF) 978-1-5015-0783-0
e-ISBN (EPUB) 978-1-5015-0776-2
ISSN 2192-2128

Library of Congress Control Number: 2019937690

Bibliographic information published by the Deutsche Nationalbibliothek
The Deutsche Nationalbibliothek lists this publication in the Deutsche Nationalbibliografie;
detailed bibliographic data are available on the Internet at http://dnb.dnb.de.

© 2021 Walter de Gruyter GmbH, Berlin/Boston
This volume is text- and page-identical with the hardback published in 2019.
Typesetting: VTeX UAB, Lithuania
Printing and binding: CPI books GmbH, Leck

www.degruyter.com

Acknowledgment

This volume offers a selection of papers that were originally delivered as part of a symposium that was concerned with conceptualizing the relationship between language and the anthropological notion of rapport. The four-day symposium was generously supported by two grants from La Trobe University: one from the School of Humanities and Social Sciences (Grant: #2015-1-STF-0005) and the other from the Linguistics Disciplinary Research Program (Grant: 2016-1-DRP-04). A wide range of themes emerged from the 20 delivered papers and the extensive discussions that occurred over these four days. This volume attempts to capture just some of the themes discussed. The remaining themes are discussed in another collection (Goebel ed. 2019. *Reimagining Rapport*. Oxford: Oxford University Press), which contains papers by Ben Rampton, Joel Kuipers, Asif Agha, Zane Goebel, Sabina Perrino, Aurora Donzelli, Michael Ewing, Nick Herriman, Monika Winarnita, and Howard Manns. Special thanks go to all those who attended the symposium and enthusiastically enriched the dialogue. These include, but are not limited to, Asrun Lio, Manneke Budiman, Yacinta Kurniasih, Harry Aveling, David Bradley, Howard Nicholas, Donna Starks, Stephen Morey, and Marija Tabain. I would also be remiss not to heartily thank Sally Bowman who made this event happen so smoothly. Finally, thanks to the School of Languages and Cultures at the University of Queensland for providing me with the needed time to put this collection together.

Contents

Acknowledgment —— V

List of Contributing Authors —— IX

Zane Goebel
1 Rapport and the Discursive Co-Construction of Social Relations in Fieldwork Settings —— 1

Debbie Cole
2 Looking for Rapport in the Metacommunicative Features of an Ethnographic Interview —— 17

Lauren Zentz
3 'Today's Episode Is Sponsored by Nü Green Tea': Rapport and Virtuoso Humour in Group Interviews —— 33

Zane Goebel
4 Understanding Rapport Through Scalar Reflexivity —— 53

Rafadi Hakim
5 Doing Ethnography Across Institutions: Rapport and Discursive Ruptures in Jakarta —— 73

Anna De Fina
6 Commentary: Rapport in Qualitative Investigation, from Researcher's Objectivity to Researcher's Reflexivity —— 87

Adam Harr
7 Sociolinguistic Scale and Ethnographic Rapport —— 97

Bernard Arps
8 The Ethnolinguistic Listener: Narrativity and Ideologies of Local Language in Urban Banyuwangi —— 111

Mikihiro Moriyama
9 The Discursive Co-Construction of Social Relations in Sundanese-Speaking Areas in West Java —— 139

Izak Morin
10   Rapport, Affinity, and Kin Terms —— 153

Dwi Noverini Djenar
11   Recognitional Reference and Rapport Building in the Author Interview —— 163

Joe Errington
12   Making Connections —— 185

Index —— 191

List of Contributing Authors

Bernard Arps
Leiden University
Leiden
The Netherlands

Debbie Cole
Utrecht University
Utrecht
The Netherlands

Anna De Fina
Georgetown University
Washington
USA

Dwi Noverini Djenar
The University of Sydney
Sydney
Australia

Joe Errington
Yale University
New Haven
USA

Zane Goebel
University of Queensland
Brisbane
Australia

Rafadi Hakim
University of Chicago
Chicago
USA

Adam Harr
St. Lawrence University
Canton, New York
USA

Izak Morin
Cenderawasih University
Jayapura
Indonesia

Mikihiro Moriyama
Nanzan University
Nagoya
Japan

Lauren Zentz
University of Houston
Houston
USA

Zane Goebel
1 Rapport and the Discursive Co-Construction of Social Relations in Fieldwork Settings

1 Introduction

Since Malinowski's (1922 [1966]: 1–25) enthusiasm for extended co-presence or 'being there' and learning and using 'native languages', the idea of rapport has received sustained attention through regular attempts to define this concept (e. g. Berreman 1972; Borneman and Hammoudi 2009b; Clifford 1988; Crapanzano 2012 [2010]; Csordas 2012 [2007]; Geertz 1973; Marcus 1998; Mead 1939; Powdermaker 2012 [1967]; Rabinow 1977; Rosaldo 1989). The notion of rapport has become a part of anthropological folk theory that sees the development of positive interpersonal relations as crucial to the anthropological endeavour. This ideology goes something like this: being co-present enables the anthropologist to learn a language of a foreign other, which in turn enables the building of positive social relations between the anthropologist and foreign others. In turn, this enables the efficient gathering of data that is then used to provide an insider's view. This 'insider's view' then forms the basis of an ethnographic product, typically a seminar or conference paper, a lecture, an article or a book manuscript.

This interpretation of rapport has been seen as over simplistic by many. For example, the links between 'being there', writing about 'being there' and ethnographic authority have been the subject of continual critiques (e. g. Clifford and Marcus 1986; Fabian 2014 [1983]). Linked to this idea of authority is the notion of objectivity, whereby the researchers are imagined to be able to reduce their influence on data if they can establish rapport with their consultants. This anthropological version of sociolinguistics' "observer's paradox" (Labov 1972) does not faithfully represent what happens in interactions (De Fina, this volume, Chapter 6). Rather than being the simple product of interaction between researcher and consultant/informant, 'objectivity' and rapport are always mediated. Social relations in the field can be mediated by what has gone on before (Berreman 1972), by the fieldworker's relationship with others in the field (e. g. Hume and Mulcock 2004b; Moerman 1988; Wagley 2012 [1960]), by others outside of the field (Erickson and Shultz 1982) and by institutional connections (Rampton 2016; Hakim, this volume, Chapter 5; Harr, this volume, Chapter 7). Much of this work indirectly

Zane Goebel, University of Queensland, Brisbane, Australia

https://doi.org/10.1515/9781501507830-001

points out that rapport is discursively created and recreated from one situation to the next, rather than being an enduring relationship between the researcher and researched during a period of fieldwork.

Even so, evidence of rapport continues to be one of the key criteria for judging the value and robustness of an ethnography in anthropology. The ethnographic turn that has increasingly characterized social inquiry in general, and sociolinguistics and applied linguistics in particular, has often uncritically adopted the idea of rapport. As a consequence, rapport has become a naturalized concept in a wide range of "how-to" textbooks on ethnography (e. g. Agar 1996; Bailey 2007; O'Reilly 2009; Wolcott 2001). In these manuals, and indeed in many recent ethnographies, rapport is often viewed as a prerequisite to be achieved before fieldworkers can start their research. At the same time, ethnographies have, with few exceptions, and despite regular pleas to do so (e. g. Borneman and Hammoudi 2009a; Clifford 1986, 1988; Fabian 2014 [1983]; Marcus 1998; Rosaldo [1989]), avoided presenting any discursive evidence of what rapport might look like in an interactional sense.

Ultimately, this erasure of co-present discursive practice, together with the uncritical acceptance of rapport as a fieldwork goal and measure, has helped to continue to hide the delicate positional work that goes on between researcher and consultant in the field. In turn, this has privileged ideas about identity as enduring over identity as emergent, as well as ideas about consultants' 'factual' accounts (i. e. denotational/referential meanings) over the connotational meanings that come with such accounts. This edited collection seeks to provide a more nuanced understanding of this 90-year-old anthropological folk concept. This will be done by providing an interactional overview of the emergence of various subject positions as both fieldworkers and consultants co-construct social relations and shared social worlds from speech event to speech event while in the field.

These papers are part of a wider ongoing discussion that emerged within a four-day symposium, "Conceptualizing Rapport", where the relationship between language and rapport received sustained intellectual attention. Many themes emerged from these discussions, and this book presents just some of them. The first theme presented in this current volume relates to the idea of common ground whereby in any interaction those involved seek to establish common referents for discussion or *common ground*. Common ground is established through a whole host of discursive practices that include the repetition of each other's utterances (Zentz, this volume, Chapter 3; Cole, this volume, Chapter 2; Djenar, this volume, Chapter 11), acknowledgment of others' discursive contributions (Harr, this volume, Chapter 7), the use and recognition of voices from elsewhere (Goebel, this volume, Chapter 4; Zentz, this volume, Chapter 3; Cole, this volume, Chapter 2; Morin, this volume, Chapter 10), and the pursuit of social sameness in terms of interests (Arps, this volume, Chapter 8; Moriyama, this volume, Chapter 9; Morin, this volume, Chapter 10; Cole, this volume, Chapter 2).

Another related theme that came out of the wider symposium discussions was the overemphasis on the positive aspects of rapport. Earlier work that tries to conceptualize rapport seemed to presuppose the positive side (e. g. the papers in Hume and Mulcock 2004b), which unwittingly creates anxieties for researchers. For example, without rapport, researchers can't do their research, finish a project, get tenure and so on, as noted by Harr and Arps (this volume, Chapter 8) and Rampton (2016). At the same time, it is not uncommon to evaluate fieldwork projects as successful, i. e. "anthropology happened", because rapport was established with the consultants. Rather than follow more than 90 years of privileging the positive aspects of rapport, in line with recent critiques (Rampton 2015), the authors in this volume point out that unexpected events or *ruptures* are a continual object and the result of discursive practice in fieldwork settings, just as they are in everyday life.

While rupture is most obvious when the foreign researcher enters a fieldwork setting (Arps, this volume, Chapter 8; Harr, this volume, Chapter 7; Goebel, this volume, Chapter 4), De Fina (this volume, Chapter 6) comments on how some of the papers in this volume problematize ideas of "native speakership" and "intercultural" that often accompany anthropological inquiry. Echoing some of the insights from pioneering studies in interactional sociolinguistics (e. g. Gumperz 1982; Scollon and Scollon 1981; Tannen 1984), Djenar (this volume, Chapter 11) and Hakim (this volume, Chapter 5) argue that while 'native speakership' presupposes a sharing of semiotic resources, this theoretical construct melts away as researcher and researched work on establishing common ground with unfamiliar folk, often in an unfamiliar communicative event.

More generally, rupture also presupposes some type of normativity that has links to the past. The Russian literary theorist Bakhtin's (1981) referred to links between past and present linguistic forms and ideologies about these forms as *intertextuality*. Linguistic anthropologists have broadened the focus of this idea to all semiotic phenomena: that is, all forms that make up human communicative activity (e. g. linguistic forms, posture, gesture, place, prosody, participant constellation, and so on), and refer to historical relations between semiotic phenomena as *interdiscursivity* (e. g. Agha 2007a; Bauman 2005; Silverstein and Urban 1996). Interdiscursivity is another theme that emerges in many of the papers in this volume, including those by Goebel, Zentz, Cole, and Hakim. In addition to highlighting the situation and participant specific nature of relations between language and those who use it (or *participation framework* for short), ideas around rupture and interdiscursivity, and the use of language to fix such ruptures and to pursue common ground, all point to the context-creating capabilities of situated discourse that we, following Arps (2016), refer to as *world making*.

In the rest of this introduction, I will focus on these five concepts—common ground, interdiscursivity, participation framework, rupture, and world making—while linking them with individual papers. I finish with a more detailed introduction to each of the ten chapters. They could be grouped in many ways, but, because each paper covers one or more of these themes, I have decided to present them in a way that starts with reports about the discursive co-construction of social relations in the field (Harr; Arps; and Moriyama), before then moving to increasingly microscopic examinations of situated discourse and their relationships to discourses in other timespaces (Morin; Djenar; Goebel, Cole; Zentz; and Hakim).

Before unpacking these five concepts further, however, it is also worthwhile pointing out that, with the exception of De Fina, all authors focus on Indonesia. We see this as a real strength of the project because contemporary anthropology and sociolinguistics see variability and complexity as the starting point for viewing language, identity, and social relations anywhere (Arnaut, Karrebæk, and Spotti 2016; Blommaert and Rampton 2015; Vertovec 2007). Thus having chapters from the same nation state that demonstrate variability is an important step in breaking down older unhelpful views that equate named nations with named communities and named languages. For example, had I chosen to invite other contributions from other countries, this would actually help to reproduce an ideology where we unintentionally view social practice from the perspective of the state rather than from participants' perspectives (Silverstein 2015).

2 The Discursive Construction of Common Ground

Common ground can be seen as mutual knowledge about place, persons, events, institutions, feelings, and so on (Enfield 2006: 422). In many encounters characterized by co-presence, what constitutes common ground is interactionally negotiated through agreement about referents (Enfield 2006; Hanks 2006). In such encounters, common ground is established one speaker turn at a time. When some of the semiotic forms that constitute a speaker's utterance (say Speaker A or SA for short) are recognized and responded to by another speaker, we refer to this as *uptake*. In cases where there is no uptake by another (say Speaker B or SB for short), SA may choose to take another speaking turn (e. g. Agha 2007a; Sacks, Schegloff, and Jefferson 1974). The papers in this volume all examine uptake, so, rather than discuss lack of uptake any further, here I will simply list some of the work that examines how lack of uptake is treated in everyday communicative practices. Within conversation analysis, lack of uptake is treated under ideas of *repair* and *preference* (Bilmes 1988; Liddicoat 2007), while in linguistic anthropology some of the social consequences of lack of uptake are treated in works on *gossip* (e. g. Besnier 2009; Goebel 2010). In the rest of this chapter, I will just focus on cases where there is uptake of some of the semiotic fragments—i. e. linguistic signs, prosody, gesture, space, etc.—found within a turn.

In cases where transcriptions of recorded interactions are available, as in the papers by Morin (this volume, Chapter 10), Djenar (this volume, Chapter 11), Goebel (this volume, Chapter 4), Cole (this volume, Chapter 2), and Zentz (this volume, Chapter 3), we can examine how common ground is interactionally established. Studies in a number of languages, including Indonesian, show that repetition (though usually not replication as precise copy) of fragments of a prior speakers' utterance is one way of establishing common ground, and in some cases feelings of social sameness (e. g. Berman 1998; Bjork-Willen 2007; Bucholtz and Hall 2004; Enfield 2009; Goebel 2010, 2015; McCarthy 2003; Tannen 1989). Conversational analytic studies, as in the case of Djenar (this volume, Chapter 11), see repetition as a form of *alignment*, while the further use of signs (including gesture, linguistic, and prosodic) for establishing social sameness and/or positive social relations is referred to as *affiliation* (e. g. Lindström and Sorjonen 2013; Steensig 2013; Stivers 2008).

CA uses of alignment and affiliation differ and overlap with concepts and terms used in linguistic anthropology, especially *role alignment* and affiliation. Drawing on Agha (2005, 2007a, 2011), *role alignment* is defined as the use of signs to display, perform, model, and ultimately align with models of personhood from other times, places, and participation frameworks or *chronotopes* (Agha 2007b; Blommaert 2016; Goebel and Manns 2018). For example, a person wearing a ten gallon hat engages in role alignment with multiple models of personhood. Which model, however, is only determined through subsequent interaction. Affiliation is more a shorthand term, rather than a developed concept. It is used for describing utterances that display or enact belonging, often to a particular named community. In the hat-case above, a query or compliment might engender affiliative responses, such as I'm a Texan, I'm a cowboy, or I want to be seen like one of these, etc. In this book we will distinguish affiliation in the CA sense from affiliation in the linguistic anthropological sense (which also overlaps with role alignment) by referring to utterances about affiliation as *acts of belonging*.

What makes such distinctions relevant to the idea of rapport is that alignment, role alignment, and acts of belonging manifest themselves very differently from one setting to the next, a point made by both Errington (this volume, Chapter 12) and De Fina (this volume, Chapter 6). This observation problematizes the idea that rapport is some sort of positive affective disposition that is carried from one setting to the next by the fieldworker and consultant, as evidenced in Arps' and Djenar's papers (this volume, Chapters 8, 11). Arps provides reports of his interest in and observations of an emerging institutionalized language, Osing, and performances of Osing which he shared with his other consultants and many of the wider community living in Banyuwangi, East Java. In his case, uptake of his interest in Osing was manifest in a host of encounters during his fieldwork, but was not evidence of rapport as an enduring phenomena. Instead, this uptake was evidence of a situated agreement on a referent, Osing and musical tastes, and an evaluation of its importance to those with whom he interacted. While Arps' interactions with inhabitants of Banyuwangi were typically in Indonesian, in part because local language ideologies did not have a place for a foreign Osing speaker, in other areas of Indonesia, local languages played more of a role in the establishment of common ground.

In rural West Java, where Moriyama (this volume, Chapter 9) conducted his area studies work, the use and uptake of semiotic fragments stereotypically associated with a local language, in this case Sundanese, helped in establishing and maintaining social relations. Similarly, in Central and East Java, both Zentz (this volume, Chapter 3) and Cole (this volume, Chapter 2) reported that the use of semiotic fragments associated with Javanese helped to establish and maintain situated social relationships with consultants. In contrast, Harr (this volume, Chapter 7) reports that an interest in a language of Flores, Lio, was enough to establish common ground between himself and his consultants. While the negotiation of common ground occurred through language use, the establishment of common ground revolved around the uptake of a whole host of topics, including ideas about language usage (*language ideologies*), other events, places, persons, feelings, and so on. Like Arps, Moriyama's interest in music helped achieve situational common ground. In a sense, this was a precondition of rapport. Sharing similar histories in relation to rural upbringing, tastes in terms of the value of rice in one's diet, spiritual beliefs about rice harvests, and having families were also referents for the establishment of common ground between Moriyama and his consultants. Interest in other cultural practices, such as poetry, also figured heavily in the establishment of common ground between Cole and the contemporary Indonesian poet Zawawi.

The papers by Morin (this volume, Chapter 10), Djenar (this volume, Chapter 11), Goebel (this volume, Chapter 4), Cole (this volume, Chapter 2), and Zentz (this volume, Chapter 3) offer up-close examinations of interaction during interviews with research participants. Morin examines a series of interviews with university colleagues and with a religious leader in his hometown of Jayapura in Papua. In addition to showing how common ground is established through repetition of utterance fragments—in this case of *Melayu Papua* 'Papuan Malay' (PM), especially kin terms—his analysis of these interviews shows how interviewees move from engaging in *role alignment* to *acts of belonging*. In the first case, this is done via acknowledging membership in the group of people who speak PM. In the second case, this is done through talk that identifies both interactants as members of a group who value PM.

Djenar (this volume, Chapter 11) moves through a series of interviews with various authors of teen literature in Jakarta, with the first five interview extracts showing how both Djenar and her interviewees established common ground by engaging in alignment through the repetition of other authors' names and utterances such as *teenlit dan ciklit* 'teen literature and female teen literature'. In her last two examples, Djenar moves to an analysis of role alignment and belonging. In her interview with Kirana, Djenar aligns with an educated social type through reference to her own studies, as well as inhabiting this social type—or engaging in belonging—through an evaluation of another teacher as *paling pinter* 'the smartest' of her university cohort.

Zentz (this volume, Chapter 3) focuses on interviews with a group of university students from a private Christian University in Central Java. Through looking at a series of interviews involving essentially the same group of participants, we are able to see how semiotic fragments used to establish common ground in one interview are imitated in subsequent interviews to establish an interpretive frame (Goffman 1974) for subsequent interactions between these speakers. The relationship between semiotic fragments used in one speech event and another as noted earlier is often referred to as interdiscursivity. Research on repetition and role alignment tells us that interdiscurvity is not be relegated to relationships between forms used in one face-to-face conversation and another (Goebel 2017; Inoue 2006). In this work, interdiscursivity can also refer to relationships between semiotic forms used in other chronotopes. We are treated to examples of this phenomena in Zentz's paper where she shows how relationships between linguistic fragments associated with the genre of a television talk show, such as *pemirsa* 'viewer' and *saksikan kami bersama* 'experience with us', are initially used and receive initial uptake by one participant (Nisa). In subsequent interactions—both within one interview and also in subsequent interviews—we see these fragments being reused as one participant, Angelo, inhabits the role of talk show host and commercial persona.

Through these interactions, common ground about specific social practices and the personas involved in them is established within a small group (or small participation framework). In this case, mutual understanding about what constitutes an interview, a talk show, and a commercial is established, as well as how those involved in such events speak and perform. Ultimately, Zentz's paper shows, in minute detail, how the imitation of linguistic forms and social practices within an ephemeral community discursively co-construct shared understandings of these forms, while maintaining and building social relations within this setting. In doing so, Zentz also provides insights into the discursive construction of rupture and its relationship with world making.

3 Rupture and World Making

Interviews have increasingly become part of the life worlds of many of the worlds' population (e. g. Cameron 2000; Gubrium and Holstein 2003), especially as populations are more regularly and more intensively connected via transportation and communication infrastructures (e. g. Castells 1996; Harvey 1989; Wallerstein 2004). Even so, for some, interviews in general and the presence of nosey foreign researchers in particular are still a relatively uncommon communicative activity in the sphere of face-to-face interaction, as pointed out by Harr (this volume, Chapter 7), Arps (this volume, Chapter 8), Zentz (this volume, Chapter 3), and Cole (this volume, Chapter 2). Uncommonness, unusualness, strangeness, deviance, and so on are all ways of talking about things that are not normative, while helping reproduce ideas of what is normal. Scholars who work on conversational narrative, for example, have pointed out that talk about nonnormative practices or rupture is a common part of human interaction in general and story-telling in particular (e. g. Bruner 1991; De Fina 2003; Georgakopoulou 2007; Labov and Waletzky 1967; Ochs and Capps 2001). While talk about rupture helps those involved in the telling reinforce common ground on what is seen as normative among particular participant constellations, at the same time, talk about rupture is a form of *world making*.

In the papers presented here, world making is discussed in a number of senses, although rupture is common to all discussions. World making is seen as the co-constructed understandings between researcher and consultant about where the researcher fits within the life worlds of their consultants, as in the papers by Harr (this volume, Chapter 7), Cole (this volume, Chapter 2), and Hakim (this volume, Chapter 5). Drawing on the classic works of Geertz (1973 [1972]) and Hymes (1975), Harr (this volume, Chapter 7) theorizes how understandings about life worlds are co-constructed through the use of semiotic forms from other scales. Such understandings can often be identified through reference to the rupture that precedes an anthropologist's "breakthrough into rapport".

Engaging with critiques of interviews, especially the idea that interviews are much more than the sum of the referential information provided by the interviewee (e. g. Briggs 1986, 2007; De Fina and Perrino 2011; Koven 2014), Goebel, Cole, and Zentz (this volume, Chapters 4, 2, 3) examine initial ruptures in their own and their consultant's life worlds as they interactionally establish reasons for an interview. Goebel points out the need to pay reflexive attention to the interdiscursive connections between his interviewees' performances and wider circulating ideas about ethnic and bureaucratic personhood. After pointing out how her consultant frames their talk as an interview, Cole then trace the interdiscursive links between her long-term interactions with the Indonesian poet Zawawi. In doing so, she provides keen insights into how semiotic resources from the past and elsewhere are imitated across speech situations to engage in role alignment and belonging. These activities establish common ground between Cole and Zawawi, which subsequently provide a frame for interpreting future performances of poetry, while also contributing to ongoing world making for this participant constellation.

Hakim (this volume, Chapter 5), reports on his interactions with other Indonesians during his time working within a non-government organization based in Jakarta. As with more general points about human contact in Indonesia and how complex histories of contact problematize unitary models of language (Goebel 2010), Hakim points to the variety of understandings about kin terms in Jakarta. He shows how the use of fragments of address in email communication can receive uptake in ways that are not intended, leading to rupture and attempts at correcting such rupture (i. e. world making). Taking a larger sample of social life, Arps (this volume, Chapter 8) describes a number of fascinating cases of how fragments of Osing, normally associated with private ethnic spaces, are used to make an Osing-speaking world in the normally public space of public transport and to make new speakers of Osing from Indonesians of Chinese ancestry, who are commonly stereotyped as nonspeakers of ethnic languages.

4 The Chapters

Taking up Briggs' (1986) invitation to pay more attention to interviews and the context that surrounds them, Cole's chapter takes a long-term view of her 15-year relationship with the Indonesian poet Zawawi. She does so as a way of understanding what it is that the interviewer and interviewee are doing to build rapport from one speech situation to the next. Cole argues that rapport is situation-specific and that different clusters of semiotic forms are used by researcher and interviewee to establish common ground and to engage in role alignment and belonging. These clusters of semiotic resources include: pitching-matching; re-performing the interlocutor's words and phrases; explicit meta-talk about the context-appropriate identity roles of the participants; and defining and explaining vocabulary items that are not immediately understood by the interlocutor.

Drawing on one year's fieldwork carried out in a small city in Central Java, Zentz's chapter provides an intimate look at the awkwardness of research interviews and how humour can be used to overcome such awkwardness. Her analysis focuses on interdiscursivity, especially the connections between the genre of talkback television and the use of semiotic fragments from this genre within and across a series of group interviews with university students. In looking at these connections, which typically manifest themselves as imitations of semiotic fragments from prior events, Zentz shows how such imitations help build an interpretive frame that is used to construct social relations in the field over time. In doing so, Zentz demonstrates how, through the use of multiple semiotic resources, some associated with named languages, researcher, and participants co-construct varying levels and types of relationship in the field, including student—teacher, researcher—informant, foreigner—local, language learner—language expert, and varying levels of friend or confidante.

In Chapter 4, Goebel examines how traces of government policy and ongoing negative media representations about Indonesian bureaucrats find their way into interviews that he conducted during fieldwork in a government office in Semarang, Indonesia, using 2003–2004 data. In examining this interdiscursivity, he reflexively teases out how a career bureaucrat and head of a department recontextualizes various sign configurations to engage in role alignment and acts of belonging with the alter-ego of emerging figures of bureaucratic personhood, i. e., the exemplary public servant. In doing so, Goebel shows how role alignment and acts of belonging are discursively achieved via the recontextualization of signs of ethnic (in this case, signs of Javanese-ness) and bureaucratic personhood.

In Chapter 5, Hakim challenges the notion of fieldwork as one that is delineated by formal, institutionally authorized research projects, or by the putative temporal framework of being "away in the field." Consistent with arguments made in the previous chapters, Hakim argues that rapport isn't some type of enduring relationship, but rather one that is interdiscursively constituted through anticipatory and retroactive contemplations of spatiotemporally contextualized and contextualizing interactions (i. e. world making). He develops this argument by looking at pronominal reference found in a series of emails exchanged when working in a nongovernment organization based in Jakarta and embedding his developing understanding of this usage in the institutionally authorized project of being a graduate student.

De Fina's commentary in Chapter 6 discusses the chapters by Cole, Zentz, Goebel, and Hakim. In pointing to some of the interactional reasons for a failure to adequately define the notion of rapport in the literature, she points to the importance of looking at the details of talk for reflexively understanding social relations, and their inderdiscursive links with other events, people, and places. In doing so, De Fina highlights how this relates to concerns for objectivity in social inquiry and to ideas around intercultural encounters more generally.

In Chapter 7, Harr Draws on nearly three years of fieldwork in the highlands of Flores island, Eastern Indonesia, to examine how his interest in local language practices are interpreted and used to establish rapport with consultants. He argues that rapport is established through cooperative discursive moves that invoke and align semiotic forms that have associations with local, national, and global scales. In this sense, rapport is a seen as a situated intersubjective understanding about a world created in a particular interaction, rather than an enduring affective disposition between researcher and consultant.

Drawing on 20 years work in the town of Banyuwangi, East Java, and building on theories of world making (Arps 2016), Arps critiques some of the key ideological features underlying the idea of rapport. Focusing on the complex linguistic repertoires of three families from Banyuwangi, he argues that linguistic understandings of language as a unitary construct are not useful for understanding human interaction in general and interaction between researcher and consultant in Banyuwangi in particular. In Banyuwangi, ideologies around one language, Osing, involve hearing the language being spoken by others rather than speaking it. This ideology helps explain Arps' own use of Indonesian in his interactions with members of these families and its appropriateness for world making and the pursuit of common ground.

Moriyama reports on his 30-plus years of work in Sundanese speaking areas of West Java with a Sundanese speaking family. He points out that through sharing interests in Sundanese poetry, novels, shorts stories, music, and Sundanese language, this common ground enables him to develop long-lasting relations with this family. Indonesian and Sundanese are part of Moriyama's repertoire and within particular participant constellations are seen as appropriate. Even so, he also points out that the social value of Sundanese has changed over this 20-year period, obliging him to learn and use different types of Sundanese to negotiate common ground with other Sundanese he encountered during his fieldwork.

Working in his hometown of Jayapura (located in Papua, Indonesia), Morin examines interview data gathered during fieldwork that he carried out from January 2015 to December 2015. Building on Marshall Sahlins (2013 [2013, 2011]) concept of *mutuality of belonging* as it relates to kinship, this chapter links these ideas to the linguistic anthropological concept of belonging as it relates to the situated use of Papuan Malay. In doing so, the chapter challenges widely held understandings of two terms, *amber* and *komin*, two words from Biak language that are now widely used in Papuan Malay in West Papua to distinguish migrants or foreigners (non-Papuans) from Papuans. This is done by showing how kin terms associated with these concepts can be used to create contexts (i. e. engage in world making).

In Chapter 11, Djenar builds on a body of work in Conversation Analysis which examines how we refer to people in everyday interaction (Stivers, Enfield, and Levinson 2007). She examines person reference in three interviews conducted with Jakarta-based authors of Indonesian teen fiction. Djenar shows that referring to persons and achieving recognizability of persons, books, and publishers in the literary world is a means of not just establishing common ground, but also of engaging in role alignment and acts of belonging. Ultimately, the chapter highlights that this type of discursive works helps to establish the type of productive working relationships in the field described by Hume and Mulcock (2004a) and Marcus (1998: 122–123), while pointing to the situation-specific nature of these relationships.

In the final chapter, Errington comments on the chapters by Harr, Moriyama, Morin, and Djenar to draw out two themes that relate to the mediation of "affective surplus" between researcher and consultant in and out of the field. On the one hand, he points to the situation-specific nature of rapport and its relationship with ongoing dialogic pursuits of social sameness or *adequation* (Bucholtz and Hall 2005), while on the other he relates this to how the authors represent such surpluses.

References

Agar, Michael. 1996. *The professional stranger: An informal introduction to ethnography*. San Diego: Academic Press.
Agha, Asif. 2005. Voice, footing, enregisterment. *Journal of Linguistic Anthropology* 15(1). 38–59.
Agha, Asif. 2007a. *Language and social relations*. Cambridge: Cambridge University Press.
Agha, Asif. 2007b. Recombinant selves in mass mediated spacetime. *Language & Communication* 27(3). 320–335.
Agha, Asif. 2011. Large and small scale forms of personhood. *Language & Communication* 31(3). 171–180.
Arnaut, Karel, Martha Karrebæk & Massimiliano Spotti. 2016. Engaging superdiversity: The poiesis-infrastructure nexus and language practices in combinatorial spaces. In Karel Arnaut, Martha Sif Karrebæk, Massimilo Spotti & Jan Blommaert (eds.), *Engaging superdiversity: Recombining spaces, times and language practices*, 3–24. Bristol: Multilingual Matters.
Arps, Ben. 2016. *Tall tree, nest of the wind: The Javanese shadow-play Dewa Ruci performed by Ki Anom Soeroto. A study in performance philology*. Singapore: NUS Press.
Bailey, Carol. 2007. *A guide to qualitative field research*. London: Pine forge press.

Bakhtin, Mikhail. 1981. *The dialogic imagination: Four essays*. Translated by Caryl Emerson & Michael Holquist. Edited by Michael Holquist. Austin: University of Texas Press.
Bauman, Richard. 2005. Commentary: Indirect indexicality, identity, performance: Dialogic observations. *Journal of Linguistic Anthropology* 15(1). 145–150.
Berman, Laine. 1998. *Speaking through the silence: Narratives, social conventions, and power in Java*. New York: Oxford University Press.
Berreman, Gerald. 1972. *Hindus of the Himalayas: Ethnography and change*. 2nd edn. Berkeley: University of California Press.
Besnier, Niko. 2009. *Gossip and the everyday production of politics*. Honolulu: University of Hawai'i Press.
Bilmes, J. 1988. The concept of preference in conversation analysis. *Language in Society* 17. 161–181.
Bjork-Willen, Polly. 2007. Participation in multilingual preschool play: Shadowing and crossing as interactional resources. *Journal of Pragmatics* 39(12). 2133–2158.
Blommaert, Jan. 2016. Chronotopes, scales and complexity in the study of language in society. In K. Arnaut, M. Karrebæk, M. Spotti & Jan Blommaert (eds.), *Engaging superdiversity: Recombining spaces, times and language practices*, 47–62. Bristol: Multilingual Matters.
Blommaert, Jan & Ben Rampton. 2015. Language and superdiversity. In K. Arnaut, Jan Blommaert, Ben Rampton & M. Spotti (eds.), *Language and superdiversity*, 29–59. New York: Routledge.
Borneman, John & Abdellah Hammoudi. 2009a. The fieldwork encounter, experience, and the making of truth: An introduction. In John Borneman & Abdellah Hammoudi (eds.), *Being there: The fieldwork encounter and the making of truth*, 1–24. Berkeley: University of California Press.
Borneman, John & Abdellah Hammoudi (eds.). 2009b. *Being there: The fieldwork encounter and the making of truth*. Berkeley: University of California Press.
Briggs, Charles. 1986. *Learning how to ask: A sociolinguistic appraisal of the role of the interview in social science research*. Cambridge: Cambridge University Press.
Briggs, Charles. 2007. Anthropology, interviewing, and communicability in contemporary society. *Current Anthropology* 48(4). 551–567.
Bruner, Jerome. 1991. The narrative construction of reality. *Critical Inquiry* 18(1). 1–21.
Bucholtz, Mary & Kira Hall. 2004. Theorizing identity in language and sexuality research. *Language in Society* 33(4). 469–515.
Bucholtz, Mary & Kira Hall. 2005. Identity and interaction: A sociocultural linguistic approach. *Discourse Studies* 7(4–5). 584–614.
Cameron, Deborah. 2000. *It's good to talk*. London: Sage.
Castells, Manuel. 1996. *The rise of the network society*. Cambridge, MA: Blackwell Publishers.
Clifford, James. 1986. Introduction: Partial truths. In James Clifford & George Marcus (eds.), *Writing culture: The poetics and politics of ethnography*, 1–26. Berkeley: University of California Press.
Clifford, James. 1988. *The predicament of culture*. Cambridge, MA: Harvard University Press.
Clifford, James & George Marcus (eds.). 1986. *Writing culture: The poetics and politics of ethnography*. Berkeley: University of California Press.
Crapanzano, Vincent. 2012 [2010]. "At the heart of the discipline": Critical reflections on fieldwork. In Antonius Robben & Jeffrey Sluka (eds.), *Ethnographic fieldwork: An anthropological reader*, 547–562. Malden, MA: Wiley-Blackwell.
Csordas, Thomas. 2012 [2007]. Transmutation of sensibilities: Empathy, intuition, revelation.

In Antonius Robben & Jeffrey Sluka (eds.), *Ethnographic fieldwork: An anthropological reader*, 540–546. Malden, MA: Wiley-Blackwell.
De Fina, Anna. 2003. *Identity in narrative: A study of immigrant discourse*. Amsterdam: John Benjamins Publishing Company.
De Fina, Anna & Sabina Perrino. 2011. Introduction: Interviews vs. 'natural' contexts: A false dilemma. *Language in Society* 40(Special Issue 01). 1–11.
Enfield, Nicholas. 2006. Social consequences of common ground. In Nicholas Enfield & Stephen Levinson (eds.), *Roots of human sociality: Culture, cognition and interaction*, 399–430. Oxford: Berg.
Enfield, Nicholas. 2009. Relationship thinking and human pragmatics. *Journal of Pragmatics* 41(1). 60–78.
Erickson, Frederick & Jeffrey Shultz. 1982. *The counselor as gatekeeper: Social interaction in interviews*. New York: Academic Press.
Fabian, Johannes. 2014 [1983]. *Time and the other: How anthropology makes its object*. Reprint edn. New York: Columbia University Press.
Geertz, Clifford. 1973. *The interpretation of cultures*. New York: Basic Books Inc. Publishers.
Geertz, Clifford. 1973 [1972]. Deep play: Notes on the Balinese cockfight. In Clifford Geertz (ed.), *The interpretation of cultures*, 412–452. United States: Basic books.
Georgakopoulou, Alexandra. 2007. *Small stories, interaction and identities*. Amsterdam: John Benjamins Publishing Company.
Goebel, Zane. 2010. *Language, migration and identity: Neighborhood talk in indonesia*. Cambridge: Cambridge University Press.
Goebel, Zane. 2015. Common ground and conviviality: Indonesians doing togetherness in Japan. *Multilingual Margins* 2(1). 46–66.
Goebel, Zane. 2017. Imitation, interdiscursive hubs, and chronotopic configuration. *Language & Communication* 53. 1–10.
Goebel, Zane & Howard Manns. 2018. Chronotopic relations and scalar shifters. *Tilburg Papers in Cultural Studies* Working paper number 204. 1–31.
Goffman, Erving. 1974. *Frame analysis: An essay on the organization of experience*. Cambridge, MA: Harvard University Press.
Gubrium, Jaber F. & James A. Holstein (eds.). 2003. *Postmodern interviewing*. Thousand Oaks, California: Sage.
Gumperz, John. 1982. *Discourse strategies*. Cambridge: Cambridge University Press.
Hanks, William. 2006. Joint commitment and common ground in a ritual event. In Nicholas Enfield & Stephen Levinson (eds.), *Roots of human sociality: Culture, cognition and interaction*, 299–328. Oxford: Berg.
Harvey, David. 1989. *The condition of postmodernity: An enquiry into the origins of cultural change*. Oxford: Blackwell.
Hume, Lynne & Jane Mulcock. 2004a. Introduction: Awkward spaces, productive places. In Lynne Hume & Jane Mulcock (eds.), *Anthropologists in the field: Cases in participant observation*, xi–xxvii. New York: Colombia University Press.
Hume, Lynne & Jane Mulcock (eds.). 2004b. *Anthropologists in the field: Cases in participant observation*. New York: Colombia University Press.
Hymes, Dell. 1975. Breakthrough into performance. In Dan Ben-Amos & Kenneth Goldstein (eds.), *Folklore: Performance and communication*, 11–74. The Hague: Mouton.
Inoue, Miyako. 2006. *Vicarious language: Gender and linguistic modernity in Japan*. Berkeley: University of California Press.

Koven, Michèle. 2014. Interviewing: Practice, ideology, genre, and intertextuality. *Annual Review of Anthropology* 43(1). 499–520.
Labov, William. 1972. *Sociolinguistic patterns*. Oxford: Basil Blackwell.
Labov, William & J. Waletzky. 1967. Narrative analysis. In J. Helm (ed.), *Essays on the verbal and visual arts*, 12–44. Seattle, WA: University of Washington Press.
Liddicoat, Anthony. 2007. *An introduction to conversation analysis*. London: Continuum.
Lindström, Anna & Marja-Leena Sorjonen. 2013. Affiliation in conversation. In Tanya Stivers & Jack Sidnell (eds.), *The handbook of conversation analysis*, 350–369. Malden, MA: Blackwell Publishing Ltd.
Malinowski, Bronislaw. 1922 [1966]. *The argonauts of the western pacific: An account of native enterprise and adventure in the archipelagoes of Melanesian New Guinea*. London: Lowe and Brydone (Printers) Ltd.
Marcus, George. 1998. *Ethnography through thick and thin*. Princeton, NJ: Princeton University Press.
McCarthy, Michael. 2003. Talking back: "Small" interactional response tokens in everyday conversation. *Research on Language & Social Interaction* 36(1). 33–63.
Mead, Margaret. 1939. Native languages as fieldwork tools. *American Anthropologist* 41(2). 189–205.
Moerman, Michael. 1988. *Talking culture: Ethnography and conversation analysis*. Philadelphia: University of Pennsylvania Press.
Ochs, Elinor & Lisa Capps. 2001. *Living narrative*. Cambridge: Harvard University Press.
O'Reilly, Karen. 2009. *Key concepts in ethnography*. Los Angeles: SAGE.
Powdermaker, Hortense. 2012 [1967]. A woman going native. In Antonius Robben & Jeffrey Sluka (eds.), *Ethnographic fieldwork: An anthropological reader*, 92–102. Malden, MA.: Wiley-Blackwell.
Rabinow, Paul. 1977. *Reflections on fieldwork in Morocco*. 2nd edn. Berkeley: University of California Press.
Rampton, Ben. 2015. Conviviality and phatic communion? *Multilingual Margins* 2(1). 83–91.
Rampton, Ben. 2016. Fieldwork rapport and the position of sociolinguistics. *Working Papers in Urban Language & Literacies, Paper No. 195*.
Rosaldo, Renato. 1989. *Culture and truth: The remaking of social analysis*. Boston: Beakon Press.
Sacks, Harvey, Emanuel A. Schegloff & Gail Jefferson. 1974. A simplest systematics for the organization of turn-taking for conversation. *Language* 50. 696–735.
Sahlins, Marshal. 2013. *What kinship is – and is not*. Chicago: University of Chicago Press.
Scollon, Ron & Suzanne Wong Scollon. 1981. *Narrative, literacy, and face in interethnic communication*. Norwood, N.J.: Ablex Pub. Corp.
Silverstein, Michael. 2015. How language communities intersect: Is "superdiversity" an incremental or transformative condition? *Language & Communication* 44. 7–18.
Silverstein, Michael & Greg Urban (eds.). 1996. *Natural histories of discourse*. Chicago: University of Chicago Press.
Steensig, Jakob. 2013. Conversation analysis and affiliation and alignment. In Carol Chapelle (ed.), *The encyclopedia of applied linguistics*, 1–6. New York: Blackwell Publishing Ltd.
Stivers, Tanya. 2008. Stance, alignment, and affiliation during storytelling: When nodding is a token of affiliation. *Research on Language and Social Interaction* 41(1). 31–57.
Stivers, Tanya, Nicholas Enfield & Stephen Levinson. 2007. Person reference in interaction. In Nicholas Enfield & Tanya Stivers (eds.), *Person reference in interaction*, 1–20. Cambridge:

Cambridge University Press.

Tannen, Deborah. 1984. *Conversational style: Analyzing talk among friends*. Norwood, New Jersey: Ablex.

Tannen, Deborah. 1989. *Talking voices: Repetition, dialogue, and imagery in conversational discourse*. Cambridge: Cambridge University Press.

Vertovec, Steven. 2007. Introduction: New directions in the anthropology of migration and multiculturalism. *Ethnic and Racial Studies* 30(6). 961–978.

Wagley, Charles. 2012 [1960]. Champukwi of the village of the Tapirs. In Antonius Robben & Jeffrey Sluka (eds.), *Ethnographic fieldwork: An anthropological reader*, 143–154. Malden, MA: Wiley-Blackwell.

Wallerstein, Immanuel. 2004. *World-systems analysis: An introduction*. Durham: Duke University Press.

Wolcott, Harry F. 2001. *The art of fieldwork*. Walnut Creek, Calif.: AltaMira Press.

Debbie Cole
2 Looking for Rapport in the Metacommunicative Features of an Ethnographic Interview

1 Introduction

In his book, *Learning How to Ask*, Briggs (1986) argues that we should study the interview ethnographically to understand issues of power between interviewer and interviewee. Such an ethnography involves four phases: Phase 1. Learn how to ask; Phase 2. Design an appropriate methodology; Phase 3. Be reflexive in the interviewing process; and Phase 4. Analyze the interview. Within the fourth phase, Briggs proposes an analytical process that looks beyond the referential content of utterances. He proposes a two-step procedure: first, map the structure of the interview as a whole before looking at the utterances in particular, and second, abstract away from the referential content of the utterances to look at metacommunicative features. We can find these features by focusing on contextualization, both within the interview event itself and across events and texts that precede and follow the interview. Another way to observe metacommunicative features is to focus on the non-referential elements of the interview event.

Briggs' proposal has had an important influence on interview research that has followed the publication of his book. A recent special issue of *Language in Society* on interviews (De Finna & Perrino 2011) and an *Annual Review of Anthropology* article on interviewing (Koven 2014) provide good overviews of how many of Briggs' suggestions from 1986 have been put into practice. In particular, scholars reflecting on interviews as a method for collecting language data have taken his advice to focus on the relationship between power, roles, and footing. We've also followed Briggs' suggestion to include ethnographic details of interview events in our writing, in some cases describing events and interactions that occurred before and after the recording of an interview.

However, some of Briggs' explicit suggestions for how to analyze interview data remain largely absent from our scholarly practices. Even though we sometimes write about the preparation we do before and texts we produce after an interview, details of how the interview event led to particular text productions that followed are largely absent. We also don't tend to produce detailed maps of the structure of an interview we are analyzing. Almost completely missing from our anal-

---
Debbie Cole, Utrecht University, Utrecht, The Netherlands

https://doi.org/10.1515/9781501507830-002

yses is a focus on the non-referential, metacommunicative aspects of our interviews. Though we sometimes write that we *should* be focusing on metacommunication, published analyses of what is happening in the interview, in terms of footing for example, largely focus on words and their syntactic structures along with their linked meanings and on how these referential language fragments are used to accomplish changes in role, voice, or alignment. Rarely do we discuss prosody, body language, and gaze or the way the site for the interview event is set up.[1]

Within the broader field of communication studies, however, research focusing on the metacommunicative features of interviews and other face-to-face interactions provides some useful pointers for how we might focus on metacommunication in the ethnographic study of rapport. For example, interview partners that match the pitch and amplitude of their voices communicate "social similitude" and "cohesiveness" (Gregory et al. 1993). Interlocutors who are sensitive to rhythmic patterning can convey enthusiasm and the feeling of achieving intimate contact in an interaction (Cowley 1994). Rhythmic patterning can also be used to perform *phonetic empathy* or the feeling that the speaking partners are "speak[ing] with one voice" (Abercrombie 1967, cited in Cowley 1994). In classroom contexts, teachers and students who match their utterance pitches, intonation contours, and rhythms communicate alignment and affiliation within the familiar initiation–response–feedback (IRF) exchange (Hellerman 2003: 90).

Researchers contributing to a recent special issue of *Language & Communication* devoted to the theory of Communication Accommodation Competence also provide some useful pointers. They found that adaptation, accommodation, and the ability to adopt the interlocutor's perspective are "essential to…developing rapport, and satisfaction" (Pitts & Harwood 2015: 92). They also note that rapport and sensitivity to cultural and linguistic differences between speakers are linked in highly skilled communicators, and that rapport is "built up utterance by utterance throughout an interaction and often requires a significant amount of verbal reassurance and repetition" (Pitts & Harwood 2015: 93). Tellingly, throughout the studies in these special issues, there is a constant echo of Briggs and other linguistic anthropologists like Silverstein (1981) and Hill (2006) who have argued that anthropologists tend to ignore the importance of the non-verbal channel in organizing social interactions. This point is made again strongly and clearly in a recent *Annual Review* piece on interviewing in which Koven warns against "erasing the more interactional, context-dependent features of interview talk" (Koven 2014: 501).

---

[1] Zane Goebel's diagrams of the way focus-group participants are seated to view and discuss television programs conducted in Japan are a clear exception (Goebel 2015: 179).

It is within this sketch of our methodological history that this chapter attempts to accomplish two goals. The first is to apply the analytical method proposed by Briggs (1986) to an interview that was experienced as rich in rapport to see whether applying it helps us to identify which metacommunicative elements contributed to that experience. The second is to lay some groundwork for future studies that could bring together converging theories and divergent methodologies for understanding rapport across a range of language-focused disciplines. As the application of Briggs' phases 1, 2, and 3 are prevalent in prior ethnographic studies of interviews, here we focus on phase 4 to document how contextualization and non-referentiality contributed to how the poet Zawawi Imron (my interviewee) and I built COMMON GROUND (Goebel, 2015, and this volume, Chapter 1) in an interview.

2 A Focus on Contextualization

Elsewhere, I have written about the poem "Keroncong Air Mata" (*Song of Tears*), about how Zawawi Imron performed the poem using multiple voices, and about how his performance embodied adequation in the enactment of a 'diverse Indonesian' identity (Cole 2004, 2010). I have also written about how I compared what Zawawi told me (in the same interview to be examined here) about his intended referents for the performed voices in his poem to how listeners to a recording of his performance interpreted those voices (Cole 2014). The latter piece demonstrated how, under certain conditions, common ground can be established across time and space even without the co-presence of the performer and the perceiver. Here, we follow Briggs' suggestion to focus on contextualization. We begin by zooming in on the context immediately surrounding the interview event to clarify when, where, and under what conditions the interview took place, because Briggs has suggested that this information may be directly relevant to how the interview unfolds, how it is experienced and remembered by the participants, and to how interviewers learn to listen. We then zoom out to document how events and texts that preceded the interview provided a context for the interview itself, enabling us to quickly establish common ground.

2.1 The Context Immediately Surrounding the Recording

Zawawi and I had arranged to meet in Surabaya on 9 May 2002, a date when we would both be visiting the city for other reasons. I was there for a Fulbright event, and he had stayed an extra night beyond his original plans so that our paths would cross. In Surabaya, the Fulbright Foundation had put up all the Fulbright students currently in Indonesia (both those of us coming from the US and those of us going to the US) in the five-star Hotel Majapahit, a luxurious accommodation in a remolded colonial building at which we students gaped and giggled in awe. Zawawi and I had met briefly only once before at a poetry festival in Solo. When we met in the hotel lobby, he greeted me like an old friend, and we went to the hotel café for lunch.

Knowing that my dissertation topic was public performances of Indonesian poetry, Zawawi engaged me immediately in a poetry discussion. He knew poets from all over the world, most of whom I had never heard of. He talked at length about Robert Frost, an American poet I was quite familiar with, citing lines and offering translations into Indonesian. After eating, we moved to my assigned suite to begin the formal interview. Although the private sitting room within the suite had couches and chairs, we chose to sit on a rug on the floor around a little coffee table. I had made two copies of a list of questions I wanted to ask, one for each of us. Up until that point, we had been talking in an easy, informal way with me taking the role of respectful youth talking to a respected elder. At the moment that the interview was supposed to begin, however, I found it difficult to switch into the appropriate mode. When I clumsily directed his attention to his copy of the questionnaire, Zawawi interrupted with, "You start by asking the questions first!"

Once the interview was over and Zawawi had autographed one of his books I had brought with me, we found we still had some time before his bus left for Madura. Zawawi suggested we go to the Gramedia bookstore nearby. Conscious that I would like to repay him for his time and information, I agreed thinking perhaps there would be something I could purchase for him there. We crossed the busy boulevard together on foot and navigated our way into the shopping plaza where the bookstore was located. Once inside, it became clear that Zawawi was looking for something in particular. Besides writing poetry, he also enjoyed painting and was fond of a particular Dutch artist whose work he wanted to study. He found a large, heavy coffee-table book of the artist's work, which he presented to me to purchase. This was both a relief and a surprise: a relief because I would be able to repay his time and attention and thereby avoid accruing too large a social debt, and a surprise because of the directness of his request. I had grown accustomed to the more indirect hints often performed by my Javanese friends and colleagues back in Yogyakarta, my home base in Indonesia. With the purchase completed, we walked together to the bus stop where Zawawi boarded the bus. We waved goodbye to each other until the bus took him beyond my view.

2.2 Contextualizing the Interview Within Prior Events and Texts

Zooming out from the discursive and physical contexts immediately surrounding the interview event, we now follow Briggs' advice to look at how the interview text is connected to prior texts and events leading up to the moment of the interview. The topical focus of the interview was Zawawi's 13-minute performance of the poem, "Keroncong Air Mata" (*Song of Tears*), which I recorded him reading at a benefit event for woman's health in Yogyakarta in September of 2001. Zawawi's composition process for the poem was ongoing, as I learned in the interview, and several versions of it had been performed by the time I heard it. At the time of our interview, there was no published text of the poem. During the months of late 2001, I listened to the recording repeatedly and transcribed it. This transcription provided the visual reference from which we worked during the interview.

In April 2002, I met Zawawi at the International Poetry Festival in Solo. At that event, we had been sitting on the floor of a large lecture hall within earshot of each other. Zawawi had engaged neighbouring members of the audience in joking conversation, and at the encouragement of a friend who had travelled to Solo with me, I introduced myself and asked if he would grant me an interview at a future date. We exchanged contact information, and a follow-up phone call from my house in Jogja to his house in Sumanep, Madura confirmed our meeting time and place at the Hotel Majapahit on 9 May. These prior texts and events are listed in (1) in chronological order.

(1) *The interview within the contexts of prior texts and events:*
1. Multiple versions of the poem are composed and performed
2. Poem is performed and recorded in Jogjakarta
3. Recording is transcribed
4. Zawawi and Debbie meet at the International Poetry Festival in Solo
5. Debbie and Zawawi make an interview appointment by phone
6. Questionnaire is created
7. Zawawi and Debbie have lunch in the Hotel Mahapahit
8. Interview is conducted and recorded, questionnaire is filled in, and observations are written down

The events leading up to the interview, as well as the immediately adjacent contexts surrounding the start and end of the interview, gave Zawawi and me the opportunity to interact using different modes of communication and to perform various "figures of personhood" (Agha 2011). By the time we took on the roles of interviewer and interviewee, we had built up a repertoire of shared references that came in part from my close listening to his poem and in part from an awareness of our common experiences at previous poetry events and at the lunch we had just shared.

2.3 Contextualizing the (Un)Familiar in Establishing Common Ground

Perhaps the prior contexts leading up to this interview, as well as the context of the interview itself, are quite different from those leading up to the prototypical academic or research interview. We get the idea from reading studies based on interview data that they often occur in an institutional setting where one of the interview partners arrives at the work place of the other (the *opposite* of 'common ground' in one of our lay senses of the word), and in which only one person has the possibility to wonder at the discovery of a new environment or to be uncomfortable in an unfamiliar space. In such settings, we may imagine that the interview interaction is bounded by the opening and the closing of the door to the room in which the interview takes place, rather than starting with lunch in a hotel café and ending with a shopping trip to bookstore. Should such personal prior and post events have actually occurred (and in some cases they undoubtedly do), they are absent from our presentations of our method, in part because such interactions would imply differing levels of familiarity with our interviewees and familiarity is not supposed to play a role in our data collection. Given pressures on qualitative research to resemble as closely as possible the criteria of objectivity, reliability, and replicability of quantitative approaches, we attempt to select "neutral" interview sites and make much of our attempts to keep the line of questioning and interactional structure the same across interviews. I recognize such attempts as well from my own experiences being the interviewee for academic research projects and from reading student thesis work.

In the interview with Zawawi, however, both contextual familiarity and contextual unfamiliarity contributed to the richness of our shared experience. We were both unfamiliar with the space we were in: Neither of us lived in Surabaya, it was the first time for both of us to be in that hotel, and we had only exchanged a few sentences prior to meeting for the interview. But we also shared a deep familiarity with the text of the poem we were there to discuss. (It is possible that given the repeated times I listened to it to transcribe it that, other than Zawawi, I had heard that poem more than anyone else on the planet.) We were both aware of this, and we chose to make use of this awareness to establish referential common ground both in orienting to the topic of the interview and in orienting to the space we were in. As we will see in the next section, however, much of the work we did to establish common ground was done using non-referential means.

3 A Focus on Non-Referentiality

We turn now to a focus on some of the non-referential elements audible on the recording of the interview, beginning with a comparison of the metacommunicative elements present at the end and at the beginning of the interview.

3.1 Ending in Rapport After a Rocky Start

In the last few seconds of an almost hour-long recording, Zawawi signed a copy of one of his books, which I had brought with me. He asked me for the date "*tanggal berapa sekarang?*" (what's the date today?), I told him it was the ninth (*tanggal sembilan*), and as he wrote, he said, "*nol sembilan mei*" (zero nine May). Listening to this excerpt 15 years later, I notice how it sounds like an intimate exchange: We were speaking softly without variation in pitch or amplitude and with audible space between our utterances. Although nothing very interesting is happening referentially (all we're doing is agreeing on the date), the prosodic, metacommunicative ambiance at the close of the interview is gentle and intimate.

In contrast, the prosodic atmosphere at the beginning of the recording could be described as turbulent and uncertain. The recording starts with me confirming that the equipment is working, and following my clumsy direction of Zawawi's attention to copies of the questions we each had in front of us, Zawawi steps in to explain how the interview should run.

(2) *The turbulent and uncertain beginning*

Debbie
ayo   let's go.
Zawawi
ayo   let's go.
Debbie
dari 'top' dari atas di sini   from the 'top' from the beginning here.
Zawawi
a, anda yang bertanya-lah dulu   y, you start by asking the questions first.
Debbie
Ok...Oh!   Ok...Oh!
Zawawi
Seperti kita, anda bertanya kenapa dibaca   It's like we, you ask why is it read like this
begini kenapa begitu, gitu loh kan?   why like that, isn't that right?

Debbie
Ok   Ok.
Zawawi
uh huh   uh huh
Debbie
Jadi dari awal mau ditanyain kalau   So from the beginning I wanna ask you
mengapa...   how, why...

The start of this interview continues to surprise and embarrass me, just as it did at the time: After I verified the functioning of the equipment, I failed to take on my appropriate role which left Zawawi unable to take on his. I sound uncertain as I fumble for the Indonesian word for "top". When Zawawi interrupted me, he was insistent and loud, with a sharp rise in amplitude and pitch. I responded with a high pitched "Oh!", like I was surprised to hear that I was supposed to ask the questions, to which Zawawi responds with a clear explanation of how I should go about interviewing him.

3.2 Building Rapport Within Shifting Roles and Alignments

Although the rocky start to this interview could have resulted in an uncomfortable struggle through the questions, the actual outcome was quite the opposite. Even as I uttered my first question about why it is important to read poetry aloud "in Indonesia", Zawawi was already encouraging me "*ya, ya, ya*" (yes, yes, yes). He took a breath and repeated the phrase "*di Indonesia ini*" (here in Indonesia) from my question, then paused while he seemed to decide where to begin. When he began to answer, he was no longer sounding like he was scolding. He first answered my question by talking about Islam and how religious teachings are conveyed through song, taking an example from his home island Madura. After about a minute, he started singing, and he sang again about a minute later. In fact, he answered my first question twice, first with the information he wanted me to know about his identity as a Muslim Madurese, and then he began again, at almost three minutes into the interview, with a more direct focus on contemporary poetry and his choices within the national context.

He began both answers with the phrase "*di Indonesia ini*" (here in Indonesia), demonstrating both a willingness to answer my question and the liberty he felt in accomplishing his own rhetorical goals. Acoustically, the two instances of "*di Indonesia ini*" are quite different. The first utterance is louder and lower pitched, the second softer, higher pitched, and with palatalization on the /si/ sequence in the word "Indonesia". He is serious, focused, and in the process of making a decision in the first instance. In the second, he is delighted and happy: We can hear him smiling.[2]

From just the first three minutes of the recording, several factors seem to have played a role in our rapport building. One is the felt freedom of both participants to enact multiple identity categories (American, Javanese, linguist, Indonesian, Madurese, Muslim, poet, performer). A second is the felt freedom to perform multiple pairings of social roles (respectful youth/respected elder, clumsy child/scolding parent, knowledgeable teacher/curious student, interviewer/interviewee, social scientist/religious poet). It may be crucial that these different pairings required alignments with a range of different imagined communities or communities of practice that entailed multiple asymmetrical power alignments for each of us. A third factor appears to be the willingness of both participants to adjust their linguistic behavior to participate in accomplishing the other's goals for the interview, with one strategy for signalling this willingness being the repetition of the other's words or phrasing.

3.3 Performing Rapport While Recontextualizing Voices

My goal for the interview was to ask Zawawi to explain the functions and indexicalities of the various voices he used in his performance. Methodologically, I had set this up by creating a list of the words and phrases where I had heard shifts in genre, timbre, tone, and articulation in the chronological order in which he had performed them. We each had a copy of the list, and we worked through them together in order, moving on to the next item on the list when we were both satisfied with the explanation. Because of this goal, most of what we did during the interview was to contextualize Zawawi's poem within the interview event and within the broader picture of Indonesian oral-literacy practices. The three examples discussed here specifically demonstrate the metacommunicative aspects of the contextualization process that were simultaneously functioning to build rapport.

A recurring metacommunicative shift in this interview was out of speaking and into singing. The first occurred with the line "*di sini batu batu*" (here [there] are rocks). To direct his attention to that fragment of the poem, I sang the line as I recalled the melody from memory. He repeated it back to me, moving the pitch up slightly before continuing to perform the rest of the stanza that he had sung in the performance. As he neared the end of the stanza, he paused before the last

---

[2] I have played these two recordings for roomfuls of students who understand no Indonesian and been delighted to see several of them smile in response to hearing the recording of Zawawi's second "*di Indonesia ini*".

line, apparently waiting for me to fill it in, but when I failed to do so, not remembering the words, he completed the stanza himself. If we compare the recording of us singing the line "*di sini batu batu*" in the interview with the recording of Zawawi performing it months earlier, we hear that my singing of the line matches the tempo and melody of the original, but that Zawawi's also matches the pitch of the original, as he shifted it up into the same key he used during the performance.

In another stanza of the poem, Zawawi critiques poets using a stylized "*deklamasi*" style, which most contemporary poets had moved decidedly away from at the time of the interview. As I set up my question about that section, Zawawi already knew what was coming, and he started to laugh in anticipation of what he knew would be my imitation of his imitation of a no longer fashionable way of reading poetry. A comparison of the interview recording with the original performance reveals that my imitation matched the timing and prosodic contours of his original performance, which clearly delighted Zawawi (he laughs, and utters a "*ya!*" of recognition). We quickly became comfortable with this mode of moving through the questionnaire items and used it to identify and establish common ground for many of the voices I wanted Zawawi to explain.

These examples suggest two more factors that played a role in building rapport in this interview. The first is the explicit identification of and reference to a shared prior text. The second is the performance of prosodic mirroring or matching. Perhaps a feature of the question–response process that was occurring simultaneously as we moved through the voices is worth noting here. Throughout the process, Zawawi paused when he saw me writing something down, and he repeated and sometimes spelled words for me if he saw me hesitate as I filled in the spaces on my copy of the questions. That we could both see everything the other had in front of them may have been an important aspect of the felt rapport. On a couple of occasions when Zawawi was explaining something, he also initiated a common pedagogical routine in Indonesian classrooms where the teacher begins a statement and leaves an audible space after a sharply rising intonation to prompt the students to fill in the right answer aloud. These observations suggest that the use of slower speech and pausing to ensure the interlocutor's understanding and the prosodic cueing of the interlocutor to demonstrate understanding also contributed metacommunicatively to building rapport.

3.4 The (Non-)Referentiality of Common Ground

This section has documented how Zawawi and I established common references and orientations using non-referential means. Within and across the turn-taking cycles that characterize the interview speech genre, we regularly imitated each other prosodically. We also established common reference to a prior text by performing intonational patterns present in those prior texts and by licensing each other's imitations of them. This licensing, or acceptance, of the other's prosodic imitations extended not only to establishing shared reference to a prior text, but also to the ongoing negotiation and performance of various roles and alignments.

To follow Briggs' methodological recommendations, I have been focusing on the metacommunicative elements of the interview and have tried to avoid discussing its referential content. But a recurring theme in Zawawi's answers to my questions about *why* he used voices in his performances was that doing so facilitated a closeness with the audience. His whole point was that the prosodic indexicality of the voices he performed functioned to remove the distance between him as the poet as speaker and his audience as hearers. An analysis of the referential content of this interview reveals that he argued that the way he builds rapport when he reads poetry is by performing the prosodic characteristics of different Indonesian voices.[3] Going back through the recording to listen for how we enacted rapport metacommunicatively within the interview, however, I was surprised that I had not previously noticed the self-referentiality of how Zawawi conveyed his argument to me. The prosodic imitations and indexicalities of the text that we were discussing and which originally took place within the frame of a poetry performance were the same behaviors that we were enacting within the frame of the interview.

4 Reflecting on Using Briggs' Method: Lessons, Implications, and Limitations

Reflecting on texts and events that followed from this interview, I notice that Zawawi and I found ways to sustain contact and exchange well past the time when I returned to the US and despite the fact that Zawawi didn't use email or have a web presence. When I returned for another year of fieldwork in 2007, I snail mailed Zawawi a copy of one of Ofelia Zepeda's recordings of her poetry in O'odham and English (Zepeda 1997) because Zawawi had told me over lunch that he was fascinated by the sound of Native American place names. This favor had to be repaid, and as his daughter happened to be living in Jojga at the time, he sent her and her husband to my house to deliver the only painting of his she had in her possession: a wall-sized depiction of the *kaaba* in Mecca on a background of bright green, which we hung in our dining room for the duration of our stay. Later, my in-

---

[3] Several of his statements about this became the cornerstones of arguments I have made in previous publications (Cole 2010; Cole 2014), though I didn't use the word "rapport" in those pieces.

teractions with Zawawi led me to focus on his poetry while working on an anthology of 20th-century Indonesian poetry, making sure one of my co-editors heard the recording of "Song of Tears" and that I was the one who translated his poems selected for inclusion in the English version of the anthology.

There were many other recordings of poetry performances and many other interviews in my dissertation data. But no other interview or connection to a poet that was established as part of my fieldwork on poetry in 2001 has remained the focus of my scholarly work like Zawawi's has. Reanalyzing the interview following Briggs' suggestions made me realize how important the rapport we built in the interview was in influencing my choice to continue to work on the poem. I wouldn't have done it as joyfully, or maybe not at all, if the interview hadn't played out the way it did.

(3) *The effects of rapport on events and texts beyond the interview event:*
1. Ofelia Zepeda's poetry CD mailed to Zawawi in Madura in 2007
2. Zawawi's daughter delivers a painting to our house in Jogja in 2008
3. Recording of "Song of Tears" played for co-editor Dorothea Rosa Herliany in 2010
4. Zawawi's poems translated for inclusion in the *Lontar Anthology of Indonesian Poetry* in 2016–2017
5. Interview analyzed for paper presented at the Conceptualizing Rapport Symposium in 2016
6. Current chapter written

4.1 Lessons Learned

I now understand why the long call to turn our attention away from referentiality in our analyses continues to be a struggle. It is so easy to slip back into a focus on referential content. Even though I set out to purposefully listen for the metacommunicative elements of this interview, I had to stop after only the first couple of minutes because I found that I was continuing to write down the words and phrases that formed the subject of our discussion, even though I had done all of that before and was already working from an elaborate understanding of the referential content of our talk. I had to start over multiple times. Once I started to focus on what was going on metacommunicatively, however, it became clear that almost every moment of the recording contains non-referential information that is functioning to do much of what we are accomplishing linguistically.

Only after eventually being able to focus on the non-referential elements of the interview could I notice that I uttered the second phrase on the recording

"*Iya sudah*" (yes, it's ready) in an Indonesian accent that was phonetically influenced by Javanese—with long, drawn-out vowels and breathy (or slack) voicing on my /d/, a distinguishing characteristic of Javanese-influenced Indonesian (Thurgood 2004). I also realized that the confusion I'd been embarrassed about at the beginning of the interview started with me accidentally switching into English "dari *top*" using the Indonesian word for "from" (dari) but the English word "top", which I pronounced as an Indonesian word (/tap/ rather than /tʰɔp/. It was while I was correcting myself, perhaps unnecessarily, to use the Indonesian word *atas* that Zawawi stepped in. To map and analyze everything that went on metacommunicatively would take a great deal more space and time than is available here. I understand why we tend to avoid doing this.

I can also understand why, as writers, we would want to avoid documenting the many details that *could* be seen from following Briggs' advice to first fully map the interview structure, something I was unable to fully accomplish or partially represent here. We tend to write focused pieces that make an argument for theory or document an interesting phenomenon, and it's not clear in the middle of mapping the structure how such work will ultimately contribute to our understanding of whatever it is we've set as our research question or theoretical focus. The fact that it also takes up lot of time and space could explain the absence, if not in practice then at least in publication, of evidence that Briggs' method of interview analysis has been followed in the way he laid it out.

Doing this kind of analysis also offers clues as to why we don't focus our analyses on non-referentiality. For one, we don't explicitly collect the kinds of data that provide evidence of the way the interactions are experienced. Though we record audio and sometimes video, we do not necessarily take pictures of our surroundings or keep autographs or other material items exchanged as gifts, or if we do, we don't think of them as data. I found Zawawi's autograph and the poem he wrote out for me by hand on the hotel stationery in my 'data files' while writing this, but I never considered them as data before. That we ate together, I think, is another important factor in our ability to establish rapport. What a focus on non-referentiality makes clear, however, is that there is so much that could be mapped and so many metacommunicative elements in our recordings that could be tracked and analyzed if we approached our data and text-making practices in the ways Briggs suggests.

4.2 Implications and Limitations

What do these data and the application of Briggs' method to them imply for understanding rapport in future fieldwork encounters? From a zoomed-out perspective, one thing we see is that rapport is not only built up within the event where we think of ourselves as collecting data. It occurs across the whole stretch of time we are in the field and can extend beyond it. This implies that we might attune ourselves to the possibility of rapport building in interactions that we may not consider to be part of our data collection methodology. From a zoomed in perspective, we see that rapport can be performed through imitations, or prosodic matching and repetitions based on shared access to prior texts. In our field sites, we can be on the lookout for opportunities to do this with others with whom we hope to build rapport, and when we hear or see others doing this, it might be a cue that our interlocutor is trying to build rapport with us.

It also appears that rapport can be established rather quickly. Despite the fact that we had only exchanged a few sentences before the day we met for this interview and despite me getting off on the wrong foot during the interview itself, within a couple of minutes, elements of rapport-building can be detected in the interaction. These data also serve as a reminder that our metacommunicative repertoires are large, and given that interviews typically shut down the opportunities for performing our widest range of roles and voices, we might consider how we could build in opportunities for this range to emerge in an interview setting.

The many limitations of this study also point to possible directions for future interdisciplinary research collaborations. We might work with communication studies scholars who do technical phonetic analyses to recover empirical evidence of affect (like smiling) to understand where and how non-referential phonetic information functions in an interview or in other interactions in which rapport is of interest (see work by Quené et al. 2012).[4] In such collaborations, we could share our theories of identity, contextualization, and voicing to name and categorize acoustic phenomena (as examples of iconization, adequation, fractal recursion, role alignment, etc.) to contribute to a big-picture understanding of how humans do rapport. Briggs' proposal may even point the way to analyses that we are not yet able to imagine doing: Given a different methodological focus on non-referentiality in communicative encounters, the types of possible analyses remain in uncharted territory. Perhaps the most striking thing I noticed listening to this interview from a metacommunicative perspective was while Zawawi was talking about the importance of music in human communication. He said that poetry has to be aligned with the rhythms of hearts. I'd heard him say that before on the recording, many times, but it was only by listening for non-reference that I no-

---

[4] Laughter happened throughout the interview, as did smiling. Both are acoustically recoverable, but their contribution to rapport is left unaddressed here.

ticed that while he said it, he started clicking the pen he was holding to set up a steady rhythm against which he uttered his answer to my question.

References

Abercrombie, David. 1967. *Elements of general phonetics*. Edinburgh: Edinburgh University Press.
Agha, Asif. 2011. Large and small scale forms of personhood. *Language & Communication* 31. 171–180.
Briggs, Charles. 1986. *Learning how to ask: A sociolinguistic appraisal of the role of the interview in social science research*. Cambridge: Cambridge University Press.
Cole, Deborah. 2004. *Performing 'unity in diversity' in Indonesian poetry—Voice, ideology, grammar, and change*. Tucson: University of Arizona. Dissertation.
Cole, Debbie. 2010. Enregistering diversity: Adequation in Indonesian poetry performance. *Journal of Linguistic Anthropology* 20(1). 1–21.
Cole, Debbie. 2014. Mobilizing voices across representational boundaries: Some considerations for local values and functions. *International Journal of the Sociology of Language* 227. Special issue "Language and borders: international perspectives", Glenn Martinez, issue editor. 175–192.
Cowley, Stephen J. 1994. Conversational functions of rhythmical patterning. *Language & Communication* 14(4). 353–376.
De Fina, Anna, & Sabina Perrino, 2011. Introduction: Interviews vs. 'natural' contexts: A false dilemma. *Language in Society* 40(Special Issue 01). 1–11.
Goebel, Zane. 2015. *Language and superdiversity*. Oxford: Oxford University Press.
Gregory, Stanford, Stephen Webster & Gang Huang. 1993. Voice pitch and amplitude convergence as a metric of quality in dyadic interviews. *Language & Communication* 13(3). 195–217.
Hellerman, John. 2003. The interactive work of prosody in the IRF exchange: Teacher repetition in feedback moves. *Language in Society* 32. 79–104.
Hill, Jane. 2006. The ethnography of language and language documentation, In Jost Gippert, Nikolaus P. Himmelmann & Ulrike Mosel (eds.), *Essentials of language documentation* (Trends in Linguistics, Studies and Monographs 178), 113–128. Berlin & New York: Mouton de Gruyter.
Koven, Michele. 2014. Interviewing: Practice, ideology, genre, and intertextuality. *Annual Review of Anthropology* 43. 499–520.
Pitts, Margaret J. & Jake Harwood. 2015. Communication accommodation competence: The nature and nurture of accommodative resources across the lifespan. *Language & Communication* 41. 89–99.
Quené, Hugo, Gün Semin & Francesco Foroni. 2012. Audible smiles and frowns affect speech comprehension. *Speech Communication* 54. 917–922.
Silverstein, Michael. 1981. The limits of awareness. *Sociolinguistic Working Paper* 84. Austin, Texas: Southwest Educational Development Laboratory.
Thurgood, Ella. 2004. Phonation types in Javanese. *Oceanic Linguistics* 43(3). 277–295.
Zepeda, Ofelia. 1997. *Jewed 'I-Hoi/earth movements*. Tucson: Kore Press.

Lauren Zentz
3 'Today's Episode Is Sponsored by Nü Green Tea': Rapport and Virtuoso Humour in Group Interviews

1 Rapport, Linguistic Performativity, and the Foreign Teacher–Researcher

In this chapter, I demonstrate how the co-construction of humorous digressions in a series of novel interactional frameworks contributed to the building of interactional roles, identities, and social relations during a series of focus group interviews I conducted during my research in Central Java during the 2009–2010 academic year. To do so, I rely on micro-interactional sociolinguistic analysis (Goodwin and Alim 2010; Jefferson 2004) in applying theories of intertextuality or interdiscursivity (Bakhtin 1981; Wortham 2005; Bauman 2005), enregisterment, and "figures of personhood" (Agha 2007) to our interview interactions. Throughout the aforementioned year, I was a teacher–researcher at a private Christian university in Central Java, and with my eight focal participants as well as other English majors, I navigated and constructed varying levels and types of relationship including student–teacher, researcher–informant, foreigner local, language learner–language expert, and varying levels of friend or confidant. Such relations represent what is commonly referred to as "rapport" in anthropological literature (Geertz 1973; Hume and Mulcock 2004; Marcus 1998).

Our relationships were constructed through trans-/polylinguistic interactions (García 2010; Jørgenson 2008). I borrow from these theories to define "language use as the *performance* of differentially available *resources* located in or away from complex centers and peripheries" (Zentz 2017: 6, italics in original; see also Blommaert 2005, 2010; Blommaert et al. 2005; Goebel 2015; Pennycook 2007). Together in- and outside of interview frames, we used language forms generally associated with the named languages English, Indonesian, and Javanese, and various registers within these categories. Using these linguistic resources, we explained ideas and vocabulary to each other; joked together and teased each other; addressed each other as insiders and outsiders to the Central Javanese context and to the global English-speaking community; and discussed the dynamic nature of language use, learning, and shift locally and in Indonesia more broadly.

Lauren Zentz, University of Houston, Houston, USA

https://doi.org/10.1515/9781501507830-003

The nature of my relationship with these students was not typical in comparison to how they related to the other English Department instructors. While I was most certainly one among their instructors, I also, due to my researcher role, spent a lot of time with many of the students outside of classes grabbing lunch or dinner together, playing basketball, drinking coffee, going to their churches, and participating in various department-related activities. As one research participant once told me, my relationship with her and other students was like a half-peer, half-teacher relationship with relatively undefined role expectations[1]:

(1)
Dian
Awhile back with [American instructor], I also didn't feel close because we didn't ever communicate outside of class, but with Lauren, ya, I feel closer because we often, communicate outside of class.
Lauren
Yeah.
Dian
and you're like a friend.
Lauren
yeah, yeah.
Dian
but like with professors we're more what ya. ya close, close, only, what ya, there's a feeling what is it we have to respect them because they're professors,
Lauren
okay.
Dian
and, ya, it's just different.
Lauren
okay.
Dian
I mean there's not ya there's not, we're very rarely close. with professors.

(Dian, Interview 3, 02/02/2010)

Additionally, my role as foreigner, and specifically a foreigner from an English-dominant country, also brought with it some expectations: students from the department expressed to me during my year there that American instructors were seen to be more charismatic and interactive in their teaching practices than their Indonesian counterparts. I believe this was particularly associated with the younger instructors, such as myself (I was 30 at the time). So, while my American-

---

[1] I show this transcript in narrative form and only its translated version as no further detail is needed. In later transcripts, however, I use Conversation Analysis conventions (see Jefferson 2004 and Appendix A) and the original language in order to show the reader the necessary level of conversational detail in those interactions.

ness alone did not make me the more approachable person as Dian describes above (she herself claimed that there were other American instructors whom she did not feel close with), I do believe my behaviors were in accordance with certain expected attributes of American professors. Additionally, my younger age combined with my spending time with the students outside of classes, all influenced the students' felt ability to interact with me in less formal ways than they did with other faculty.

1.1 The Focus Group

Montell writes of group interviews: "A group interview [...] allows certain topics to be explored in more depth than they might be in individual interviews, as contradictory ideas prompt [participants] to elaborate on their original statements" (1999: 48). I would add that such topic exploration, wherein the participants collaboratively or contradictorily respond to questions and end up, through their own negotiations, bringing more to light for the researcher than is often possible in a one-on-one interview, is also conditioned by the relationship of the participants to each other and to the researcher.

Focus group interactions—in which I divided participants into two groups of four and held four interviews with each group over the course of the year—generally fall outside of regular norms for communication or generally accepted frame schemata in any given context. Both my role in relation to these students as described above, as well as our interactions in research interviews in front of a camera and in which I at times asked odd, obvious, and repetitious questions (Geertz 2000 [1973]: 29), led to a situation in which prototypical relationship boundaries and participation frameworks (Goffman 1974, 1979) informed our interactions, but they also had to be reconsidered and produced in novel ways in order to construct this new context.

Despite the novel circumstances, this group of students were quite used to interacting with each other on a regular basis. English Department students as peers were a relatively tight knit group—they spent lots of time with each other in and outside of classes, and so they knew each other well and interacted informally, in both Javanese and Indonesian registers. Also, by the time we started our group interviews together, the students were regularly interacting with me inside and outside of school contexts. So, while there wasn't quite a set frame for group interview interactions, there were pre-existing familiarities and interactional norms for these four students with each other and with me. As we will see in the analysis below, the students' prior relationships with each other and their relatively informal relationships with me allowed for these novel focus group interactions to be experimented with through play, particularly through playing with interactional frameworks, as well as with figures of personhood (Agha 2005, 2007) culturally available to all five of us in the group-interview situation.

In the subsequent analysis, I will focus on a combination of play and humour (Bateson 1972; Coates 2007), the voicing of figures of personhood (Agha 2005, 2007), and the intertextual/interdiscursive enregisterment of individuals as tied to certain group/conversational roles (Bakhtin 1981; Bauman 2005; Wortham 2005; Agha 2005, 2007). To briefly define these terms: Agha (2005) defines enregisterment as "a social regularity of recognition whereby linguistic (and accompanying nonlinguistic) signs come to be recognized as indexing pragmatic features of interpersonal role (persona) and relationship" (p. 57). In the following excerpts, we will see Angelo improvisationally voice a specific "figure of personhood"—a character that has no biographical identity, but is readily identifiable by all participants relying on a shared set of cultural references (Agha 2007).

In this case, the performance is one of 'TV talk show host', and specifically a talk show host who is interrupting the interview in order to advertise sponsor products to the "viewers at home" (who exist through the lens of the camera). As he repeats this performance, Angelo begins to enregister himself and to become recognized by the group as this TV talk show host persona that he keeps enacting. That is, his performances each rely *intertextually* by referring back to his previous performances; they rely on the intertextual reference to a recognizable "talk show host" persona that everyone in the group recognizes as culturally relevant; and they also rely on the group's acceptance of this performance as appropriate to the interaction and, in these cases, humorous enough to entertain at all. The importance of humour in group interactions and group development of rapport is thus salient to our analysis, and so, a brief note on how humour and play contribute to the development of rapport or solidarity over time.

1.2 Humour in Group Interactions

Coates (2007) claims that playful talk and collaborative humour are key to building solidarity in group interactions:

> [...] laughter [...] emerges as the result of humorous stories, or of bantering or teasing among participants, or when speakers pick up a point and play with it creatively. Everyday conversation exhibits spontaneous outbursts of verbal play.
> [...] Conversational participants can frame their talk as humorous by signalling 'This is play'. The notion of a 'play frame' captures an essential feature of humour—that it is not serious—and at the same time avoids being specific about the kinds of talk that can occur in a play frame: potentially anything can be funny. (2007: 31)

She further notes, citing Jefferson et al. (1978):

> [...] when conversational participants collaborate in humorous talk, they achieve a display of 'not merely laughing at the same time, but laughing in the same way' (174). These insightful observations [...] suggest that laughter and intimacy are significantly linked. (Coates 2007: 44)

Additionally, Dynel (2008) describes "contestive" and "collaborative" humour, as well as "joint fantasy" in the creation of humorous scenes suspended above the reality of a given interaction. Regarding the latter, she describes (citing Hay 1995) joint fantasizing as "a humorous fantasy sequence which is a jointly produced humorous discourse on a given topic" (p. 244). Such joint fantasizing is "composed of short conversational contributions made by participants to form a coherent scene, based on the augmentation of unreality. The phenomenon observable here is that the preceding absurd proposition can always be topped, i. e. wittily outdone" (Dynel 2008: 244, cit. Kotthoff 2007).

For the rest of this paper, I will focus specifically on a sequence of excerpts featuring Angelo's moments of initiating a "talk show" frame and assuming a "talk show host" persona, or figure of personhood. While I exclude many relevant conversational moments, it remains my aim to provide a *thick description* of the events (Geertz 2000 [1973]). This is done in order to show how this character was built up, reinforced, and taken to the height of absurdity and hilarity, or how this entire sequence led to Angelo's enregisterment (Agha 2007) as a "brand ambassador" in Interview 2, and subsequently a marketing expert in Interview 3. In Interview 2, where most of the work in enregistering this persona was completed, Angelo's shifts into "talk show host" were met with laughter in early instances, then sarcasm and humorous exasperation, and finally with the group joining in on the activity. In doing so, they attempted to take Angelo's increasingly ridiculous frame shifts "over the top", or to the most absurd extent possible, perhaps in an attempt to get him to stop. The excerpts below will all be presented in Jefferson's (2004) style of Conversation Analysis[2] transcription (see Appendix A for specific transcription norms) in an attempt to capture the group's detailed interactions in constructing these humorous moments.

---

[2] Different from Goebel (2005, 2010, 2015), I do not indicate different languages in my transcripts. This is partially in the interest of not further cluttering already complex transcriptions, partially driven by the fact that some language forms cannot necessarily be attributed to one language, and partially due to wariness about my own ability to differentiate where one language form ends and another begins. Instead of marking languages in the transcripts, then, I talk in the texts surrounding the transcripts about language forms that are indexical of various named languages where relevant.

2 Performing for the Camera

Angelo first performed his talk show host persona at the beginning of the first group interview, by switching into a higher pitched and highly formal and fluent standard TV Indonesian. His performance evoked laughter and contestation:

(2)
Angelo
1   ini acarane, ini acara apa sih? ini apa ini,   this is the show, what show is this? this
2   mau talk show atau apa?   what this, you want a talk show or what?
Lauren
3   sudah? okay   ready? okay
Angelo
4   pemirsa, saksikan kami bersama nara   viewers, we're here with our interviewee
5   sumber yaitu ibu [Nisa's full name],   Mrs. [Nisa's full name], please. Later
6   silakan. nanti kita akan bicara tentang   we'll be talking about women's influence
7   pengaruh wanita dalam, (Novita looks up   in, (Novita looks up from phone with
8   from phone with smile and playfully   smile and playfully imitates a slap to
9   imitates a slap to Angelo's shoulder)   Angelo's shoulder)
Nisa
10 opo: what?
All
11 @@@   @@@
Satriya
12 'Gelo, tanya gue dulu dong   'Gelo, ask me first man
Nisa
13 hih, kowe ki kok @@@   hih, why are you @@@

(Interview 1, 10/27/2009)

In the above excerpt, Angelo and others negotiated frames, from an informal peer-to-peer frame into talk-show advertisement frame, through their use of different language varieties. In lines 1–2, Angelo speaks in an informal Indonesian with Javanese suffixation (*acara* is associated with Indonesian, the *-(n)e* possessive suffix is associated with Javanese). In line 4, Angelo switches registers—and with it, body language, by facing the camera and sitting more upright—into a highly formal 'television Indonesian' involving more clear elocution, a higher pitch in voice intonation, and words associated with formal Indonesian, lacking any Javanese affixation. When Angelo pauses to try to figure out what "influence of women" he'll talk about, Nisa immediately cuts in to challenge his entire frame change. She does this by using a Javanese word, *opo* (what), with simultaneous increased volume, deepened pitch, and a lengthened final vowel, to signal that this 'what' is not just a question, but a challenge to the game Angelo has taken up. The group collectively laugh—beginning an interdiscursive string of laughter that both encourages Angelo's performances and also makes this a ratified group activity—at the playful frame negotiation that is taking place. Then Satriya takes up Angelo's performance in a moment of meta-pragmatically describing what should be the next step in the talk show frame (line 12): He should be asked an interview question. This is also a commentary on the talk show frame as Satriya speaks informally, too (instead of in a TV talk show register), here with the first person singular pronoun *gue*, associated with Jakarta urban youth culture and generally classified as a word in informal Indonesian, and *dong*, an emphatic particle also associated with youth and informality. Nisa further challenges the frame in line 13, again in informal Javanese. This challenge, combined with group laughter at the absurd frame that has been introduced into the situation, end the general play frame and act as a segue into the beginning of the formal interview wherein I take on 'researcher' role and the students take on 'informant' role.

Angelo's talk show host persona was not taken up again in Interview 1—this first instance above might be seen as a "testing of the waters" for how acceptable play is within the interview setting. But in the second interview, he opened the recording again with a performance, for us and the camera, as if he were hosting a talk show sponsored by Nü Green Tea, a product which he happened to be carrying with him.

The bottle of tea had become a small topic of conversation between himself and Nisa just as I was setting the camera to record. As I moved back toward the group, Angelo turned to the camera and acted as if he were advertising the tea product. This, subsequent to his performance in the Interview 1, would serve interdiscursively to begin to develop a sequence of acts in which Angelo began to take on a persona as talk show host (Agha 2005, 2007; Bauman 2005; Wortham 2005) and also to insert us into a frame of 'absurdity' each time he transitioned to this frame. Eventually by the end of Interview 2, and through much polyphonic play and dissent within the group, this series of acts would culminate in Angelo's self-labelling as "brand ambassador" just prior to Excerpt 5 below (I have excluded its original utterance for space considerations. It is echoed by Nisa, though, in Excerpt 5, line 18). This would later feed into his and the group's interdiscursive reliance in Interview 3 on his performances in Interview 2 in order to position Angelo as a relative expert in advertisement and marketing, when I asked the group to engage in a task of creating advertisements for various products.

We now turn to Angelo's first performance in Interview 2. As I sat down with the group after setting the camera to record, Angelo started us off by turning to the camera and engaging the 'viewer' in a sponsorship advertisement before the official 'show' (interview) was to begin. By engaging in this performance, he again evoked our collective shared knowledge of how an Indonesian TV host speaks or performs, and he also interdiscursively referred back to his initial performance in Interview 1 (Excerpt 2 above). The performance was met with laughter from Nisa and me and a commentary by Nisa on his behavior, referencing Angelo's previous performance in stating that he was not yet over his obsession with being a TV presenter:

(3)
Angelo
1   okay pemirsa, xx episode hari ini   okay viewers, xx today's episode is
2   disponsori oleh nu green tea.   sponsored by nu green tea.
Nisa and Lauren
3   @@@   @@@
Satriya
4   nu green ↑tea, =   nu green ↑tea, =
Angelo
5   = nu green ↑tea, =   = nu green ↑tea, =
Satriya
6   = satu xx,   = one xx,
7   [↓xx   [↓xx
Angelo
8   [enak dan sehat.   [good and healthy.
Lauren
13 @@   @@
Nisa
14 @@@((covering mouth)) obsesi presenter   @@@ ((covering mouth)) his presenter
15 nggak kesampaian.   obsession isn't finished.
                                              (Interview 2, 12/18/2009, 00:11)

Again, in this excerpt we see Angelo's assumption of a formal television Indonesian, and this is again accompanied by a change in posture and a raise in the pitch of his voice. We also see here that Satriya joins in with the same register, repeating "nu green tea" after Angelo says it and then attempting to help advertise it. Again Nisa plays a monitor role by trying to bring the performance to an end, using Indonesian but here with an informal *nggak* as well as the informal prefix *ke-* and suffix *-an*. With these linguistic behaviors in combination with the interdiscursive role performances described in Excerpt 2, we see the group start to develop a set of roles: Angelo leads in the development of a frame of 'talk show advertisement', and Satriya takes this play up (perhaps acts as an accomplice) and joins in, lending to the development of a joint fantasizing that is fast becoming absurd.

The females of the group, however, contest this play. Nisa essentially polices Angelo's behavior by playfully chastising him (lines 14–15), using Indonesian in order to direct her comment toward me/the group, but to have Angelo as a *ratified overhearer* (Goffman 1979) so that he will get the message. Novita often avoids participation when the talk show frame is begun: she sometimes rolls her eyes, sometimes looks at her phone, and sometimes playfully slaps Angelo to tell him to stop playing around. These behaviors all essentially demonstrate that she will not be a part of such digressions from the "real" task at hand. These roles can also be seen to align with gender: the females are trying to stay "on task", while the males are toying with the main frame of our activity.

Twenty-five seconds after Excerpt 3, a brief teasing bout between Angelo and Satriya ends with Angelo saying, "At least I wasn't left behind by my girlfriend," relying on his knowledge that Satriya's girlfriend had returned home to another island for the break between semesters. The conversation then turns to Satriya's girlfriend's origin. Nisa and Novita comment on its distance from Central Java and then I provokingly state, "Why don't you just go visit her?" This suggestion is met with shocked surprise, demonstrated by laughter (this is also building an interdiscursive link across these absurd moments, seen in the previous two excerpts, here beginning to crescendo, and by Excerpt 5 reaching a climax) and jaw-dropping, and an explanation that such a visit would violate the respect due to her parents.

Such a comment seems to evoke a level of absurdity that then begins to build. I next elevate the absurdity of this imagined scenario by stating (line 1 below), "So just stay at a hotel!" My statement is met with further shock, performed with laughter and a high pitched scream by Nisa. Immediately following this, Angelo interrupts the conversation, turns to the 'viewers at home' and waves his hands in front of the group (lines 15–18): "Viewers, this is getting scandalous. I warn you this is just getting more and more scandalous. Stay with us on the talk show...Stay with us on the talk show with Nü Green Tea." This provokes more laughter from Nisa and me (lines 19 & 21) and arguably further increases the level of absurdity at play while also serving to stop the conversational digression. This break allows Novita to insert, "That's enough, that's enough," (line 23) and Nisa to follow up with "What are we talking about?" (line 25) which returns the floor to me and leads to my switching for the first time in the interview into a frame of asking formal research interview questions.

(4)
Lauren
1   tinggal dihotel aja   just stay at a hotel
Satriya
2   eh?   eh?
Angelo
3   [tinggal di hotel]   [stay at a hotel]
Lauren
4   [tinggal di hotel] aja   [just stay at a hotel]
Satriya
5   [@@@   [@@@
Nisa
6   [AAAH   [AAAH

All
7   ((overlapping talk, Novita quiet checking
8   phone))
Satriya
9   [((raises hands palm up at chest level))
10 apa?]
Lauren
11 [@@@ no not with her] not with her
Nisa
12 [okay @@ ((grabs own head with both
13 hands and wiggles it side to side))
Lauren
14 ((gesturing away from body)) xxx
Angelo
15 (waving hands, leaning forward toward and
16 looking at camera) pemirsa xxxxx semakin
17 seru interview hari ini. saya perhatikan
18 semakin seru aja, tetap di talk show.
Nisa and Lauren
19 @@@
Angelo
20 tetap di talk show bersama nu green tea
Lauren
21 @@@
Satriya
22 ((points winks at camera twice))
Novita
23 ((putting phone away)) sudah, sudah.
Nisa
24 ((shrugging shoulders, hands facing up at
25 face level)) what are we talking about?
Lauren
26 okay. anyway. uh first I want to ask...

((overlapping talk, Novita quiet checking phone))

[((raises hands palm up at chest level)) what?]

[@@@ no not with her] not with her

[okay @@ ((grabs own head with both hands and wiggles it side to side))

((gesturing away from body)) xxx

((waving hands, leaning forward toward and looking at camera)) viewers xxxxx more and more scandalous today's interview. I warn you this is getting more and more scandalous, stay with us on the talk show.

@@@

stay with us on the talk show with nu green tea

@@@

((points winks at camera twice))

((putting phone away)) enough, enough.

((shrugging shoulders, hands facing up at face level)) what are we talking about?

okay. anyway. uh first I want to ask...
(Interview 2, 18 December 2009, 01:28)

Here, control of the conversational frame is dominated again by the same two players: Angelo interrupts an already absurd conversation and elevates (or at least redirects) the absurdity by initiating talk show frame (line 16) with its concomitant features (formal TV Indonesian, raised pitch, upright posture, looking at camera). Again Nisa aligns herself with me in laughter and then contests his frame manipulation and tries to bring us back on task, here using English (which also indicates alignment with me, line 23). Whereas previously in Excerpt 2 she used Javanese to make a commentary to the other research participants on their behavior (*kowe ki kok*), and in Excerpt 3 she used informal Javanese-Indonesian to make a comment on Angelo's behavior (*obsesi presenter nggak kesampaian*); in this instance, she used English in a move that was less a commentary on others' behavior (though she did make this commentary through gesture in line 24) and more a directive to bring us down from absurdity and put us back on task—back into research interview frame—and return control of the conversation to Lauren, the researcher.

Such digressions happen four more times over the next 35 minutes, until peaking at one final break of the interview frame, which draws the group into high hilarity. As a serious conversation is taking place about outlying/peripheralized islands and their economic and human rights situations as members of the Indonesian nation, Angelo manages to insert his advertisement into the conversation one last time. Nisa expresses exasperation (line 9: "AH") that Angelo keeps sneaking this in to the conversation, but then she joins in the play by saying that no other brands besides Nü Green Tea should be advertised. But then Angelo uses a laughter break to reach into his bookbag, pull out a bottle of water, and then chime back in (line 24), "Don't worry, beyond Nü Green Tea I also have Aqua," again outdoing or outwitting both his interlocutors and his previous performances.

This leads to an eruption of laughter at the absurdity of the situation and the unexpected prop that Angelo has pulled out of his bag. The whole group laughs loudly, and as the laughter wanes I initiate applause at his very well-timed, culminating comic performance. As a denouement Satriya, who has not participated much in this sequence, adds "I also have a product here" (line 53). This receives laughter, and he moves on to just pull out the next random thing in his bookbag (lines 51–52), which essentially serves to indicate the level of absurdity that the group has achieved. Upon this Nisa attempts again to rein the interview back in and return control to me, requesting the closing of this frame and a return to interview frame, starting in Javanese (line 60 *wis wis*)—here she was most likely directing her speech just at her peers—and then transitioning to Indonesian to expand her group of message recipients to me (line 60 *cukup cukup*...): "...enough enough. This is becoming all advertisements. Let's move on."

(5)
Satriya
1   [ey:@@ those people who rule this   [ey:@@ those people who rule this country=
2   country=
Nisa
3   =↓yu: =
                                                   ↓yu:
Satriya
4   violate their rights, as the citizens.   violate their rights, as the citizens.
Novita
5   °yea. jadi bagaimana kiat kita untuk°   °yea. so what can we do to° ((looking at
6   ((looking at Nisa)) @@@   Nisa)) @@@

Nisa
7   ((shaking head))   ((shaking head))
Satriya
8   xxxx   xxxx
Satriya, Novita and Nisa
9   @@@   @@@
Angelo
10 sebagai bentuk kepedulian, nu [green tea   for your information, nu [green tea donates
11 menyumbangkan
Nisa
12   ((frowns))[AH@@@   ((frowns))[AH@@@
Satriya
13   [@@@   [@@@
Lauren
14   [@@@   [@@@
Angelo
15 @@ ((showing open palm to indicate five))   @@ ((showing open palm to indicate five))
16 [lima ratus rupiah xxxx   [five hundred rupiah xxxx
Nisa
17 ((higher pitch))   ((higher pitch))
18 [AH@@@ (.) brand ambassador @@   [AH@@@ (.) brand ambassador @@
Angelo
20   [bagi, daerah-daerah   [to, isolated regions who
21 terpencil yang membutuhkan ↑sumber   need ↑water↓resources.
22 ↓daya air.
Nisa
23 @@ satu liter @ untuk sepuluh.   @@ one liter @ for ten.
Novita
24 [nggak sepuluh. [satu liter untuk [sepuluh   [not ten. [one liter for [ten (?)water.
25 (?)air.
Angelo
26 [itu,   [itu jadi,   [jadi: [that,   [that makes, [makes: not nu green
27 bukan nu green tea itu jadi ce↑thit.   tea that makes ce↑thit.
Nisa
28 ce↑thit@@. ((side glance to camera))   ce↑thit@@. ((side glance to camera)) °don't
29 °jangan sebut merek lain, ya?°   mention other brands, ya?°
Lauren
30 @   @
Novita
31 @@   @@
Angelo
32 tapi gapa-apa, ((reaching into bag)) selain   but no worries, ((reaching into bag)) beyond
33 nu green tea, saya juga punya aqua [yang   nu green tea, I also have aqua [that xxxx
34 xxxx
All
35   [@@@   [@@@
36 ((uproarious))   ((uproarious))

Angelo
37 yang xxx satu- satu a- sepuluh liter [air   that xxx one- one a- ten liters [of clean
38 bersih   water
Lauren
39   [@@ =   [@@ =
Angelo
40   =   = for
41 untuk satu liter aqua yang anda beli.   one liter of aqua that you buy.
Satriya
42 xx [xx   xx [xx
Angelo
43   [aqua, satu untuk kita, [xxx   [aqua, one for us, [xxx
Nisa
44   [ke°saks [a   [°no [fair°
45 wae°
Angelo
46   [untuk   [for
47 semuanya.   everyone.
Satriya
48 xxxx   xxxx
Angelo
49 satu dari kita untuk semuanya.   one from us for everyone.
Nisa
50 kesaksa ((L starts clapping hands and rest   no fair ((L starts clapping hands and rest
51 join)) @@@ (.) ((Sat reaches into bag and   join)) @@@ (.) ((Sat reaches into bag and
52 pulls out small phone))   pulls out small phone))
Satriya
53 saya juga punya produk ini @@   I also have a product here @@
Nisa
54 [((covering up Sat's product with hands)) o   [((covering up Sat's product with hands)) o
55 jangan jangan @@@@@   don't don't @@@@@
Angelo
56 [@@@   [@@@
Satriya
57 @@@ sa- affordable for you ah: juga, ada   @@@ sa- affordable for you ah: also, I have
58 flas disk juga   a flash disk too
Nisa
59 ((Nisa pushes Sat's hand back into his   ((Nisa pushes Sat's hand back into his bag))
60 bag)) oalah wis wis cukup cukup. jadi iklan   oalah enough enough enough enough.
61 semua. ((turns to L and waves hands   everything is becoming a commercial.((turns
62 toward self, inviting L)) lanjut, lanjut.   to L and waves hands toward self, inviting
                                                                L)) continue, continue.
Lauren
63 ((shaking shoulders)) @@@ lanjut? apa.   ((shaking shoulders)) @@@ lanjut? apa. so,
64 so, okay. ini. kalau orang biasanya bilang...   okay. this. if people usually say...
                                                                (Interview 2, 18 December 2009, 37:20)

Two more brief instances of Angelo's talk show host occur before the interview ends for the evening, and by our third interview together, Angelo had developed a reputation for himself as the "brand ambassador" and marketing executive of the group. At the beginning of the third interview, I asked the group to create pretend advertisements for various types of products (inspired by Meadows 2009). Angelo immediately jumped on this to say "oh easy" (Excerpt 6 below, line 3). Nisa followed along, though somewhat jokingly (with an eye roll) as she stated "that's already Angelo's specialty" (line 5), and Satriya did similarly by referring to Angelo's previous performances to build on this one: "last time Fresh Tea, now Tong Tji" (line 8). This collective work, and the fact that right after this the group did let Angelo take the lead on dreaming up advertisements—not as a TV talk show host but as himself—only helped him continue to build and expand interdiscursively on his previous performances. Only now, he was able to transition the character away from the talk show figure of personhood, and to transform it into an aspect of his "real" self: He, Angelo, was the group's marketing expert, and the group did not contest this. The following excerpt introduces his transition from talk show host persona to "Angelo the marketing expert", when I introduce the task. Angelo subsequently dominates the group's creation of an advertisement for a body wash (not shown below), and for the rest of their ad-making exercises.

(6)

Lauren
1   today I'm going to ask you to create a tv
2   advertisement.

today I'm going to ask you to create a tv advertisement.

Angelo
3   o gampang. ((Nov smiles, turns left to play
4   slap Ang on the forearm))

o easy. ((Nov smiles, turns left to play slap Ang on the forearm)).

Lauren
4   @@

@@

Nisa
5   o lha Angelo sudah ((rolls eyes)) ahlinya

o gosh Angelo this is already ((rolls eyes)) his specialty.

Lauren
6   iya, sudah kemarin sudah dibuat di
7   interview.

yeah, he already last time did this in the interview.

Satriya
8   kemarin fresh tea, sekarang tong tji.[3]

last time fresh tea, now tong tji.

(Interview 3, 7 July 2010, 00:42)

---

[3] Tong Tji is another brand of prepared tea.

Finally, Angelo had to call in sick for the final interview, and our consequent lack of advertisement expertise for the day did not go unnoticed:

(7)
Novita
1	Friday, nanti Friday dikumpulin.	Friday, on Friday it will be collected.
2	((Nov+Nis speak together at low volume))	((Nov+Nis speak together at low volume))
3	((Sat gives peace sign to camera))	((Sat gives peace sign to camera))

Lauren
3	since Angelo is not here to do an iklan then	since Angelo is not here to do an advertisement then xx @@
4	xx @@	

All
5	@@@	@@@

(Interview 4, 24 May 2010, 00:22)

3 Conclusion

In the above sequences, much of the group's humour was contestive—Angelo broke the frame of interaction and shifted the discourse in another direction, Novita often gave him a playful slap on the arm to tell him to stop, and Nisa generally tried to bring the group back to a research frame. These "absurd" frames often consisted of much "outdoing" or "outwitting"—sometimes of the others, and sometimes of Angelo's own prior performance. There were also, though, collaborative moments: Satriya especially was a willing accomplice, and Nisa willingly laughed along before trying to bring the group back into interview frame. The group's laughter as a whole crescendoed across sequences into a pinnacle moment of hilarity (Excerpt 5). Intertextually across interactions and interviews, Angelo's performances and the group's laughter over them, contestation of them, and even co-construction of his produced fantasy generated a shared experience, a shared conversational frame, and a shared set of references and interdiscursively constructed identities that turned us into an in-group based on exclusive shared experiences over time. This aligns with the suggestions of Coates (2007) and Jefferson et al. (1978) in Section 1.2 that laughter and intimacy are tightly interlinked.

Regarding language use, the group members facilely navigated language forms and the indices associated with them in constructing our conversational frames and our in-group identity characteristics. In transitional frames—as the interviews began or ended, and in any asides they made to each other—participants were most likely to mix a variety of features associated with Javanese and Indonesian, and occasionally English (see Excerpt 7 line 1, *nanti* Friday *dikumpulin*), in order to communicate quickly and comfortably with each other. In 'research-interview' frame, the group spoke in either formal Indonesian (with many Javanese features mixed in) or formal English (often mixed with Indonesian) in order to convey their points clearly to me, a nonspeaker of Javanese and a learner of Indonesian. And in talk show frame, the language choice was a 'pure' formal, television appropriate Indonesian, associated not only with the linguistic features of such TV Indonesian, but also with more formal postures, higher pitched voices and looking straight into the camera to indicate that the speaker (namely Angelo) was communicating with a television public.

To relate this all to ethnography and rapport: The ethnographer's relationship with her research participants usually charts unfamiliar terrain because it violates the delineations of most relationship paradigms for which people hold cognitive-frame schemata. In the interactions above, the group's collective experience accumulated over these four interviews, based on our previous interactions with each other, our shared linguistic resources, and our shared cultural knowledge, through humour and joint fantasizing as the group built on the relationships that we already had with each other and toyed with novel and uncertain interactional frames. In doing so, we created a set of shared experiences over the course of a year in which we enregistered emergent behaviors and personae to which we five together could interdiscursively refer. Such a tightly woven set of shared experiences and identifiable personae signalled a level of intimacy and rapport, delineated by a specific set of co-constructed lived experiences that we exclusively shared together.

Appendix A. Transcription Conventions

For the detailed data transcriptions, I have relied primarily on the conventions provided in Jefferson (2004). I paraphrase Jefferson's conventions here, providing examples of the symbols as I have used them in data presentations in this text.

= latching speech	no pause between the end of one speaker's statement and the beginning of the other's speech	
	78 Lauren: be<u>tul</u> ya =	
	79 Satriya: = °ya°	
[overlapping speech]	speakers talk at the same time	
	7 like personality atau, [kebanggaan:]	
	8 Satriya: [I feel like] oh- no.	
((nonverbal information))	description of non-speech actions that are meaningful to interaction	

↑↓	remarkable shift in pitch
	40 Novita: ((looking up at ceiling with a big grin on her face))
	6 Nisa: karena: mungkin kita bisa menggunakan bahasa: indo↑nesia:, to replace °apa ya (.) bahasa kromo°
CAPS	spoken louder than surrounding speech
	43 = [um]
	44 Nisa: [HOW][CAN YOU SPEAK]
	45 Satriya: [>just because]
question mark?	phrase-final rising intonation
	1 Lauren: dan apakah kamu merasa seperti,(.) apa (.) berubah kalua pakai bahasa inggris?
period.	phrase final falling intonation
	28 I don't know.
comma,	non-sentence final falling intonation
	64 un- I can understand more English than Indonesia, sometimes I feel guilty because,
°degree signs°	the phrase at hand is produced more quietly than surrounding speech
	9 to replace °apa ya (.) bahasa kromo°
xx	unintelligible speech
	35 Sat: xxxx
	36 Ang: one from us for everyone.
@@	laughter pulse
	27 terlalu cewek. I don't know.
	29 Lauren: @@@
-	word is cut off
	53 I myself admit that I: I have l- I have °<lost my love>°,
:	lengthened sound
	58 Lauren: o:kay
underline	underlined syllable(s) are emphasized
	24 *slowing down and up

References

Agha, Asif. 2005. Voice, footing, enregisterment. *Journal of Linguistic Anthropology* 15(1). 38–59.

Agha, Asif. 2007. *Language and social relations*. New York: Cambridge University Press.

Bakhtin, Mikhail M. 1981. Discourse in the novel. In Michael Holquist (ed.), *The dialogic imagination*, 259–422. Austin, TX: University of Texas Press.
Bateson, Gregory. 1972. *Steps to an ecology of mind*. London: Paladin.
Bauman, Richard. 2005. Commentary: indirect indexicality, identity, performance: Dialogic observations. *Journal of Linguistic Anthropology* 15(1). 145–150.
Blommaert, Jan. 2005. *Discourse: A critical introduction*. New York: Cambridge University Press.
Blommaert, Jan. 2010. *The sociolinguistics of globalization*. New York: Cambridge University Press.
Blommaert, J., N. Muyllaert, M. Huysmans & C. Dyers. 2005. Literacy and the production of locality in a South African township school. *Linguistics and Education* 16. 378–403.
Coates, Jennifer. 2007. Talk in a play frame: More on laughter and intimacy. *Journal of Pragmatics* 39. 29–49.
Dynel, Marta. 2008. No aggression, only teasing: The pragmatics of teasing and banter. *Lodz Papers in Pragmatics* 4(2). 241–261.
García, Ofelia. 2010. Education, multilingualism and translanguaging in the 21st century. In Tove Skutnabb-Kangas, Robert Phillipson, Ajit K. Mohanty & Minati Panda (eds.), *Social justice through multilingual education*, 140–158. Tonawanda, NY: Multilingual Matters.
Geertz, Clifford. 2000 [1973]. Thick description: Toward an interpretive theory of culture. In Clifford Geertz (ed.), *The Interpretation of cultures*, 3–30. New York: Basic Books.
Goebel, Z. 2005. An ethnographic study of code choice in two neighborhoods in Indonesia. *Australian Journal of Linguistics* 25(1), 85–107.
Goebel, Z. 2010. *Language, migration, and identity: Neighborhood talk in Indonesia*. New York: Cambridge University Press.
Goebel, Z. 2015. *Language and superdiversity: Indonesians knowledging at home and abroad*. New York: Oxford University Press.
Goffman, Erving. 1974. *Frame analysis. An essay on the organization of experience*. New York: Harper and Row.
Goffman, Erving. 1979. Footing. *Semiotica* 25(1–2). 1–29.
Goodwin, Marjorie H. & Samy Alim. 2010. "Whatever (neck roll, eye roll, teeth suck)": The situated coproduction of social categories and identities through stancetaking and transmodal stylization. *Journal of Linguistic Anthropology* 20(1). 179–194.
Hay, Jennifer. 1995. Only teasing. *New Zealand English Newsletter* 9. 32–35.
Hume, Lynne & Jane Mulcock. 2004. Introduction: Awkward spaces, productive places. In Lynne Hume & Jane Mulcock (eds.), *Anthropologists in the field: Cases in participant observation*, xi–xxvii. New York: Columbia University Press.
Jefferson, Gail, Harvey Sacks & Emanual Schegloff. 1978. Notes on laughter in the pursuit of intimacy. In Graham Button & John R. E. Lee (eds.), *Talk and social organisation*, 152–205. Clevedon: Multilingual Matters.
Jefferson, Gayle. 2004. Glossary of transcript symbols with an introduction. In Gene H. Lerner (ed.), *Conversation analysis: Studies from the first generation*, 13–34. Philadelphia, PA: John Benjamins.
Jørgenson, J. Normann. 2008. *Languaging: Nine years of poly-lingual development of young Turkish-Danish grade school students*. Vol. 1. Copenhagen: University of Copenhagen Faculty of Humanities.
Kotthoff, Helga. 2007. Oral genres of humor: On the dialectic of genre knowledge and creative authoring. *Pragmatics* 17(2). 263–296.

Marcus, George E. 1998. *Ethnography through thick and thin*. Princeton, NJ: Princeton University Press.
Meadows, Bryan. 2009. Capital negotiation and identity practices: Investigating symbolic capital from the 'ground up'. *Critical Discourse Studies* 6(1). 15–30.
Montell, Frances. 1999. Focus group interviews: A new feminist method. *NWSA Journal* 11(1). 44–71.
Pennycook, Alastair. 2007. The myth of English as an international language. In Sinfree Makoni & Alastair Pennycook (eds.), *Disinventing and reconstituting languages*, 90–115. Clevedon: Multilingual Matters.
Wortham, Stanton. 2005. Socialization beyond the speech event. *Journal of Linguistic Anthropology* 15(1). 95–112.
Zentz, L. 2017. *Statehood, scale and hierarchy: History, language and identity in Indonesia*. Bristol, UK: Multilingual Matters.

Zane Goebel
4 Understanding Rapport Through Scalar Reflexivity

1 Introduction

Drawing on a long tradition of work on reflexivity in anthropology, especially as it relates to rapport, and an equally long tradition of work on semiotics, scale and narrative, this paper looks at the scalar nature of the reflexive processes that I went through as I sought to understand an interview. After bringing together work on reflexivity, rapport, scale, semiosis, and narrative, I describe how my interpretation of this interview with a civil servant from a government office in Indonesia required me to regularly jump scale (both in terms of timespace and participation framework) between interview data and two other data sets that provided insights into chronotopic configurations found within bureaucratic and ethnic register formations. I will refer to this type of reflexivity as "scalar reflexivity". I point out that this type of reflexivity is useful for understanding how instance of represented speech in an interview can be related to the concept of rapport.

2 Reflexivity, Rapport, and Language

Anthropologists have a long history of being reflexive about the nature of rapport and on writing about the development, maintenance, and dissolution of anthropologist–consultant relationships (e. g. Berreman 1972; Clifford 1988; Crapanzano 2012 [2010]; Geertz 1968, 1973; Hume and Mulcock 2004; Marcus 1998, 2015; Powdermaker 1967; Rabinow 1977; Rosaldo 1989; Wagley 1960). In many ways this reflexivity aligns with Goffman's (1969 [1959]) earlier insights about the presentation of self, where rapport is the outcome of communicative practices of impression management. While being able to imitate communicative practices relating to impression management require anthropologists to do things such as imitate local languages, dress and act like one's subjects, engage in deep hanging out, and so on, with the exception of Moerman's (1988) work we typi-

---

Acknowledgement: I thanks all the members of the symposium for their invaluable comments, which have helped me sharpen my ideas. I was able to analyze much of the data presented here because of a generous grant from the Australian Research Council (DP130102121).

Zane Goebel, University of Queensland, Brisbane, Australia

https://doi.org/10.1515/9781501507830-004

cally only have reports of language use rather than any nuanced analysis of the relationship of language use to rapport. More recent invitations to focus upon the relationship of language to rapport seem to have received no uptake (Borneman and Hammoudi 2009; Robben 2012 [1995]). This lack of attention continues in contemporary work where rapport-building in complex multilingual settings is seen as important, but no analysis of language use are presented (e. g. Hoffman and Tarawalley 2014; Middleton and Cons 2014). In this section I point out how attention to situated interaction and its relationships with other semiotic phenomena—that is, Silverstein's (1985: 220) "total linguistic fact"—can provide insights into the construction of one dimension of rapport, trust.

As part of a larger intellectual effort to study language in social life, linguistic anthropologists and sociolinguists have pointed out that all language use is inherently reflexive: always requiring us to look backwards to understand situated instances of language use (e. g. Agha 2007a; Jaworski, Coupland, and Galasiński 2004; Lucy 1993). One stream of this work studies enregisterment and language ideology formation (e. g. Goebel 2015; Inoue 2006; Miller 2004; Urban 2001; Wortham 2006). Agha (2007a) points out that these process require several elements. They require use of particular types of deictics, especially those that remove the deictic anchoring of interaction in a way that reconfigures particular characteristics of situated personhood to a more general model of personhood. This process also requires constant imitation—i. e. not replication as precise copy (Lempert 2014)—of these models and associated ways of speaking and being, large one-to-many participation frameworks that provide the infrastructures for imitation (e. g. school classrooms, mass media), and valorisation of these infrastructures and imitations by powerful authoritative figures (e. g. celebrities, presidents, bosses, government institutions, media organizations, etc.).

Another stream of work that focuses on interviews and the narratives found within them highlights the reflexive nature of situated language use (e. g. Briggs 1986; De Fina and Perrino 2011; Koven 2014; Rampton 1995). For example, we know that interviews afford interviewees opportunities to position themselves as certain types of people to achieve certain goals, such as convincing a researcher about their prowess in a certain activity or their moral sensibilities in relation to other events or discourses (De Fina 2003; Modan and Shuman 2011; Wortham, Mortimer, Lee, Allard, and White 2011). This positioning work can be done through a performance of the event that is reported in ways similar to conversational story-telling (e. g. De Fina and Perrino 2011; Ochs and Capps 2001).

These types of performances are often referred to as reported talk, constructed dialogue, or represented talk/speech (e. g. Agha 2007a; Clift and Holt 2007; Tannen 1989). This type of talk creates cross-chronotope alignments (e. g. Agha 2007b; Perrino 2011; Silverstein 2005). Cross-chronotope alignment is the situation where the then-and-there of the story in comparison to the here-and-now of the ongoing story-telling event is temporarily brought into the same timespace. Bringing about such alignments through the use of represented speech can also create a sense of authenticity to the story by turning those in the storytelling event into bystanders in the narrated event. In this case, cross-chronotope alignment adds what I refer to as *believability* to a story by making the audience a type of witness to the event being narrated.

In line with Silverstein's (1985: 220) notion of the "total linguistic fact", others have emphasised the importance of reflexively for exploring the connections between these interactions and the semiotic configurations that have emerged from processes of enregisterment in different timespaces (e. g. Errington 1998; Rampton 2006; Wortham 2006), or what Blommaert and colleagues refer to as different *scales* (Blommaert 2015; Blommaert, Westinen, and Leppänen 2015). This type of reflexivity requires us to demonstrate the indexical potentials created by processes of enregisterment at different scales and their relationship to the imitation of fragments from these registers in situated interaction. In short, to interpret such interactions we need to regularly jump scale. I refer to this reflexive process as *scalar reflexivity*. Scalar reflexivity enables us to move towards a picture of the total linguistic fact as it relates to understanding rapport.

3 Changing Chronotopes of Bureaucratic Personhood

As I returned to my fieldwork data in 2013, one thing that struck me was *Pak*[1] Ismail's (my main consultant) proclivity to engage in self-praise about his abilities as a bureaucrat in my first interview with him. My prior years of fieldwork in Semarang neighborhoods suggested that self-praise was typically inappropriate (Goebel 2010). This "strangeness" piqued my interest in bureaucratic chronotopes that circulated during the period of my fieldwork. In turn, this engendered an instance of scalar reflexivity that involved reading local archived online Indonesian newspapers from the period of my fieldwork (July 2003–February 2004). As I read through front page stories from this period, what was striking was the regular and

---

[1] Pak is a kin term use to index both respect and familial relationships. I use it here to indicate my relationship with Ismail.

negative reportage about bureaucrats. This reportage contrasted with media coverage from the mid to late 1990s that only positively represented bureaucrats and their role in nation building. This idea of bad bureaucrats and poor governance thus engendered a further scalar jump, this time back to the mid- to late-1990s, although here I will only touch on this period before taking a more detailed look at some of newspaper stories from the 2003–2004 period.

Prior to 1998, Indonesian civil servants were part of the political machine and typically positively represented in news programs as well-respected and helpful nation-builders. This model of bureaucratic personhood began to be reconfigured with the collapse of President Suharto's authoritarian regime in May 1998. A confluence of factors helped to create a more deviant model of personhood that we regularly see and hear about today. These factors included: a severe economic downturn that occurred after the Asian financial crisis of 1997 onwards (Forrester 1999; Thee Kian Wie 2001); sustained pressure from the IMF and World bank since the mid-1990s to reform the bureaucracy (Camdessus 1998; Poverty reduction and economic management unit 2003; World Bank private sector development unit East Asia and Pacific region 2001); uptake of these "discourses of good governance" by Indonesian leaders, senior bureaucrats, and within government departments within the Indonesian government (Assegaf 2002; Habibie 1999; Kementerian Pendayagunaan Aparatur Negara 2002, 2003, 2004; Lindsey 2002; Rohdewohld 2003); deregulation of the media, which included the relaxation of previously heavy-handed censorship laws that stopped any form of criticism of the government and its bureaucracy (Kitley 2000; Sen and Hill 2000); and big-bang democratization and decentralization (Aspinall and Fealy 2003; McLeod and MacIntyre 2007).

During the election campaign for local parliamentary seats that started in 2003, issues of "good governance" also became very prominent in the local and national newspaper media. To get some sense of just how often these ideas were imitated in the local public sphere during the period of my fieldwork, we can look at the online front page stories of the Semarang based newspaper, *Suara Merdeka* "Voice of Freedom". With the help of an Indonesian research assistant, we browsed the front pages of over a thousand online stories from *Suara Merdeka* in 2013 and downloaded those that negatively reported about civil servants and the civil service. Chart 1 gives a quantitative view of these stories relative to other stories. Many of these stories imitated the themes about bureaucratic personhood found in World Bank and International Monetary Fund documents (e. g. Poverty reduction and economic management unit 2003), as well as within mountains of administrative policies and memos within the Indonesian government (Assegaf 2002; Habibie 1999; Kementerian Pendayagunaan Aparatur Negara 2002, 2003, 2004; Lindsey 2002; Rohdewohld 2003).

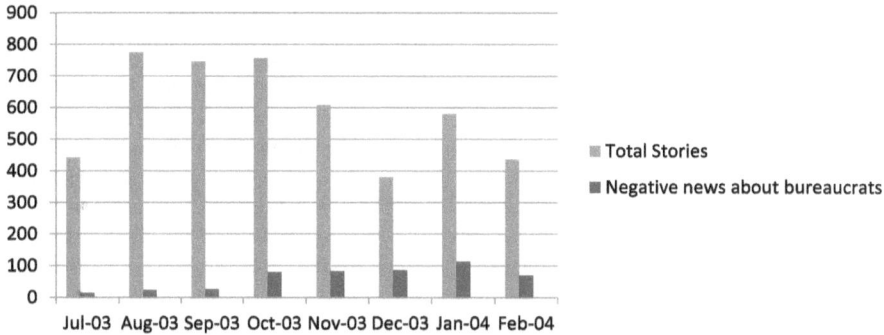

Chart 1: Online newspaper representations of bureaucratic personhood.

In a recent paper (Goebel 2017), I examined around one hundred of these stories and pointed out that they formed and circulated multiple chronotopes of Indonesian civil servants. These chronotopes were inhabited by civil servants whose activities and moral dispositions included the following: nepotism; (lack of) responsible behavior toward a public; lack of efficiency; being absent without leave; being too proud, arrogant, or conceited; not serving the people; engaging in collusive practices; participating in endeavors that waste money; being involved in political activities; and (not) helping to improve public prosperity. The construction of these categories was aided by constant imitation of prior characteristics, the adding of new characteristics, the quotation or reporting of speech by authoritative figures, and the use of certain deictics that helped to generalize these characteristics to all civil servants.

In reading these stories, what was striking was how much of the content seemed to also be part of the content of my first interview with *Pak* Ismail. I've selected just two of these stories, those that relate to evaluation (ex. 1) and misuse of money (ex. 2), because these characteristics are invoked in the interview texts that I will look at shortly (ex. 3, 4, and 5). Excerpt 1 below is from a story that was published on 16 June 2003 in *Suara Merdeka*. Of note is how all bureaucrats' work is seen as needing to be evaluated (lines 9–13), although just exactly how this evaluation is to be carried out is not discussed.

(1)

1	Lebih dari 13.000 pegawai negeri sipil	More than thirteen thousand civil servants
2	(PNS) di lingkungan Pemerintah	(PNS) from within the regional government
3	Kabupaten (Pemkab) Karanganyar akan	(Pemkab) of Karanganyar will be tidied
4	ditertibkan...."Pengembangan sistem	up...."The development of a system of
5	dengan memberikan penghargaan dan	rewards and punishments for staff who do
6	hukuman bagi staf yang berprestasi dan	well and perform poorly or are regularly
7	bermasalah atau mangkir juga perlu untuk	absent without leave also need to increase
8	meningkatkan motifasi kerja," tandasnya.	their motivation to work", he said firmly.
9	"Kami akan membuat evaluasi terhadap	"We are going to evaluate the efficiency of
10	kinerja para pejabat dan staf masing unit	senior bureaucrats and their staff in their
11	kerja guna mengetahui seberapa jauh	respective departments so that we
12	tanggung jawab mereka dalam	understand how responsible they are in
13	melaksanakan tugasnya," tandas dia....	undertaking their duties", he firmly said.

(Source: G8-78 2003)

In another story published on 20 August 2003, an excerpt of which appears below (ex. 2), a number of the characteristics from prior stories were imitated. This story is an opinion piece written by an academic from the Faculty of Social Sciences and Politics at the prestigious government funded institution, Diponegoro University. Like excerpt 1, this text imitates multiple characteristics from past stories, including inappropriate use of time and money, as well as offering a new one, commitment to work (lines 3–4). What "commitment to work" means is only slightly fleshed out through the contrasting of the prioritization of money and appearance (*gengsi*) over working to do a good job (lines 11–14).

(2)

1	Saya melihat, dilema yang paling	I see the most basic dilemma is the
2	mendasar adalah perilaku disiplin dari	discipline of bureaucrats, especially in
3	aparat birokrasi, terutama disiplin	regards to time, money, and commitment.
4	terhadap waktu, anggaran, dan komitmen.	
5	Perilaku disiplin ini memang sulit	Discipline is indeed hard to maintain....
6	ditegakkan... Pengertian masyarakat	[Because] the people's understanding of
7	dalam konteks tertentu, termasuk juga	discipline in certain contexts, including
8	unsur birokrasinya. Artinya,	within the bureaucracy [is unclear]. What
9	kebutuhannya untuk berprestasi sangatlah	is understood is that the need for
10	rendah sehingga mereka lebih suka	achievement is very low while in contrast
11	berprinsip "gengsi lebih penting daripada	they have the principle "putting on airs
12	prestasi" atau "uang lebih berharga	and graces is more important than
13	daripada kerja". Dengan dorongan prestasi	achievement" or "money is more
14	yang rendah didukung pengendalian diri	important than work". A low push for
15	yang lemah, lahirlah perilaku birokrasi	achievement supports weak self-
16	yang tidak berdisiplin.	monitoring, giving birth to undisciplined bureaucrats.

(*Amirudin 2003*)

Engaging in this type of scalar reflexivity—that is, jumping scale from the interview to newspaper reportage helped me to interpret many of *Pak* Ismail's instances of self-praise. We might say that through engaging in self-praise *Pak* Ismail was engaging in scalar reflexivity himself by using emblems of bureaucratic personhood—in this case certain characteristics that were part of an emerging bureaucratic chronotope—to present a self that did not inhabit this chronotope. When we take a closer look at how *Pak* Ismail presented a bureaucratic self that was unlike those found in newspapers, what was also striking was how *Pak* Ismail performed these presentations of self. In many of these performances, *Pak* Ismail used represented speech, often signaled through the use of fragments of Javanese. This required me to engage in another instance of scalar reflexivity, this time in relation to ethnic chronotopes in Indonesia in general, and Javanese ones in particular.

4 Ethnic Chronotopes in Indonesia

Indonesia is well-known for having hundreds of ethnolinguistic groups who are typically associated with specific territories. While these ethnolinguistic chronotopes predate the Dutch colonial period, their imitation has been upscaled since colonial periods, especially since the heavy investment in infrastructures of imitation (e. g. schooling and mass media) that began in the late 1960s (e. g. Errington 1998; Goebel 2010, 2015; Sneddon 2003; Wolff and Poedjosoedarmo 1982). Here I move from this brutal summary of the enregisterment of ethnic registers in general to those specifically relating to Javanese. This more specific picture of Javanese registers, their associated chronotopic configurations, and the indexical potentials of the signs that constitute them provides insight into some of the semiotic resources required when engaging in scalar reflexivity, especially for interpreting *Pak* Ismail's use of fragments of Javanese for reporting talk.

One variety of Javanese associated with the royal courts of Solo and Yogyakarta has benefited greatly from the investment in infrastructures of imitation described above. The well-described Javanese "speech levels" (e. g. Geertz 1960; Wolff and Poedjosoedarmo 1982) or "speech styles" (Errington 1988) were imitated during the Suharto period in school textbooks, radio and television (Errington 1998, 2000; Goebel 2007, 2010; Kurniasih 2007). These imitations helped to enregister chronotopes of Javanese speakerhood, including chronotopes associated with vocabulary sets described as ngoko (N), madyá (M) and krámá Javanese (K), which were identifiable by the presence or absence of particular words and affixes, as in Table 1.

Table 1: Examples of words and affixes indexical of Javanese speech levels.

Krámá	Madyá	Ngoko	Gloss
meniko	niki	iki	this
	niku	kuwi	that
	niko	kaé	that over there
menopo	nopo	opo	what
wonten	enten	ono, neng	there is/are, in/at/on
badhé	ajeng	arep	will/wish/intend

Adapted from Wolff and Poedjosoedarmo (1982:30).

In addition to the main vocabulary sets, there are two others. These raise the status of one interlocutor in relation to another. The first, labelled *krámá inggil* (KI), literally 'high Javanese', consist of words and terms of address that honor or elevate the addressee and his or her actions (Wolff and Poedjosoedarmo 1982). The second set, called *krámá andhap* (KA), consists of words that humble the speaker and his or her actions. The ways in which these vocabulary sets can be exchanged is summarized in Diagram 1. Many later studies suggest that the symmetrical exchanges shown in a) and b) of Diagram 1 are just as common as the asymmetrical exchanges in c) (e. g. Bax 1974; Goebel 2010; Smith-Hefner 1983). What also seems common in these, and latter studies, is that Javanese forms can interactionally have multiple meanings because of their indexical relationships with other contexts. For example, symmetrical exchange of *ngoko* can not only presuppose a familiar equal relationship but one where labor, help, goods or even animosity are expected to be exchanged reciprocally (Berman 1998; Errington 1995, 1998; Goebel 2010).

---

a) Interlocutors familiar and of same status   **NGOKO** ⟷ **NGOKO**
b) Interlocutors unfamiliar and of same status **KRÁMÁ** ⟷ **KRÁMÁ**
c) ***NGOKO*** used by status superior (in terms of age, occupation, education,
   ↓ ↑   wealth, noble background)
  KRÁMÁ used by status inferior (often plus self-effacing **KRÁMÁ ANDHAP** forms and other-elevating **KRÁMÁ INGGIL** forms)

Diagram 1: Symmetrical and Asymmetrical Exchanges of Javanese.

Symmetrical exchange of *krámá* forms of type b) in Diagram 1 can index unfamiliarity between interlocutors, ceremonial speech, polite noble speak, or public addresses to a co-ethnic public (Bax 1974; Errington 1995, 1998; Goebel 2010;

Smith-Hefner 1983). Asymmetrical exchanges of the type found in c in Diagram 1 also presupposes unequal exchanges in other areas of social life, as well as expectations of patronage by those who give respect via *krámá* forms, but receive *ngoko* in return (Berman 1998; Dewey 1978; Errington 1998; Goebel 2014). The usage of vocabulary from different sets can thus potentially invoke these types of relationships, as well as the chronotopes associated with them. In short, use of certain vocabulary can also engender scalar reflexivity, both for the participants and the researcher. In the following section, I show how this works by paying close attention to two excerpts from an interview with *Pak* Ismail.

5 Scalar Reflexivity: From Interview to Javanese Bureaucratic Chronotopes and Back

The fragment represented as excerpt 3 below is extracted from the first interview that I recorded with *Pak* Ismail, the section head of a government department in Semarang where I had been conducting my fieldwork since early August 2003. I made this recording in early November 2003, just before three in the afternoon, and after I had been hanging around the office for about an hour listening to and observing conversational interactions. Two features of *Pak* Ismail's talk struck me as quite different from the interviews about language in the office that I had conducted with two other head of departments and most of *Pak* Ismail's staff in the months prior to this interview, and the use of these features also differed compared to subsequent interviews with *Pak* Ismail. These features included regular self-praise and over 50 instances of represented speech in this 40-minute interview. I typically conducted my interviews with *Pak* Ismail and others in his office in Indonesian (plain font), although I had some ability in Javanese (bold font), as *Pak* Ismail and others were aware. The talk in excerpt 3 ensues after I asked about how *Pak* Ismail trained his staff to be leaders.

(3)
Pak Ismail
1   dan itu prosesnya a penyiapan itu tidak
2   secara khusus . tapi sambil jalan proses .
3   dengan lemparan lemparan pekerjaan . **iki**
4   tolong dirampungi . **iki** tolong selesaikan .
5   pada saat dia melaksanakan itu sering
6   saya mengadakan rapat staf. itu juga
7   jarang dilakukan birokrat . saya rapat staf
8   itu hampir dua minggu sekali .

And that process, um, of preparation is not done formally, but while, while [we] work, [I] give out tasks "please get **this** done, please finish **this**". During the time he/she does these [tasks] I often hold a staff meeting, [something] which is rarely done by bureaucrats, I hold a staff meeting almost every two weeks.

Zane

9	he e:m .	Yes.

Pak Ismail

10	meting staf . khusus bagian saya =	A staff meeting, specifically for my section.

Although my question about how Ismail trained his staff was oriented to via his answer about his regular convening of fortnightly meetings, I didn't expect him to compare his practice to other heads who rarely convened meetings (lines 6–7). In trying to understand *Pak* Ismail's presentation of self here, we can note that it contrasts with the emerging chronotopes of bureaucratic personhood discussed earlier (e. g. excerpt 1). Here *Pak* Ismail positions his practices and thus himself as exemplary through his report of holding staff meetings to monitor the progress of tasks given to staff (lines 3–6). What is also interesting here is how *Pak* Ismail goes about convincing me that he actually engages in mentoring. In this case, and in subsequent excerpts, we see that *Pak* Ismail supports his claims through the use of represented speech (lines 3–4). In doing so, *Pak* Ismail brings me into this past event as a witness to his practices.

This chronotopic shift is achieved through his prior description of his actions (lines 1–3), which keeps me and *Pak* Ismail in the interview timeframe. The subsequent use of ngoko Javanese deictic *iki* "this" (line 3) helps bring about a chronotopic shift. This use of Javanese is followed by requests, *tolong dirampungi* 'please finalize' and *tolong selesaikan* 'please finish', which provide an example of *Pak* Ismail enacting these practices by transporting him into the past as the one engaging in the practice and asking for things to be finished, and transporting me there as a witness to these practices. It is also important to note that here and in many other parts of the interview, *Pak* Ismail's use of fragments of ngoko Javanese further increased the believability of his accounts because they represented the close relations he had with his staff (Goebel 2016b).

In excerpt 4, *Pak* Ismail continues his presentation of a self that contrasts with the selves that inhabited the bureaucratic chronotopes discussed in excerpts 1 and 2. This piece of talk occurs nearly directly after the talk in excerpt 3. The deleted part is where I (over)enthusiastically ask about the possibility of recording the meetings he describes in excerpt 3.

(4)

Pak Ismail

1	[iya = nda masalah . itu	Yes, no problems. [Meetings are held
2	sering . saya dua minggu sekali saya	often,] I do it every two weeks.
3	lakukan itu .	

Zane

4	o:: .	I see.

Pak Ismail
5   bisa sifat rapat staf itu saya memberikan
6   pengarahan .

The meeting can have the characteristic of giving direction.

Zane
7   he em =

Yes.

Pak Ismail
8   = directing (1.1) >saya punya tugas
9   ini ini . tolong kita selesaikan> . anda
10 selesaikan ini . >anda ini ini ini> . atau
11 kadang . dua arah .

Giving direction. "I have these tasks, please let's finish them, you this, this and this" or sometimes two directional

Zane
12 he em .

Yes.

Pak Ismail
13 #saya# inginnya begini . @anda maunya
14 apa@ . #atau# >kadang kadang> satu arah
15 . dari mereka .

"I want this. What do you want?" or sometimes one directional, from them.

Zane
16 he em .

Pak Ismail
17 saya hanya @buka tutup@ . ok keluhan
18 anda **opo** [@**opo**

I just open and close [the meeting]. "OK **what** problems do you have, **what** [problems]?"

Zane
19   [he em .

Yes.

Pak Ismail
20 saya tampung@ .

I take it in.

Zane
21 he em (1.3) @he em@ .

Yes, go on.

Pak Ismail
22 @itu yang saya lakukan@ .

That is what I do.

Zane
23 he em .

Yes.

Pak Ismail
24 di tiga kabag di sini . hanya saya .

Among the three section heads here, it is just me [who does this].

Zane
25 he eh he eh

Yes, go on.

Pak Ismail
26 di sekda dari sembilan biro (1.0) itu .
27 tidak ada kabag yang melakukan @itu@ .

Amongst the nine bureaus in the Area Secretariat, there are no other department heads who do this.

In excerpt 4, *Pak* Ismail continues to position his practices as exemplary in relation to other department heads in his office (lines 24–27). As with excerpt 3, we can interpret this and subsequent sequences of self-praise as orienting to the chronotopic configurations of bureaucrats discussed in excerpts 1 and 2. For example, we can see the need to evaluate staff found in newspaper stories (e. g. excerpt 1) is imitated via Ismail's accounts of using meetings to give directions (lines 5–10), engage in joint monitoring (lines 11–14) and self-monitoring (lines 14–18). In the talk that immediately follows that represented in excerpt 4, there are also accounts of his practices of rewarding and disciplining staff as they carry out their tasks. For reasons of space I won't include the full transcript, but for those interested a published version of this extended talk can be found in excerpts 5.2 and 5.3 in Goebel (2016b) and in excerpt 3 in Goebel (2016a). The main point here is that engaging in scalar reflexivity through scale jumping between this interview and newspaper reportage helped me to interpret many of the instances of self-praise that I initially found difficult to understand.

When taking a close look at how *Pak* Ismail presents a bureaucratic self that was unlike those found in newspapers, what is also striking is how *Pak* Ismail performed these presentations of self through the use of represented speech. In excerpt 4 there are three instances of represented talk (lines 8–10, 13–14, and 17–18), which again achieve a chronotopic shift from reporting about practices in the "here and now" of the interview to performing specific examples of these practices in the "then and there". At the same time, this chronotopic shift brings me into this meeting to listen to his exchanges with staff. These representation of talk add believability (in this case saying something like "believe me, I really do hold fortnightly meetings"). How he does this is interesting, too, because it contrasts with other ways he interactionally pulls off represented talk. In the case at hand, it is the alternation between how one utterance is delivered in relation to the previous ones that help index a chronotopic shift.

More specifically, the delivery of narrative-like orienting information from lines 1–7 does not have the variations in tempo and pitch that start on line 8 after a longish pause. On lines 8–10 *Pak* Ismail speeds up his tempo (indicated by ">" surrounding the utterance that is spoken faster) then slowing down before speeding up again. Contrasts with prior talk continue to help index chronotopic shift. For example, by slowing down his talk, *Pak* Ismail temporarily brings us back into the interview timespace on lines 10–11, before then using increased volume (indicated by "#" surrounding the word or utterance), normal volume, and decreased volume (indicated by "@" surrounding the work or utterance), to bring us into the timespace of the narrated event on lines 13–14.

Chronotopic shift back to the "here and now" of the interview then follows; this time it is brought about through a contrast of slightly different delivery features; a raised volume on *atau* "or" (line 14), followed by a lowering of volume and an increase and decrease in tempo on lines 14–15. In this case, contrast in tempo and volume, reference to a they/them in line 15 (*mereka*) rather than the "you" (*anda*) used in line 13 also assist chronotopic shift. Finally, one last chronotopic shift, this time back into the narrated event, is again achieved through a contrast of volume and reference to a "you" on line 18. As with excerpt 3, there is also a use of *ngoko* Javanese form, *opo* "what". As I have argued elsewhere (Goebel 2016a), this indexes close interpersonal relations between *Pak* Ismail and his staff. For the purpose of this paper, however, the point is that in order to interpret cases where fragments of Javanese are used we need to engage in another instance of scalar reflexivity. In this case, I have jumped scale from the interview to the long and ongoing durée of ethnic chronotopes in general, and Javanese ones in particular.

In the following excerpt (5), we see *Pak* Ismail presenting a self that is unlike corrupt or money-hungry bureaucrats. This talk follows that represented in excerpt 4 and is preceded by another sequence of self-praise that is followed by two further instances of represented talk. In this case, it is his use of honorific language with staff, his thanking behaviors, the use of material rewards that he uses to motivate his staff to continue to do a good job, and how they think about this. Unlike the previous excerpts, this talk is not directly related to my question, which checks my understanding about whether one can praise staff while they are present.

(5)

Pak Ismail
1 >makanya> . kalau . pak zane ke rumah   So if you [come] to my house, I would
2 saya . saya bilang rumah saya gubug .   say my house is ramshackle. Others at my
3 #setingkat esjlon saya::# (1.0) itu   level, have to have two-storey houses,
4 rumahnya harus tingkat . [standarnya =   that is the standard.
Zane
5   [hm   I see, I see.
6 hm:: =
Pak Ismail
7   = di semua kabag itu (laughs) =   In all the [other] heads of department.
Zane
8   = hm::   I see, yes, yes.
9 [heeh heeh =
Pak Ismail
10 [gitu (laughs) . tapi rumah saya biasa   It is like that. But my house is very plain.
11 biasa saja =
Zane
12   = he eh he eh (1.1)   Yes, go on.
Pak Ismail
13 #karena# saya bekerja . me::motto motto   Because I work using the Javanese motto,
14 jawa . jadi >orang jawa toh ada motto   so Javanese you know have a motto like
15 nya> begini . >anda bekerja . pertanyaan   this "You are at work, the first question is
16 pertama . ini anda cari **jenang** apa   are you after a **name** or a **sweet**?"
17 **jeneng**> .

Zane

18	hm: (1.0) **jenang** atau? =	Yes, a **sweet** or

Pak Ismail

19	= **jeneng** =	A **name**

Zane

20	= **jeneng** .	A name,
21	#bedanya apa# .	what is the difference?

Pak Ismail

22	jeneng itu kan kalau diindonesiakan kan .	**Jeneng** right if in Indonesian is name
23	nama [name .	right, name.

Zane

24	[aha: heeh heeh .	I get it, yes, go on.

Pak Ismail

25	**jenang** itu nama makanan . #**dodol**# .	**Jenang** is the name of a food [also called] **dodol**.

One minute of talk deleted where *Pak* Ismail explains that those who seek money are like those who seek something sweet, but will not have a good name. In contrast, if you seek a good name, money will follow although not a lot. *Pak* Ismail notes that his motto is "*cari jenang*" (seek a good name) and because of that he helps anyone who asks.

Pak Ismail

26	>saya yakin suatu saat dia punya **gawé**	I am certain that next time he
27	dia punya program dia punya proyek> .	[acquaintances just named] have some
28	butuh orang pemda (1.0) >kenapa susah	sort of **event** or a program or project and
29	susah **ning kono ono wong sing enteng**	they need a local government person,
30	**entengan ono wong sing** gampangan **ono**	[they will think] "Why go through hassles
31	**wong sing apikan**> . Ismail (laughs)	when [we] **have someone who is easy going, someone who is** easy [to work with], **there is a great person**, Ismail."

In the talk in excerpt 5, *Pak* Ismail promotes himself as someone who is not interested in personal enrichment, unlike other bureaucrats and heads of department, which is evidenced by his simple house (lines 2–7). He justifies this practice by first citing his belief in a Javanese philosophy that people should be interested in making a good name for themselves, rather than trying to enrich themselves (line 13 onwards). Note that this has interdiscursive links with the representation of bureaucrats described in excerpt 2. *Pak* Ismail clarifies his statement by saying that once a person has a good name (done by being helpful and accommodating to all), then some additional money will follow. In representing himself as someone who has enacted this philosophy, he sees the benefits of such an approach as making him the first person to be approached when there is a problem to be solved (lines 28–31). The way he does this has both similarities and differences with his talk in excerpts 3–4.

The way he self-praises is similar insofar as he follows an account with represented talk that brings about a chronotopic shift. This shift, which again brings me into another time and place as a witness, is achieved via a change in tempo (line 28) and the use of *ngoko* Javanese to report the thoughts of a number of his acquaintances (lines 29–31). This chronotopic shift differs to his earlier shifts because it is both about others' thoughts and because these thoughts are directly about *Pak* Ismail's exemplariness, rather than an example of him enacting his practices. While reporting talk also adds believability to his accounts, the use of *ngoko* Javanese has the potential to further increase the believability of his account. Its use here potentially indexes the type of intimate interpersonal relationship that he has with colleagues who might require his help.

6 Conclusion

Drawing on a wide range of scholarship in anthropology and linguistic anthropology on rapport, reflexivity, semiosis, and narrative, this paper has detailed how I moved toward producing an account of "the total linguistic fact" (TTLF) required to interpret interview data that I gathered as part of fieldwork in an Indonesian government office. I offered two concepts for helping to explore TTLF, namely *scalar reflexivity*, defined as the researcher's movement between different timespaces to understand the indexical potentials of semiotic forms used in situated interaction, and *believability*, defined as the ways in which consultants perform versions of self as a way of convincing the researcher about the truthfulness of their accounts.

In addition to the timespace of the interview, I focused on two other timespaces, the registers that formed within these timespaces, and the chronotopic configurations that emerged as part of these register formations. These included a rapidly reconfigured chronotope inhabited by the bureaucrat who needed to be constantly surveilled because they could not be trusted to do their job. This rapid reconfiguration was a result of confluence of factors including regime change, relaxation of media censorship laws, political and fiscal decentralization, and democratization that occurred between the period of 1998 and 2004, an ongoing election campaign, and pressure from the World Bank and the IMF to operationalize good governance. The chronotope of Javanese-ness in contrast, had its genesis in the Dutch colonial period and been subsequently imitated via waves of infrastructures of enregisterment, such as print media, schools, radio, television and so on.

I engaged in scalar reflexivity by jumping scale between interview data and configurations of bureaucratic and ethnic personhood as a way of helping interpret how one career bureaucrat presented himself in interviews as unlike the personas who inhabited widely circulating bureaucratic chronotopes of the 2003–2004 period. His presentations of self, in Goffman's (1969 [1959]) sense, gained believability through the use of represented talk that often relied upon the use of emblems from widely circulating Javanese chronotopes. Engaging in this type of reflexivity (i. e. scalar reflexivity) and examining the construction of believability provides a vantage point for understanding one dimension of rapport—truth—and its relationship to language use. In this case, we saw how rapport is discursively constructed and how its construction, at least for consultants, has much of its motivation and building materials located in another timespace.

References

Agha, Asif. 2007a. *Language and social relations*. Cambridge: Cambridge University Press.
Agha, Asif. 2007b. Recombinant selves in mass mediated spacetime. *Language & Communication* 27(3). 320–335.
Amirudin. 2003. Disiplin birokrat kendala gubernur. *Suara Merdeka*, 20 August.
Aspinall, Edward & Greg Fealy (eds.). 2003. *Local power and politics in Indonesia: Decentralisation and democratisation*. Singapore: Institute of Southeast Asian Studies.
Assegaf, Ibrahim. 2002. Legends of the fall: An institutional analysis of Indonesian law enforcement agencies combating corruption. In Tim Lindsey & Howard Dick (eds.), *Corruption in Asia: Rethinking the good governance paradigm*, 127–146. Annandale, N.S.W.: Federation Press.
Bax, Gerald William. 1974. *Language and social structure in a Javanese village*. Tulane, USA: Tulane University PhD thesis.
Berman, Laine. 1998. *Speaking through the silence: Narratives, social conventions, and power in Java*. New York: Oxford University Press.
Berreman, Gerald. 1972. *Hindus of the Himalayas: Ethnography and change*. 2nd edn. Berkeley: University of California Press.
Blommaert, Jan. 2015. Chronotopes, scales, and complexity in the study of language in society. *Annual Review of Anthropology* 44. 105–116.
Blommaert, Jan, Elina Westinen & Sirpa Leppänen. 2015. Further notes on sociolinguistic scales. *Intercultural Pragmatics* 12(1). 119–127.
Borneman, John & Abdellah Hammoudi. 2009. The fieldwork encounter, experience, and the making of truth: An introduction. In John Borneman & Abdellah Hammoudi (eds.), *Being there: The fieldwork encounter and the making of truth*, 1–24. Berkeley: University of California Press.
Briggs, Charles. 1986. *Learning how to ask: A sociolinguistic appraisal of the role of the interview in social science research*. Cambridge: Cambridge University Press.
Camdessus, Michael. 1998. The IMF and good governance. In *Address to Transparency International*. Paris, France, 21 January. Accessed at https://www.imf.org/external/np/speeches/1998/012198.htm on 12 August 2015: IMF.
Clifford, James. 1988. *The predicament of culture*. Cambridge, MA: Harvard University Press.
Clift, Rebecca & Elizabeth Holt. 2007. Introduction. In Elizabeth Holt & Rebecca Clift (eds.),

Reported talk: Reporting speech in interaction, 1–15. Cambridge: Cambridge University Press.
Crapanzano, Vincent. 2012 [2010]. "At the heart of the discipline": Critical reflections on fieldwork. In Antonius Robben & Jeffrey Sluka (eds.), *Ethnographic fieldwork: An anthropological reader*, 547–562. Malden, MA.: Wiley-Blackwell.
De Fina, Anna. 2003. *Identity in narrative: A study of immigrant discourse*. Amsterdam: John Benjamins Publishing Company.
De Fina, Anna & Sabina Perrino. 2011. Introduction: Interviews vs. 'natural' contexts: A false dilemma. *Language in Society* 40(Special Issue 01). 1–11.
Dewey, Alice. 1978. Deference behaviour in Java: Duty or privilege. In S. Udin (ed.), *Spectrum: Essays presented to Sutan Takdir Alisjahbana on his seventieth birthday*, 420–428. Jakarta: Dian Rakyat.
Errington, Joseph. 1988. *Structure and style in Javanese: A semiotic view of linguistic etiquette*. Philadelphia: University of Pennsylvania Press.
Errington, Joseph. 1995. State speech for peripheral publics in Java. *Pragmatics* 5(2). 213–224.
Errington, Joseph. 1998. *Shifting languages: Interaction and identity in Javanese Indonesia*. Cambridge: Cambridge University Press.
Errington, Joseph. 2000. Indonesian('s) authority. In Paul V. Kroskrity (ed.), *Regimes of language: Ideologies, polities, and identities (advanced seminar series)*, 205–227. Santa Fe, NM: School of American Research.
Forrester, Geoff (ed.). 1999. *Post-Soeharto Indonesia: Renewal or chaos?* Bathurst, N.S.W.: Crawford House Publishing.
G8-78. 2003. Tiga belas ribu lebih pns di karanganyar ditertibkan. *Suara Merdeka*, 16 June.
Geertz, Clifford. 1960. *The religion of Java*. Chicago: The University of Chicago Press.
Geertz, Clifford. 1968. Thinking as a moral act: Ethnical dimensions of anthropological fieldwork in the new states. *Antioch Review* 28(2). 139–158.
Geertz, Clifford. 1973. *The religion of Java*. New York: Basic Books Inc. Publishers.
Goebel, Zane. 2007. Enregisterment and appropriation in Javanese-Indonesian bilingual talk. *Language in Society* 36(4). 511–531.
Goebel, Zane. 2010. *Language, migration and identity: Neighborhood talk in Indonesia*. Cambridge: Cambridge University Press.
Goebel, Zane. 2014. Doing leadership through signswitching in the Indonesian bureaucracy. *Journal of Linguistic Anthropology* 24(2). 193–215.
Goebel, Zane. 2015. *Language and superdiversity: Indonesians knowledging at home and abroad*. New York: Oxford University Press.
Goebel, Zane. 2016a. Rapport and believability in interviews. Published under creative commons licence.
Goebel, Zane. 2016b. Represented speech: Private lives in public talk in the Indonesian bureaucracy. *Pragmatics* 26(1). 51–67.
Goebel, Zane. 2017. Imitation, interdiscursive hubs, and chronotopic configuration. *Language & Communication* 53. 1–10.
Goffman, Erving. 1969 [1959]. *The presentation of self in everyday life*. London: Allen Lane The Penguin Press.
Habibie, Bacharuddin Jusuf. 1999. *Instruksi presiden republik Indonesia nomor 7 tahun 1999 tentang akuntabilitas kinerja instansi pemerintah* [The Republic of Indonesia Presidential directive number 7, 1999]. Jakarta: Presiden Republik of Indonesia.

Hoffman, Danny & Mohammed Tarawalley. 2014. Frontline collaborations: The research relationship in unstable places. *Ethnography* 15(3). 291–310.

Hume, Lynne & Jane Mulcock. 2004. Introduction: Awkward spaces, productive places. In Lynne Hume & Jane Mulcock (eds.), *Anthropologists in the field: Cases in participant observation*, xi–xxvii. New York: Colombia University Press.

Inoue, Miyako. 2006. *Vicarious language: Gender and linguistic modernity in Japan*. Berkeley: University of California Press.

Jaworski, Adam, Nikolas Coupland & Dariusz Galasiński (eds.). 2004. *Metalanguage: Social and ideological perspectives*. Berlin: Mouton, Walter de Gruyter.

Kementerian Pendayagunaan Aparatur Negara. 2002. *Keputusan menteri pendayagunaan aparatur negara [decree of the ministry of national administrative capacity]: Tentang pedoman pengembangan budaya kerja aparatur negara [policy guidance about the development of work culture within the national administration], 25/kep/m.Pan/4/2002*. Jakarta: Kementerian Pendayagunaan Aparatur Negara.

Kementerian Pendayagunaan Aparatur Negara. 2003. *Keputusan menteri pendayagunaan aparatur negara [decree of the ministry of national administrative capacity]: Tentang pedoman penyelenggaraan pelayanan publik [policy guidance about the carrying out of public services], 63/kep/m.Pan/7/2003*. Jakarta: Kementerian Pendayagunaan Aparatur Negara.

Kementerian Pendayagunaan Aparatur Negara. 2004. *Keputusan menteri pendayagunaan aparatur negara [decree of the ministry of national administrative capacity]: Tentang pedoman penyusunan indeks kepuasan masyarakat unit pelayanan instansi pemerintah [policy guidance about the creation of a publick satisfaction indexs in relation to carrying out of public services by specific government departments], kep/25/m.Pan/7/2003*. Jakarta: Kementerian Pendayagunaan Aparatur Negara [Ministry for National Adminstrative Capacity].

Kitley, Philip. 2000. *Television, nation, and culture in Indonesia*. Athens: Ohio University Press.

Koven, Michèle. 2014. Interviewing: Practice, ideology, genre, and intertextuality. *Annual Review of Anthropology* 43(1). 499–520.

Kurniasih, Yacinta. 2007. Local content curriculum 1994: The teaching of Javanese in Yogyakarta schools. In *First International Symposium on the Languages of Java (ISLOJ), 15–16 August*. Graha Santika Hotel, Semarang, Indonesia.

Lempert, Michael. 2014. Imitation. *Annual Review of Anthropology* 43(1). 379–395.

Lindsey, Tim. 2002. History always repeats? Corruption, culture and 'Asian values'. In Tim Lindsey & Howard Dick (eds.), *Corruption in Asia: Rethinking the good governance paradigm*, 1–23. Annandale, N.S.W.: Federation Press.

Lucy, J. A. (ed.). 1993. *Reflexive language: Reported speech and metapragmatics*. Cambridge: Cambridge University Press.

Marcus, George. 1998. *Ethnography through thick and thin*. Princeton, NJ: Princeton University Press.

Marcus, George 2015. Reflexivity and anthropology. In James Wright (ed.), *International encyclopedia of the social and behavioural sciences*, Elsevier Ltd.

McLeod, Ross & Andrew MacIntyre (eds.). 2007. *Indonesia: Democracy and the promise of good governance*. Singapore: Institute of Southeast Asian Studies.

Middleton, Townsend & Jason Cons. 2014. Coming to terms: Reinserting research assistants into ethnography's past and present. *Ethnography* 15(3). 279–290.

Miller, Laura. 2004. Those naughty teenage girls: Japanese kogals, slang, and media assessments. *Journal of Linguistic Anthropology* 14(2). 225–247.
Modan, Gabriella & Amy Shuman. 2011. Positioning the interviewer: Strategic uses of embedded orientation in interview narratives. *Language in Society* 40(Special Issue 01). 13–25.
Moerman, Michael. 1988. *Talking culture: Ethnography and conversation analysis*. Philadelphia: University of Pennsylvania Press.
Ochs, Elinor & Lisa Capps. 2001. *Living narrative*. Cambridge: Harvard University Press.
Perrino, Sabina. 2011. Chronotopes of story and storytelling event in interviews. *Language in Society* 40(Special Issue 01). 91–103.
Poverty reduction and economic management unit. 2003. Indonesia: Combating corruption in Indonesia, enhancing accountability for development: World Bank.
Powdermaker, Hortense. 1967. *Stranger and friend: The way of an anthropologist*. 2nd edn. London: Secker and Warburg.
Rabinow, Paul. 1977. *Reflections on fieldwork in Morocco*. 2nd edn. Berkeley: University of California Press.
Rampton, Ben. 1995. *Crossing: Language and ethnicity among adolescents*. London: Longman.
Rampton, Ben. 2006. *Language in late modernity: Interaction in an urban school, studies in interactional sociolinguistics*. Cambridge: Cambridge University Press.
Robben, Antonius. 2012 [1995]. The politics of truth and emotion among victims and perpetrators of violence. In Antonius Robben & Jeffrey Sluka (eds.), *Ethnographic fieldwork: An anthropological reader*, 175–190. Malden, MA.: Wiley-Blackwell.
Rohdewohld, Rainer. 2003. Decentralization and the Indonesian bureaucracy: Major changes, minor impact? In Edward Aspinall & Greg Fealy (eds.), *Local power and politics in Indonesia: Decentralisation and democratisation*, 259–274. Singapore: Institute of Southeast Asian Studies.
Rosaldo, Renato. 1989. *Culture and truth: The remaking of social analysis*. Boston: Beakon Press.
Sen, Krishna & David T. Hill. 2000. *Media, culture and politics in Indonesia*. Oxford: Oxford University Press.
Silverstein, Michael. 1985. Language and the culture of gender: At the intersection of structure, usage and ideology. In Elizabeth Mertz & Richard Parmentier (eds.), *Semiotic mediation*, 220–259. Orlando, FL: Academic Press.
Silverstein, Michael. 2005. Axes of evals: Token versus type interdiscursivity. *Journal of Linguistic Anthropology* 15(1). 6–22.
Smith-Hefner, Nancy. 1983. *Language and social identity: Speaking Javanese in Tengger*. Michigan: University of Michigan PhD thesis.
Sneddon, James. 2003. *The Indonesian language: Its history and role in modern society*. Sydney: University of New South Wales Press.
Tannen, Deborah. 1989. *Talking voices: Repetition, dialogue, and imagery in conversational discourse*. Cambridge: Cambridge University Press.
Thee Kian Wie. 2001. Reflections on the new order 'miracle'. In Grayson Lloyd & Shannon Smith (eds.), *Indonesia today: Challenges of history*, 163–180. Singapore: Institute of Southeast Asian Studies.
Urban, Greg. 2001. *Metaculture: How culture moves through the world*. Minneapolis, MN: University of Minnesota Press.
Wagley, Charles. 1960. Champukwi of the village of Tapirs. In Joseph B. Casagrande (ed.), *In*

the company of man: Twenty portraits of anthropological informants, 397–415. New York: Harper and Row Publishers.

Wolff, John & Soepomo Poedjosoedarmo. 1982. *Communicative codes in Central Java*. New York: Cornell University.

World Bank private sector development unit East Asia and Pacific region. 2001. Indonesia: World bank group private sector development strategy (report no. 21581-ind): World Bank.

Wortham, Stanton. 2006. *Learning identity: The joint emergence of social identification and academic learning*. Cambridge: Cambridge University Press.

Wortham, Stanton, Katherine Mortimer, Kathy Lee, Elaine Allard & Kimberly Daniel White. 2011. Interviews as interactional data. *Language in Society* 40(Special Issue 01). 39–50.

Rafadi Hakim
5 Doing Ethnography Across Institutions: Rapport and Discursive Ruptures in Jakarta

1 Introduction

In this chapter, my aim is to illustrate how my interactions with fellow Indonesians outside of a formal research context also consist of negotiations about the discursive roles that speakers, including myself, perform in relation to others. Through the variable understandings of kin terms and pronominal address in Jakarta, a multi-ethnic city, I will demonstrate how rapport, whether ethnographic or otherwise, is indeterminate and constantly transformed beyond the formal duration of field research. Even among fellow Indonesians, both ethnic identity and professional identity, for instance, are indeterminate and are subject to a substantial amount of retroactive guessing. Such forms of guesswork, I argue, are not limited to periods of formal ethnographic research: the production of ethnographic knowledge, broadly understood, relies upon the judgements and indeterminacies that speakers and researchers encounter as they navigate a heterogeneous social world. Thus, rather than always responding to a presupposed inequality in social relationships, situated forms of knowledge are also produced out of encounters where interacting parties are unsure about each other's social position. Rapport, therefore, is not an enduring form of relationality, rapport is interdiscursively constituted through retroactive and anticipatory evaluations of semiotically mediated interactions (Cole, this volume, Chapter 2; Goebel, this volume, Chapter 4; Zentz, this volume, Chapter 3). In turn, these interactions are spatiotemporally contextualized and contextualizing (Bakhtin 1986; Agha 2005, 2007): ethnographers and other social actors do not only co-produce discourse in the moment of interaction, but they also draw upon and re-evaluate these interactions as ethnographic knowledge from a timespace *other than* the researcher's here-and-now.

Although critiques of the authoritative ethnographic voice have been productively used to interrogate the epistemological position of researchers vis-à-vis their ethnographic interlocutors (Clifford and Marcus 1986), much less attention has been paid to how empirical communicative practices contribute to knowledge that is derived from ethnographic fieldwork (Gal 2012; Goebel, this volume, Chap-

Rafadi Hakim, University of Chicago, Chicago, USA

https://doi.org/10.1515/9781501507830-005

ter 4). In this chapter, my aim is to demonstrate that ethnographic knowledge itself draws upon interactions beyond those that happen during formal research periods. As a graduate student, for instance, my position as a researcher is also developed through my ability to draw ethnographic examples, whether first-hand or otherwise. To draw upon social interactions as ethnographic data, however, researchers have to develop a sense of reflexivity: the ability to translate and reevaluate social interactions into ethnographically salient data that are relevant for other researchers. Such forms of reflexivity influence how researchers reframe and retell their ethnographic data to other researchers who might not be familiar with the social or linguistic contexts at play. For instance, researchers communicate their findings to each other through particular institutional channels and according to the roles that they occupy in their respective institutions, such as faculty or student (Kulick 1995). Thus, rapport as a semiotic resource is not only dependent on the specificities of a research site, but also on particular ideologies of communication among researchers themselves (Antaki et al. 2008). As I will illustrate in this chapter, an encounter with a fellow anthropologist engenders further reflexivity about the nature of rapport.

Using examples from a set of emails I exchanged with the chair of an Indonesian professional association and later discussed with a professor, this chapter asks the following questions: (1) How is rapport interdiscursively constituted through spatiotemporally contextualized and contextualizing interactions? (2) While shared 'native speakership' presupposes a sharing of semiotic resources between the researcher and the researched (De Fina, this volume, Chapter 6; Djenar, this volume, Chapter 11), how do researcher and researched work on establishing common ground in mutually unfamiliar situations?

Furthermore, my aim in this chapter is to illustrate how the ethnographic field site is perpetually open to anticipatory and retroactive evaluation not only by one's interlocutors, but also by one's collaborators in a research institution. The constant re-evaluation of social fields in one's ethnographic site thus makes the distinction between an ethnographer "in the field" and an ethnographer "at the desk" unstable and at times collapsible (Strathern 1999; Briggs 2007). Thus, I will illustrate how ethnographic rapport is invoked beyond institutionally delineated spacetimes of fieldwork and writing. While rapport has been previously theorized as the gaining of access to locally privileged knowledge (Geertz 1973; Herzfeld 1997), rapport can be questioned and contested by the multiplicity of interlocutors in both "the field" and "at the desk."

Thus, rapport as a form of relationality is produced through world-making practices by researchers and their interlocutors: the active co-construction of common social worlds with one set of interlocutors and the recounting of such worlds to another. To illustrate how such co-constructed social worlds unfold, I will outline an ethnographic example in three stages: (1) how an email exchange unfolded between myself and the chair of an Indonesian professional association; (2) how Javanese kin terms that are normatively used in the setting of Jakarta workplaces were used in these email exchanges; and (3) how the this email exchange was taken up as ethnographic data among two linguistic anthropologists.

2 Email with Mr. M

In my experience as a development worker in Jakarta before I started graduate training in anthropology, rapport with fellow Indonesians is constituted through, among others, deploying the different registers in which Indonesian and other languages are comingled (e. g. Errington 1998; Goebel 2010; Goebel 2015). These registers include particular grammatical forms, especially titles and other forms of honorifics, that are indexically salient in work relationships and other situations that involve putatively hierarchical relations (Errington 1985). However, in the world of Indonesian NGOs and development organizations, hierarchies are far from certain: A staff member or even entire projects can suddenly find their own authority superseded when they encounter shifting institutional configurations (Pollard 2009). Similarly, as a relatively young person working for an international NGO based in Jakarta, the capital, I was in an ambivalent position: I had the authority to assess the merits of the work that has been done by local partner organizations that received grants from my institution; at the same time, I was less experienced in the dynamics of Indonesian NGOs compared to older colleagues who have worked in their respective organizations for decades. This position, furthermore, obligated me to conduct audits and assessments of about 30 nonprofit organizations throughout a calendar year, which made rapport-building through face-by-face interaction often unfeasible. As a result, these professional relationships were shaped by phone calls, instant messaging texts, and e-mails more than through face-to-face interactions. In such electronically mediated interactions that are quasi-anonymous (Boellstorff 2008), the enregistered correlations between language and certain models of social relationships cannot be entirely presupposed; rather, the deployment of certain registers of language also entails unanticipated consequences in these emergent social relations.

While this email exchange took place outside of a formal research project, these unanticipated consequences form ruptures that produce uncertainties in both ethnographic work and other ways of co-producing rapport (Arps, this volume, Chapter 8; Djenar, this volume, Chapter 11; Harr, this volume, Chapter 7). During my time as an NGO staffer, the relative lack of standardized templates for electronic communication means that introducing my organization (and myself) to others requires constant guesswork. For instance, in one of my first few months of work, I was assigned to invite experts who have worked on the issue of freedom of expression to participate in a panel at an international conference. I had exchanged emails in English with the organizer of the panel and mistakenly referred to Mr. M., chair of a professional association, as "Executive Director" rather than "Chairman" in an attempt to translate the Indonesian phrase *ketua umum* (lit. 'public chairman'), a title that is commonly applied to chiefs of professional associations. In an exchange with the chair of a well-regarded professional association (excerpt 1 below),[1] I was reminded of how institutional and personal identities are indeterminate: The use of pronominal forms for self-reference and other-reference are always subject to re-evaluation and realignment.

(1)

1	**Mas** Rafadi Hakim,	**Mas** Rafadi Hakim,
2	Terima kasih atas usaha	Thank you for **NJENENGAN** [your] effort
3	**NJENENGAN** menjelaskan YYY dan	in explaining YYY and myself to the
4	saya kepada pihak panitia #.	organizers of the # conference.
5	Sekadar meluruskan beberapa hal :	Just to clarify certain things:
6	Posisi saya di YYY adalah Ketua Umum	My position at YYY is Chairman or
7	atau Presiden, bukan Executive Director...	President, not Executive Director... Of all
8	Semua pengurus YYY tidak ada yang	of YYY's members, none of us are
9	digaji. Kami semua kerja volunteer.	salaried. We all work as volunteers. The
10	Jabatan "executive director" mengesankan	title of "Executive Director" makes it
11	saya orang profesional yang digaji YYY.	sound as if I am a professional who is paid by YYY.
12	Meskipun bagian dari civil society	Although we are part of civil society, YYY
13	organization, YYY bukan LSM. YYY	is not an advocacy organization. YYY is a
14	adalah organisasi profesi @, seperti	professional association of @, like the
15	Ikatan Dokter Indonesia (IDI) atau	Indonesian Association of Medical Doctors
16	Asosiasi Advokat Indonesia (AAI).	(IDI), or the Indonesian Bar Association (AAI).
17	Penjelasan ini disampaikan supaya **mas**	I have delivered this explanation in order
18	Rafadi memahami YYY lebih baik.	for **mas** Rafadi [you] to understand YYY better.

---

1 Transcription conventions are as follows: Personal pronouns are in bold; Indonesian is unmarked; Javanese (Krámá Inggil) is in CAPS' YYY is the name of the professional association; @ is the type of professionals represented by ***; # is the name of the conference.

Here, in an e-mail otherwise set up in mostly standard Indonesian, my relationship to M., the sender, is presupposed through an exchange of pronominal forms that are nominally classified as Javanese. Nevertheless, such distinctions between Indonesian and Javanese is often irrelevant, because locally emergent semiotic registers often naturalize what appears to be switching between multiple linguistic codes (Goebel 2010; Cole 2010). At the same time, linguistic ideologies that conventionally regiment interactions in Javanese are also at play: The otherwise predominant use of standard Indonesian suggests that the few tokens of Javanese used for second-person address are particularly salient. In other bureaucratic settings, similar uses of Javanese pronominal forms do not index the speakers' lack of knowledge of Indonesian, the official language of state organizations; rather, these tokens of Javanese are meant to do relational work across persons of unequal standing (Goebel 2014).

In this context, however, M.'s lack of knowledge about my social standing reflects a particular kind of uncertainty: the tokens of Javanese that he uses to refer to me are not used because he presumes that I am a speaker of Javanese (or, by extension, a Javanese person). First, my own proper name is not immediately presupposable as an index of Javanese identity. Furthermore, my previous email exchanges with M. have not included any tokens of Javanese. Hence, M.'s use of Javanese presents a puzzle: In a multi-ethnic setting, and for an ethnically indeterminate addressee, what is the salience of these tokens of Javanese? To decode this short yet complicated email, I will discuss two of its Javanese linguistic features: (1) the use of the kin term *mas* (lines 1 and 17); and (2) the use of the second-person pronoun *njenengan* (line 3).

3 Multi-Ethnic Kin Terms

In multiethnic and multilingual settings, role alignment among speakers is a highly indeterminate process (De Fina, this volume, Chapter 6; Errington, this volume, Chapter 12), and involves ruptures in understanding when mutual fluency in multiple codes cannot be presumed. In this case, while M. simply presumed my understanding of Javanese pronominal forms, the interaction aligned our respective discursive roles because it did turn out that I can comprehend Javanese linguistic forms. In Jakarta, Javanese plays a disproportionally large role in the city's linguistic ecology. While Jakarta has a multi-ethnic populace, he can still address a large number of potential interlocutors in Javanese. Among other factors, as rural–urban migration continues from Java's agriculturally-focused hinterlands to urban centers (e. g. Repetto 1986), Jakarta's proportion of ethnic Javanese residents reached 35 % in 2003 (Suryadinata, Arifin, and Ananta 2003).

The role of Javanese linguistic tokens in Jakarta, therefore, diverges in some fundamental ways from social contexts where fluency in Javanese is widely presumed, such as Central and East Java (Cole, this volume, Chapter 2; Zentz, this volume, Chapter 3). For instance, the use of the Javanese kin term *mas* (lit. "brother"), which appears throughout this e-mail, does not place me above the sender as an older consociate, which denotational accounts of Javanese would otherwise suggest. Thus, the use of mas in this email exchange demonstrates a different kind of relational work. In Jakarta, a city that is not stereotypically associated with the homeland of the ethnic Javanese, *mas* (lit. "brother") and *mbak* (lit. "sister") are exchanged among people of different ethnicities who are non-intimates. This practice, however, is contrasted to locales where local kin terms that are emblematic of other ethnicities or standard Indonesian kin terms are used among non-intimates. A coworker who is of Batak (North Sumatran) descent later remarked to me that "this [exchange of *mbak* and *mas* happens here] because Jakarta is [virtually] majority Javanese," but "you should always use *bang* (Malay; lit. "brother") and *kak* (Malay; lit. "sister") when you're addressing people in Medan [North Sumatra]." Therefore, my position as an addressee who receives the pronominal term *mas* in this e-mail exchange does not index familiarity or coethnic solidarity, but rather a situation of relative unfamiliarity.

In the context of an email exchange, the use of *mas* indexes an encounter between non-intimates who are presumably of equal social standing. While I did reciprocate M.'s use of *mas* in a later reply to his email, the use of such kin term does not necessarily entail a linguistic debt towards the speaker who initiated the exchange. Rather, in this context, the term has lost is salience as an emblem of Javanese kinship and becomes a term that is deployed regardless of one's presumed ethnolinguistic identity.

The use of *mas* and *mbak* and its ethnolinguistically emblematic salience, however, is contested among Indonesians who live in multiethnic locales, such as the Jakarta metropolitan area. In the following example, metapragmatic discourse conducted in Indonesian about pronominal forms that are ethnolinguistically emblematic, such as *mas* and *mbak* for Javanese speakers, underlines two aspects of speakerhood: (1) ethnic identity; and (2) age. In the ensuing blog post, a student of literature based in the Sundanese-speaking city of Bogor, which lies in the greater Jakarta metropolitan area, discusses the pragmatic salience of these pronominal forms (Errington 1985):

> All respondents admit that "Mas" and "Mbak" are the pronouns of choice when they speak to those to whom they are not well-acquainted. In certain cases, such choice of pronouns

does not change even when they have been better acquainted [with their addressees]. Other pronouns are also used for addressees of different [ethnic] backgrounds (for instance, "Uda" and "Uni" for those who are from Minangkabau).
However, not everyone accepts such kinds of pronouns. At times, Koko, a respondent who hails from and grew up in Palembang [South Sumatra] admits that he does not feel comfortable being referred to as "Mas," especially by those who are well-acquainted to him. Reasons of conversational pleasantry and of politeness [which are reasons for using "mas"] are instead felt as insulting [for Koko]. Koko admits that he prefers others to call him by name or, for those younger than him, by "Pak" [(lit. "Sir")].
Such is the case with Satrio. For him, the pronoun "Mas" erases his identity as a person from Maluku. "[That happens] although my skin color and facial features already tell you that I am not Javanese". (Mubarok 2011)

The blog-post author, Husni Mubarok, does not identify his own self by ethnicity, yet he acknowledges the practice of using "Mas" and "Mbak," which, while ostensibly are Javanese linguistic forms, spread across different "[ethnic] backgrounds" (Indonesian: *latar belakang*). The semiotic uptake of these practices, however, is variable. Koko, for instance, finds the use of "mas" to be "insulting" (I: *melecehkan*) compared to the relatively unproblematic use of the standard Indonesian form "Pak" from younger speakers or the reciprocal use of first names among intimates. For Koko, however, "mas" and "mbak" are not shibboleths of ethnic differentiation, which for Satrio, who hails from the Maluku, is problematic. In this set of commentaries, "mas" and "mbak" are contrasted against forms of address that are normatively non-indexical in terms of their associations of ethnic identity: "Pak" for older men, and first names for consociates of equal social status.

The emergence of *mas* and *mbak* as unmarked pronominal forms, therefore, runs counter to the ideologically regimented position of Indonesian in official state discourse as a medium of communication across ethnic difference (Keane 2003; Goebel 2010; Zentz 2014; Goebel 2015). Instead of using standard Indonesian to communicate to non-intimates without marking ethnic affiliation, the use of *mbak* and *mas* in the Jakarta metropolitan region simultaneously serves as an ethnically unmarked form of address and as Javanese kin terms. These forms of unmarked pronominal address demonstrate the often contradictory relationship between metapragmatic discourse, or commentaries and justifications about the use of linguistic form, and metapragmatic function, or the formal features of linguistic forms themselves (see Silverstein 1979). Rather than a form of building intimacy, these modes of pronominal address that are otherwise described as forms of "politeness" or "respectfulness" towards co-ethnics serve as a way of negotiating ethnolinguistic plurality in co-producing rapport.

4 The Trouble with the Second-Person Pronoun

Although the use of *mas* in the e-mail exchange above is common even among speakers of different ethnic backgrounds in the Jakarta area, M.'s use of [*pa*]*njenengan*, a *krámá inggil* (KI) 'high Javanese' second-person pronoun (lines 2–4), remained somewhat opaque to me at that time. Nevertheless, as I will explain shortly, M.'s use of KI created a discursive rupture where I had to discursively realign myself with respect to M.'s professional identity. As an Indonesian- and Javanese-speaker who grew up in Jakarta, the exchange of Javanese kin terms, such as *mas*, was familiar to me; however, as a person who mostly communicated in standard Indonesian at work, I did not anticipate being addressed in KI. Previous scholarship on Javanese have emphasized native metadiscourse on the use KI as acts of honoring or socially elevating the addressee (Errington 1998; Wolff and Poedjosoedarmo 1982). Thus, KI is often regarded as an index of an unequal relationship between the speaker and the addressee. Nevertheless, the differences between our respective institutions (an NGO and a professional association) mean that no definite hierarchy clearly defines the social distance between us. As I finished reading his email, however, M's use of [*pa*]*njenengan* made me feel guilty of misrepresenting his proper title in his organization, because M successfully created a situation of linguistic debt. That is, M.'s ironic honorification of me, a person who initially requested his participation in a conference, means that I am obligated to mend the rupture created by my misrepresentation of M.'s professional title. Hence, a few minutes after receiving M.'s message, I quickly apologized for my mistake and mentioned that I will send corrections to the conference organizers.

Through M.'s correction and use of a KI pronoun, my experience was that of a mildly embarrassing yet interactionally normative role alignment between two non-intimates who found themselves in a multi-ethnic and multilingual setting. In such settings, the use of any particular linguistic register carries the risk of misidentifying one's addressee. Nevertheless, in the few days after I replied to M.'s e-mail, I still felt troubled not only by my own lack of knowledge about M's organization, but also by his ironic use of KI to address me. At that time, I thought that KI's effect to me as a reprimand are among the social peculiarities afforded by Javanese's multiple speech levels. Nonetheless, as with any socially situated communicative practice, this interaction was subject to retroactive evaluations that recontextualize its ethnographic specificity and render it comparable to other semiotic phenomena. As I will illustrate in the following section, although I did not initially communicate with M. for formal research purposes, this interaction retroactively becomes an object of ethnographic contemplation.

5 (Re)Contextualizing Rapport as Ethnographic Data

About two years later, a few months after I started graduate school in linguistic anthropology, I mentioned the email exchange casually as a source of embarrassment during my relatively short stint as an NGO worker. To a professor, I said that "you know you've made a mistake when you're addressed in Javanese as *panjenengan*." In reply, the professor remarked that "oh, well that's just like having someone call you 'Sir' unnecessarily when you talk in English" (Silverstein, pers. comm, 2015). It was this moment "out of the field" rather than in the field itself that reminded me how the email exchange did not only show that I was unfamiliar with professional associations. The email exchange also demonstrated that discourse becomes an object of ethnographic contemplation only insofar as it is comparable to interactions in any other language. Now doubly re-evaluated after Mr. M's correction and a professor's interpretation, the email exchange has been interdiscursively co-constructed and transformed across the multiple roles that I have inhabited: an NGO staffer and, later, a graduate student in linguistic anthropology.

At the end, however, I realized that I was not entirely sure of my own position during my initial email exchange with M. My subject position during linguistic exchanges in the so-called "field" are, rather than predetermined, negotiated at the moment of interaction as well as retroactively constituted. Rapport, as one contemplates in the here-and-now, is also a mode of reckoning about social relations in other spatiotemporal frameworks. More specifically, an ethnographer can only account for spatiotemporally situated interactions insofar as he or she retells those interactions to others beyond the duration of formal fieldwork. Interactions that are not retold, in other words, do not contribute to a collective body of ethnographic knowledge. To be able to report that one has understood interactions during ethnographic fieldwork in the past, one has to anticipate future requests to retell such interactions and, accordingly, enact oneself as an ethnographer. Thus, practices of discursive world-making extend beyond ethnographers and their interlocutors in the field, because such discursive worlds are also anticipatorily or retroactively oriented towards fellow ethnographers and scholars.

While my email exchange might be initially limited to an encounter between two institutions in Indonesia, the discursive life of this email exchange extends beyond the two institutions that were initially involved: It became an object of interest for my later study of communicative forms as a graduate student in linguistic anthropology. By doing this reflexive practice, I wish to demonstrate how metacommunicative frameworks regiment standardization but are also themselves subject to contestation: a study of group noticing sessions in the Conversation Analysis (CA) tradition, for instance, uncovers the metapragmatic frameworks that regiment scholarly analysis itself (Antaki et al. 2008). As a linguistic anthropologist, I have been trained to locate purportedly disinterested semiotic ideologies (Bauman and Briggs 2003; Kroskrity 2000): if an utterance erases its own social position, then it is an anthropologist' obligation to socially contextualize such an utterance. In many situations, such "voices from nowhere" are modernist ideologies of standardization that enable persons to speak from a culturally unmarked subject position (e. g. Woolard and Schieffelin 1994; Silverstein 1998; Gal 2006). Research questions thus start as soon as one asks how utterances are attached through some means to real persons and how these utterances connect persons and institutions as well. The ethnographer, however, also participates in these discursively mediated institutional formations. Hence, rapport between ethnographers and their interlocutors is not an enduring artefact of fieldwork; rather, it is the co-production of rapport that requires navigating ideologically mediated regimes of discourse production, whether in the field or among anthropologists themselves.

The graduate student as an ethnographer-in-training, in particular, encounters a particular ideology of rapport-building that is defined and imposed by normative paradigms of anthropological training: The possibility of succeeding or failing at creating rapport in the field produces a great amount of anxiety. Rapport, in this paradigm, is expected to "[result] in inclusion in the group and amusing post-fieldwork anecdotes" (Kulick 1995: 11). Even before formal dissertation fieldwork starts, however, graduate students in anthropology are already expected to demonstrate a certain degree of familiarity with their planned field site. Developing competence in a field language and often in a language in which relevant scholarship has been published, for instance, are prerequisites that have to be fulfilled before a student goes to the institutionally formative experience of doing dissertation fieldwork. Nevertheless, even in the early years of anthropological training, my experiences demonstrate the ways in which anthropology departments require their students to interpret and compare discursive processes beyond formally delineated fieldwork as ethnographic data. Such forms of anthropological pedagogy are key in producing normative reductions of rapport into linguistic fluency and social intimacy with interlocutors. As this volume illustrates, however, rapport involves negotiating complex interfaces between researchers themselves and their multiple interlocutors.

6 Conclusion: Rapport and the Co-Construction of Ethnography

By critically situating my account of my email exchange with M., I have demonstrated how rapport as world-making entails making ethnographic accounts of discourse available for retelling to different audiences. As a speaker of Indonesian in that email exchange, I naturalized myself as a participant in emergent semiotic registers that corresponds to the professional, quasi-bureaucratic world where M. interacts with his work colleagues (Goebel 2014), albeit disfluently. Later on, my own position as a graduate student at an American university requires me to translate his encounter into academic English. The retroactive projection of linguistic comparability became clear to me only after a conversation with a professor, rather than in my own exchange with M., the chair of the professional media association whose title I misrepresented. Thus, during these conceptually focused conversations among linguistic anthropologists, languages are made comparable to one another in terms of how they re-enact social relations as ethnographic data. As I have illustrated, however, ethnographic data is inseparable from the co-construction of a field by ethnographers, their interlocutors during fieldwork, and fellow anthropologists at universities and other institutions.

The ethnographer's sense of self while building rapport with interlocutors changes constantly, and often through mutually confusing misapprehensions (Kondo 1986; Narayan 1993; Kulick and Willson 1995). Rapport between the researcher and the researcher's interlocutors have been understood through moments that mark a temporal juncture: unfamiliarity followed by familiarity (Geertz 1973), or confusion followed by revelation (Lévi-Strauss 1974). As Geertz's famous scene of a suddenly interrupted Balinese cockfight illustrates, these junctures are often unintentional and rarely premeditated, thus questioning understandings of rapport as a modular relationship that can be built in degrees of linguistic fluency or social intimacy. In this chapter, I have illustrated how these productive misapprehensions happen even before fieldwork and also through interactions that are mediated through electronic means. Ethnographic understandings and misapprehensions, in other words, goes beyond the face-to-face interactions that a Malinowskian paradigm for fieldwork prescribes (Malinowski 1922). Although rapport might be projected as the essence of a successful ethnography, it is in fact perpetually reconstituted before, during, and after fieldwork.

References

Agha, Asif. 2005. Introduction: Semiosis across encounters. *Journal of Linguistic Anthropology* 15(1). 1–5.
Agha, Asif. 2007. Recombinant selves in mass mediated spacetime. *Language & Communication*, Temporalities in Text 27(3). 320–335. https://doi.org/10.1016/j.langcom.2007.01.001.
Antaki, Charles, Michela Biazzi, Anette Nissen & Johannes Wagner. 2008. Accounting for moral judgments in academic talk: The case of a conversation analysis data session. *Text & Talk – An Interdisciplinary Journal of Language, Discourse Communication Studies* 28(1). 1–30.
Bakhtin, Mikhail. 1986. Forms of time and of the chronotope in the novel. In Michael Holquist (ed.), *The dialogic imagination*, translated by Caryl Emerson & Michael Holquist, 84–258. Austin: University of Texas Press.
Bauman, Richard & Charles Briggs. 2003. *Voices of modernity: Language ideologies and the politics of inequality*. Cambridge, UK: Cambridge University Press.
Boellstorff, Tom. 2008. *Coming of age in second life: An anthropologist explores the virtually human*. Princeton: Princeton University Press.
Briggs, Charles 2007. Anthropology, interviewing, and communicability in contemporary society. *Current Anthropology* 48(4). 551–567. https://doi.org/10.1086/518300.
Clifford, James & George Marcus (eds.). 1986. *Writing culture: The poetics and politics of ethnography*. Berkeley: University of California Press.
Cole, Debbie. 2010. Enregistering diversity: Adequation in Indonesian poetry performance. *Journal of Linguistic Anthropology* 20(1). 1–21. https://doi.org/10.1111/j.1548-1395.2010.01045.x.
Errington, Joseph. 1985. *Language and social change in Java: Linguistic reflexes of modernization in a traditional royal polity*. Athens, Ohio: Ohio University, Center for International Studies.
Errington, Joseph. 1998. *Shifting languages: Interaction and identity in Javanese Indonesia*. Cambridge: Cambridge University Press.
Gal, Susan. 2006. Contradictions of standard language in Europe: Implications for the study of practices and publics. *Social Anthropology* 14(2). 163–181. https://doi.org/10.1111/j.1469-8676.2006.tb00032.x.
Gal, Susan. 2012. The role of language in ethnographic method. In Richard Fardon, Olivia Harris, Trevor H. J. Marchand, Mark Nuttall, Chris Shore, Veronica Strang & Richard Wilson (eds.), *The Sage handbook of social anthropology*, 38–53. Los Angeles: SAGE.
Geertz, Clifford. 1973. Deep play: Notes on the Balinese cockfight. In *The interpretation of cultures*, 412–453. New York: Basic Books.
Goebel, Zane. 2010. *Language, migration, and identity: Neighborhood talk in Indonesia*. New York: Cambridge University Press.
Goebel, Zane. 2014. Doing leadership through signswitching in the Indonesian bureaucracy. *Journal of Linguistic Anthropology* 24(2). 193–215. https://doi.org/10.1111/jola.12048.
Goebel, Zane. 2015. *Language and superdiversity: Indonesians knowledging at home and abroad*. New York, NY: Oxford University Press.
Herzfeld, Michael. 1997. *Cultural intimacy: Social poetics in the nation-state*. New York: Routledge.

Keane, Webb. 2003. Public speaking: On Indonesian as the language of the nation. *Public Culture* 15(3). 503–530.
Kondo, Dorinne. 1986. Dissolution and reconstitution of self: Implications for anthropological epistemology. *Cultural Anthropology* 1(1). 74–88. https://doi.org/10.1525/can.1986.1.1.02a00030.
Kroskrity, Paul. 2000. *Regimes of language: Ideologies, polities, and identities*. Santa Fe, N.M.: School of American Research Press.
Kulick, Don. 1995. Introduction. In Don Kulick & Margaret Wilson (eds.), *Taboo: sex, identity, and erotic subjectivity in anthropological fieldwork*, 1–28. New York: Routledge.
Kulick, Don & Margaret Willson. 1995. *Taboo: sex, identity, and erotic subjectivity in anthropological fieldwork*. New York: Routlege.
Lévi-Strauss, Claude. 1974. *Tristes tropiques*. 1st American edn. New York: Atheneum.
Malinowski, Bronislaw. 1922. *The Argonauts of the Western Pacific: An account of native enterprise and adventure in the archipelagoes of Melanesian New Guinea*. London: Lowe and Brydone (Printers) Ltd.
Mubarok, Husni. 2011. Penggunaan panggilan 'Mas' dan 'Mbak' ke sembarang orang. *Husnimubabrok* (blog). https://husnimubabrok.wordpress.com/2011/03/13/penggunaan-panggilan-%e2%80%9cmas%e2%80%9d-dan-%e2%80%9cmbak%e2%80%9d-ke-sembarang-orang/. (Accessed March 13, 2011.).
Narayan, Kirin. 1993. How native is a 'native' Anthropologist? *American Anthropologist* 95(3). 671–686.
Pollard, Amy. 2009. *Power in doubt: aid, effectiveness, and harmonization amongst donors in Indonesia*. Cambridge: University of Cambridge PhD Thesis.
Repetto, Robert. 1986. Soil loss and population pressure on Java. *Ambio* 15(1). 14–18.
Silverstein, Michael. 1979. Language structure and linguistic ideology. In Paul Clyne, William Hanks & Carol Hofbauer (eds.), *The elements: A parasession on linguistic units and levels*, 193–247. Chicago: Chicago Linguistics Society.
Silverstein, Michael. 1998. Monoglot 'standard' in America: Standardization and metaphors of linguistic hegemony. In Donald Brenneis & Ronald Macaulay (eds.), *The matrix of language: Contemporary linguistic anthropology*, 284–306. Boulder, CO: Westview Press.
Strathern, Marilyn. 1999. *Property, substance, and effect: Anthropological essays on persons and things*. London: Athlone Press.
Suryadinata, Leo, Evi Nurvidya Arifin & Aris Ananta. 2003. *Indonesia's population: Ethnicity and religion in a changing political landscape*. Singapore: ISEAS–Yusof Ishak Institute.
Wolff, John & Soepomo Poedjosoedarmo. 1982. *Communicative codes in Central Java*. Ithaca, NY: Cornell Southeast Asia Program Publications.
Woolard, Kathryn & Bambi Schieffelin. 1994. Language ideology. *Annual Review of Anthropology* 23(1). 55–82. https://doi.org/10.1146/annurev.an.23.100194.000415.
Zentz, Lauren. 2014. 'Love' the local, 'use' the national, 'study' the foreign: Shifting Javanese language ecologies in (post-)modernity, postcoloniality, and globalization. *Journal of Linguistic Anthropology* 24(3). 339–359. https://doi.org/10.1111/jola.12062.

Anna De Fina
6 Commentary: Rapport in Qualitative Investigation, from Researcher's Objectivity to Researcher's Reflexivity

A volume on rapport and the co-construction of social relations in field settings is both timely because of the kinds of reflections that it invites on the part of qualitative researchers, and symptomatic because of its signalling a significant shift that is taking place in sociolinguistic and anthropology oriented research. The latter involves a change from a view of knowledge gathering as a process of understanding emic perspectives, or to say it with Malinowski, a way "to grasp the native's point of view, his relation to life, to realize his vision of his world" (1922: 25; also see Geertz 1983), towards an approach in which reflexivity, positionality (Creswell 2013) and intersubjectivity (Gable 2014) take center stage. These concepts encompass the wide issue of the researcher's position not only in relation to informants, but also in relation to the research topic, the context and the research process more generally. Indeed, discussing rapport inevitably leads us to think of the research focused interactional encounters in which data was generated as contexts for understanding that data, and of social relations established and continuously negotiated among participants as enabling and contextualizing the type of exchanges produced, and therefore as inextricably tied to their interpretation.

The stress on the importance of directing the focus on the interactional events that are at the center of qualitative research was a fundamental preoccupation for Charles Briggs who noted more than 30 years ago, "… speech, whether contained in interviews, myths, or 'natural' conversations, provides an ongoing interpretation of its own significance (1986: 106)." As discussed by Goebel in his introduction to this volume, calls for attention to the research context and particularly to the role of participants in it, have punctuated the history of qualitative research in both anthropology and sociolinguistics. For instance, some scholars have offered critiques of the erasure of the researcher's presence in the process of investigation (see, for example, Crapanzano 1986) and of the neglect of possible implications of the researcher's identity for the establishment of relationships with interviewees (Young 2004; Al-Natour 2011; Ganga and Scott 2006). Others have talked about the need for a discussion of the *observer's paradox* (Labov 1972) as a productive starting point for an appreciation of the status of field work encounters as interactional occasions in their own right (De Fina and Perrino 2011).

Anna De Fina, Georgetown University, Washington, USA

However, these contributions have not stimulated a more in depth reflection on the concept of rapport. Indeed, rather than discussing what rapport is or is not, what impact its presence or absence can have on research processes and data collection and on what strategies people employ to create it, most researchers still see it simply as a sort of precondition for gathering meaningful data, especially when carrying out ethnographic interviews. Thus, for example, according to Heyl (2001), ethnographic interviews are:

> ... those projects in which researchers have established respectful, ongoing relationships with their interviewees, including enough rapport for there to be genuine exchange of views and enough time and openness in the interviews for the interviewees to explore purposefully with the researcher the meanings they place on events in their worlds. (p. 369)

However, if we want to take reflexivity and positionality seriously, the concept of rapport also needs to be appraised in a different light and it is to this enterprise that the four chapters on which I am providing my comments here offer an important contribution. Indeed, the authors of the four papers explicitly intended to highlight the importance of rapport for qualitative research by investigating different and important facets of it, and also by taking it as a starting point to provide insights on wider theoretical methodological issues. In the rest of this commentary, I will focus my comments on the following questions raised by the various chapters:
1. Ways in which rapport can be defined
2. Rapport as product of discursive and social work
3. Specific strategies that define rapport in different situations and across speech events
4. Relationships between various contexts, times, and scales in the appraisal of rapport

Let me start with the definition of rapport. What exactly do we mean by rapport? This is one of those concepts that are intuitively easy to grasp, but that turn out to be complex to operationalize. I imagine that we would all agree that rapport has to do with reciprocal understanding, but also with harmony and trust; however, when it gets to more specific definitions things become complicated. Such complexity is reflected in current literature. For example, Hunt states that rapport is "the process whereby the researcher becomes competent to membership by first displaying an awareness that membership is problematic and must be negotiated, and second by demonstrating a salient knowledge of the essential features by which subject members distinguish themselves from non-members" (1984: 283). In this somewhat obscure characterization, the stress is on group membership, i. e. on the perception of being part of different communities. But not all interviews or research encounters take place among members of different communities, so I suspect that rather than finding generalizable definitions it is actually better to start with our intuitive sense that rapport has to do with harmony, empathy, and trust and work our way from the bottom up. In other words, it is better to start from concrete contexts of interaction and from the analysis of what people do to collaborate or to move closer to each other and then get to definitions. This is exactly what the chapters on which I am providing a commentary do and therefore I will first reflect on what I think is their take and focus on rapport, and after that I will offer some reflections and ask some questions.

In the introduction to the volume by Zane Goebel and in the paper by Debbie Cole, there is a stress on attaining common ground as an essential element of rapport. Goebel talks about creating "common ground" and "alignment" as fundamental strategies for rapport building but also stresses that these attainments take place through the interactional work of participants and may involve a variety of strategies going from repetitions to the open expression of acts of belonging. The notion of common ground is central to Cole's chapter as well. Cole connects this construct to the communication of "social similitude" and "cohesiveness" a matching of footings, attitudes, and dispositions that is slowly built between persons even in situations when very little shared knowledge can be presupposed. In Goebel's chapter, rapport has to do with empathy and with acceptance of the subject's self-presentation on the part of the interviewer, but also on the establishment of trust. Ismail is trying to convince the interviewer that his self-presentation as a good person is truthful and he uses certain strategies (among which storytelling strategies have a central role) to attain this objective. Goebel's focus is on the informant rather than on the researcher (although, of course, he incorporates talk by both and is aware of the role of co-construction), but he shows how rapport can be analyzed at different levels in the interview: on the one hand, as the result of an attempt by the interviewee to elicit empathy and trust on the part of his interlocutor, and, on the other, as an element of the relationships that Ismail has established with his subordinates in the story-worlds that he performs throughout his tellings in the interview.

In Lauren Zentz's chapter, rapport is viewed as harmony and mutual understanding within a group. She talks about the former as being built over time and focuses on the constitution of a mutual repertoire of resources that allows members to tune in with relation to each other in a cohesive way. She analyzes a specific case in which that rapport is built through the group's response to the initiative of one of the participants and specifically his use of humor to create a fictional context in which he plays a central part as a talk-show host.

In Rafadi Hakim's chapter, the concept of rapport is once more related to the idea of "common ground" but the area to which it is applied is that of pragmatic knowledge that allows people to assume roles that are pertinent to specific interactions and reciprocally acceptable. Hakim also defines it as a form of "world making" in the sense that it consists of "the active co-construction of common social worlds" which helps people make sense of events and relations.

In brief, the notions on which these analyses are based: common ground, alignment, trust, and social similitude all point to another significant thread that ties these chapters together: the idea that rapport is not given but needs to be built through discursive and non-discursive strategies, often, as I will discuss later, over the course of various times and spaces. Indeed, the debates about the insider–outsider status of researchers (see Al-Natour 2011; Naples 1996; Coloma 2008; Smith 1999) that have at their center the possibility for "outsiders" to human communities to gain access to their knowledge or world view presuppose the existence of a direct relationship between rapport and community membership. Leaving aside the very complicated issue of what a community is and how it can be defined, the discussion of which would be beyond the scope of these comments, there is still the question of the simplification implied in a notion of rapport as a given in situations where group membership is not at stake. In all the chapters discussed here, rapport is seen as the outcome of careful and delicate work among all participants no matter how distant their relationship. Indeed, the chapters deal with situations in which researchers and subjects are at different grades of distance, from almost total strangers, like in the case of Goebel and Ismail, to almost friends as in the case of Zentz and her students. The situations depicted in the chapters present all the complexity of the continuum along which the insider/outsider status can present itself in real life and all demonstrate that rapport is not "there" but is achieved through context specific strategies. As acutely noted by Hakim, the bases for rapport are often indeterminate because people may be unsure of their reciprocal status and for this reason they have to form hypotheses on the kind of relationships that is emerging with the other party and design their own strategies of rapport creation. These situations may in fact lead to ruptures in communication and to the inability to establish rapport. Cole also notes that rapport is literally built utterance by utterance and moment by moment through a continuous process of repetition and reassurance that interactants are, so to speak, on the same wavelength. And it is in the careful and detailed description of the variety of strategies put in place by participants in different types of contexts that the chapters offer their most interesting contributions.

For example, Cole makes a strong case in her chapter for not limiting the analysis of ways in which rapport is built to linguistic strategies, and even in the case in which only language is involved, to look carefully at phenomena at the micro level. Making reference to literature from the field of communication, she underlines the importance of the "metacommunicative" level and discusses the use of subtle paralinguistic cues that go from tone of voice to "rhythmic patterning" or what she calls "phonetic empathy," that is the process of speaking in one voice, to create rapport between participants in an encounter. In her fascinating analysis of her encounter/interview with the writer Zawawi Imron, Cole describes moment by moment how both actively worked to achieve common ground through a great variety of strategies that include speaking softly, singing, and a kind of "prosodic matching" based on the issuing of prosodic cues from one party to the other. At the same time, moving swiftly and freely between various roles in order to accommodate the tone and topic of the encounter seems to be another successful strategy put in place by the two participants.

In Goebel's chapter, strategies of rapport have to do with self-presentation through both open self-praise and implicit performance of a certain kind of persona. Central to such performance is the use of reported dialogue and within it, switches from one language variety to another to signal certain kinds of relationships among the story world characters. Ismail uses chronotopic shifts from the world of the interview to the world of the story as a strategy to create coeval alignment (Perrino 2005) and to place the interviewer in the story-world as a kind of witness to the events. Thus, using reported dialogue and self-praise are ways to gain Goebel's trust and to create an atmosphere of mutual understanding.

In Zentz's chapter, strategies for rapport creation are centered on the use of humor. Angelo, one of the friends who gather for conversations and interviews with Zentz, creates humorous frames that interrupt serious moments in groups' discussions. He does so by referring to well-shared scripts about talk shows in order to transform the current conversational context into a fictional performance. But, rapport would not be created if others in the group did not offer an uptake and in that sense members of this community need to show that they get the humor and need to align to the roles required by the fictional world evoked by Angelo. Strategies here involve performance devices such as voice quality, pitch, and tempo, the use of specific elements of shared knowledge and, as in all cases, language choice. By mobilizing all of these resources, interactants are able to construct a particular social world through multiple voices.

Hakim presents an analysis in which rapport is at stake since there is a situation of potential conflict created by the erroneous use of term of address on the part of one of the interlocutors. However, participants are not involved in sustained interaction since they are exchanging emails and therefore there is no real possibility of creating trust and understanding between them. What we see there is the participant's reactions to this possible rupture: irony on one side and explanations and apologies on the other.

Each in different ways, the four chapters provide rich descriptions of strategies for rapport building or mending, but they also offer important reflections on the role of different times and spaces in these processes. In none of the four chapters, is rapport seen as something that can be constructed and or understood within the borders of a specific encounter. Cole offers a chronology of her encounters with Zawawi Imron and describes what came before the interview from which she discusses excerpts in order to explain how the poet and she relied on a series of elements in their previous experience to build common ground: From their mutual passion for poetry (which was disclosed in a previous encounter) to the imitation of poetry performances that had taken place in other moments, the two participants draw on the past to build the here-and-now. She also shows that mutuality happens turn by turn through the creation of patterns that are based on previous utterances. Finally, she draws attention to the importance of spaces and landscapes in the evolution of the interaction between the two participants as she points to the value of an autograph on a book for the kind of relationship built among the interlocutors.

Both intertextuality as a reference to prior texts and interdiscursivity as the threads that link discourses at different levels figure prominently in the chapters, and this in turn is an indication of the need to treat rapport as something that both develops and can only be appreciated within a net of semiotic relationships that are spatially and temporally discontinuous. This issue is particularly clear in the arguments presented by Goebel and Hakim. Goebel illustrates how the task of interpreting the particular self-presentation constructed by his informant, which is at the core of his attempt to create rapport, can only be carried out through what he calls "jumping scales," that is resorting to discourses about the figure of personhood of the Indonesian bureaucrat that are circulated and crafted at different scales: from the macro-scale of IMF policy to the regional scale of Indonesian policy and of press discourses. Understanding rapport therefore requires the consideration of multiple contexts and multiple elements relating them. Hakim makes the same case illustrating how the interpretation of what goes on in an interactional exchange is subject to different evaluations at various moments in time and across speech events of different kinds: from an email exchange to a conversation among academics.

Both Hakim and Cole talk about how the process of reinterpretation is constant and ongoing and therefore can be projected into the future as well. In Zentz's analysis, looking across speech events is a fundamental element as she is dealing on the one hand with the establishment of trust and intimacy within a group and of the group with the researcher and on the other with the establishment of interactional patterns based on humor that happen in a repetitive way until they become part of the groups' repertoire. Rapport then can be created in a single interactional event or across different events, spaces, and times, but in all cases can only be conceived of as emerging in relation to multiple semiotic contexts.

To summarize, these chapters analyze different ways in which rapport is built (or broken) and the various challenges that creating it poses in different interactional contexts, such as those involving one-to-one vs. multi-party communication or those involving close vs. distant relationships. What are the theoretical methodological implications of these analyses? Why is studying rapport important? One of the implications is that analyzing interviews reflexively leads to a much more in-depth understanding of the role of different contexts in the way meanings are created and interpreted. Zane Goebel illustrates how the analysis of rapport is a necessary step into the study of how processes at wider scales influence what is going on at the interactional level, while at the same time offering a key to understanding those processes from an emic perspective. His chapter shows the inadequacy of the micro–macro opposition and the need for a more nuanced account of the way different contexts interact with each other in space and time.

A second implication that can be derived from all the chapters is that interviews, like all interactional encounters, are complex events in which different roles and relationships coexist and are continuously being negotiated. This point is of enormous importance to strengthen the argument made by many researchers (see, for example, De Fina 2009, 2011; De Fina and King 2011; De Fina and Perrino 2011; Koven 2014) that interviews should neither be opposed *tout court* to "naturally occurring" interactions nor lumped together as one type of context. As such then, they provide excellent loci for understanding strategies for maintaining interactional cohesion within dyads and groups and for grasping how interactional moves relate to the construction and perception of identities.

Another implication is that we need to embrace the observer's paradox rather than shy away from it. There is a tendency among researchers to still regard the erasure of the observer as a guarantee for "objective" research. However, as I think the chapters in this volume have demonstrated, the moment an interviewer steps into a room, the possibility of that objectivity is erased. But, while some measure of non-interventionism is good—for example, it is important for interviewers to let interviewees speak and try not to put words in their mouths and to create an atmosphere in which talk can happen—non-interventionism does not equate with objectivity. I believe that the authors show that instead of sweeping the presence of the interviewer under the carpet, we should embrace it as one of the elements in our analysis. As noted by Giles, Coupland, and Coupland (1991: 1):

> research that addresses the contexts as much as the behavior of talk can tease out the ordering—motivational, strategic, behavioral, attributional and evaluative—that interactants themselves impose upon their own communicative experiences, and the ways in which the social practices of talk both are constrained by and themselves constrain goals, identities, and social structures.

Another implication of the chapters is that the question of rapport should not be seen as pertaining essentially to intercultural encounters, a tendency that I think was prevalent in the anthropological literature on rapport and that we saw was represented in the quote by Hunt. First of all, as I mentioned, not all interviews involve members of different cultures, secondly we should remember how recent sociolinguistic literature has problematized the notion of cultures as unitary blocks and of speech communities as cohesive ensembles (see, for example, Blommaert 2013). Such problematization involves not only not essentializing culture, but also not taking for granted that "cultural issues" are what is at stake in instances of negotiation among members of different national groups. We want to know what categories are mobilized by participants as accepted or problematic. Thus, in Zentz's case, it is probably the researcher status as a teacher that can be problematic for rapport building, while in Goebel's chapter it is the fact that he is not a member of the class of state employees that can lead him to prejudge his interviewee.

In any case, all the chapters point to the fact that what is relevant to participants in terms of rapport can only be uncovered through painstaking work on the details of interaction. A final implication of the analyses has to do with data validity. I have discussed the fact that reflexivity can enhance our understanding of both interactional contexts in general and specific interview environments. But, we must also consider the implications of analyses of communicative processes in interviews for the evaluation of the kinds of data that we get. Thus, as I have argued, while there is no such a thing as a sterile situation in which the observer can be erased, this does not imply that we should neglect questions of truthfulness and factuality. If, for example, as in many of the chapters analyzed, we are doing research on perceptions about social issues such as the status of language varieties or the behavior of government employees, we need to gather information that is reliable and given in good faith, and that is very difficult or impossible when there is no rapport between participants. Besides telling us whether the things that people say are spoken in good faith, the analysis of rapport will also give us a clue on the kinds of dynamics that emerge in particular situations and therefore on how those dynamics will affect the kind of data collected so that we can literally put those data in context. For example, are informants being defensive about issues? This is the case with Goebel's analysis. His interviewee was defensive and it is precisely his question of why that bureaucrat appeared to be so defensive that led him to appreciate the impact of processes at larger scales on that interview. Similar observations can be made for the analysis presented by Hakim about his email exchange with a panel organizer. It was thanks to the irony with which his interlocutor reacted to his choice of terms of address that he realized that there had been a mismatch in expectations.

To conclude, I think that the chapters collected in this section of the volume show the richness and complexity of interviews and field research contexts and demonstrate the many avenues that can be taken in the analysis of rapport, but they also point to the important implications that these kinds of analyses have for research based on interviews and for qualitative research more in general.

References

Al-Natour, Ryan. 2011. The Impact of the researcher on the researched. *MC Journal* 14(6). http://journal.media-culture.org.au/index.php/mcjournal/article/view/428. (Accessed October 10, 2017).
Blommaert, Jan. 2013. Language and the study of diversity. *Tilburg Papers in Culture Studies* 74. http://www.tilburguniversity.edu/upload/2648cf26-31f2-4138-83d3-3176cabc28b0_TPCS_74_Blommaert.pdf. (Accessed April 2, 2018).
Briggs, Charles. 1986. *Learning how to ask: A sociolinguistic appraisal of the role of the interview in social science research*. Cambridge: Cambridge University.
Coloma, Roland. 2008. Border crossing subjectivities and research: Through the prism of feminists of color. *Race, Ethnicity and Education* 11(1). 11–27.
Crapanzano, Vincent. 1986. Hermes dilemma: The masking of subversion in ethnographic description. In James Clifford & George Marcus (eds.) *Writing culture: The poetics and politics of ethnography*, 51–76. Berkeley: University of California press.
Creswell, John. 2013. *Qualitative inquiry and research design: Choosing among five approaches*. 3rd edn. Los Angeles, CA: Sage.
De Fina, Anna. 2011. "We are not there. In fact now we will go to the garden to take the rain." Researcher's identity and the observer's paradox. In Jo Angouri & Meredith Marra (eds.), *Constructing identities at work*, 223–245. New Basingstoke: Palgrave.
De Fina, Anna & Kendall King. 2011. Language problem or language conflict? Narratives of immigrant women's experiences in the US. *Discourse Studies* 13(2). 163–188.
De Fina, Anna & Sabino Perrino (eds.). 2011. Narratives in interviews, interviews in narrative studies. *Language in Society* 40. Special Issue.
Gable, Eric. 2014. The anthropology of guilt and rapport: Moral mutuality in ethnographic fieldwork. *Journal of Ethnographic Theory* 4(1). 237–258.
Ganga, Deianira & Sam Scott. 2006. Cultural "insiders" and the issue of positionality in qualitative migration research: Moving "across" and moving "along": Researcher-participant divides. *Forum: Qualitative Social Research* 7(3). http://www.qualitative-research.net/index.php/fqs/article/view/134/289#g2. (Accessed September 30, 2017).
Geertz, Clifford. 1983. 'From the native's point of view': On the nature of anthropological understanding. In Clifford Geertz (ed.), *Local knowledge: Further essays in interpretive anthropology*, 55–72. New York: Basic Books.
Giles, Howard, Nickolas Coupland & Justine Coupland. 1991 Accommodation theory: communication, context, and consequence. In Howard Giles, Justine Coupland &

Nickolas Coupland (eds.), *Contexts of accommodation. Developments in applied sociolinguistics*, 1–68. Cambridge: Cambridge University Press.

Heyl, Barbara. 2001. Ethnographic interviewing. In Paul Atkinson, Amanda Coffey, Sara Delamont, John Lofland & Lyn Lofland (eds.), *Handbook of ethnography*, 369–383. London: Sage.

Hunt, Jennifer. 1984. The development of rapport through the negotiation of gender in field work among police. *Human Organization* 43(4). 283–296.

Koven, Michele. 2014. Interviewing: Practice, ideology, genre, and intertextuality. *Annual Review of Anthropology* 43. 499–520.

Labov, William. 1972. The transformation of experience in narrative syntax. In W. Labov (ed.), *Language in the inner city: Studies in the black English vernacular*, 354–396. Philadelphia: University of Pennsylvania Press.

Malinowski, Bronislaw. 1922. *Argonauts of the Western Pacific: An account of native enterprise and adventure in the archipelagoes of Melanesian New Guinea*. London: Routledge and Kegan Paul.

Naples, Nancy. 1996. A feminist revisiting of the insider/outsider debate: the 'outsider phenomenon' in rural Iowa. *Qualitative Sociology* 19(1). 83–106.

Perrino, Sabina. 2005 Participant transposition: text and trope in Senegalese oral narrative. *Narrative Inquiry* 15(2). 345–375.

Smith, Linda 1999. *Decolonizing methodologies: Research and indigenous peoples*. Dunedin: University of Otago Press.

Young, Alford. 2004. Experiences in ethnographic interviewing about race. In M. Bulmer & J. Solomos (eds.), *Researching race and racism*, 187–202. London: Routledge.

Adam Harr
7 Sociolinguistic Scale and Ethnographic Rapport

1 Breakthrough into Rapport

In arguably the most famous narrative of ethnographic rapport, the American anthropologists Hildred and Clifford Geertz arrived as eager foreign researchers in a Balinese village in 1958 only to be ignored by virtually everyone around them. Their presence was sanctioned by a stack of visas and research permits, but, in a village of around 500 people, only their landlord and the village head would talk to them. In *Deep Play: Notes on a Balinese Cockfight*, Clifford Geertz (1972) describes moving around the village feeling vaguely disembodied—less a fully human being than "a cloud or a gust of wind" (57). The Geertzes' situation changed precipitously when they attended a cockfight that was broken up by Javanese police officers. In an unthinking moment, the foreign anthropologists ran from the police and ducked into a courtyard for a hastily assembled tea setting. When the police arrived on the scene, Geertz tells us:

> [o]ur host of five minutes leaped instantly to our defense, producing an impassioned description of who and what we were ... We had a perfect right to be there, he said, looking the Javanese upstart in the eye. We were American professors; the government had cleared us; we were going to write a book to tell Americans about Bali. And we had been there drinking tea and talking about cultural matters all afternoon and did not know anything about any cockfight" (58).

After this incident, Geertz tells us they were warmly and widely accepted by the community, who were astonished and more than a little amused that the American couple ran from the authorities rather than staying and producing their papers.

Much has been said and written about this story of a cockfight (e. g. Crapanzano 1986; Marcus 1997; Gable 2014). I propose that we can read Geertz's narrative yet again as an illustration of the relation between ethnographic rapport and the ethnographer's shifting alignments between different scales of space, time, sociality, and authority. The Geertzes arrived in Bali as highly mobile members of a

---

Acknowledgement: The paper on which this chapter is based was prepared for the Conceptualizing Rapport Symposium at La Trobe University, July 17–20 2016. The symposium was organized by Zane Goebel, and I thank him heartily for the impetus to begin this paper.

Adam Harr, St. Lawrence University, Canton, New York, USA

foreign elite under the authorization of the Indonesian Republic, their housing arranged for by the provincial government. This status enabled their presence but it also marked them as outsiders and virtual non-people to their Balinese hosts. The Geertzes' alignment with global and national scales was interrupted, however, by their immersion in an event that was resolutely Balinese. The breakthrough into rapport was precipitated by their presence at a cockfight, which Geertz tells us was:

> illegal in Bali under the Republic ... largely as a result of the pretensions to puritanism radical nationalism tends to bring with it. The elite, which is not itself so very puritan, worries about the poor ignorant peasant gambling all his money away, about what foreigners will think, about the waste of time better devoted to building up the country. It sees cockfighting as "primitive," "backward," "unprogressive," and generally unbecoming of an ambitious nation (57).

The Geertzes embody their alignment with the chronotopically "backward" and "local" scale of the cockfight when they, almost instinctively, flee from the police rather than produce the documents that would have tied them to a "progressive" Indonesian national scale. They end up in a courtyard, where their impromptu Balinese host looks the Javanese police officer "in the eye"—connoting equality despite the power differential—and trots out the Geertzes' *bona fides* as American professors with permissions from a host of government agencies. Their host, who Geertz tells us later became a key informant, indexes the Geertzes' privileged status as American scholars to trump the Javanese officer with translocal authorizations that *scale-jump* (Uitermark 2002) the now-local policeman, who is interactionally refashioned as an "upstart." Geertz doesn't say, but it seems safe to suppose that this scalar play was linguistic as well, with registers of Balinese characterizing the cockfight and some variety of Malay being the language of the confrontation with the police.

This is a dramatic example, to be sure, but I propose that ethnographic rapport is a perpetual matter of this kind of scale shifting and scale alignment. It is not simply a matter of shifting unidirectionally "up," "down," or "laterally"—from "global" to "national" to "local," or from the ethnographer's "local" to an informants' "local"—but of dancing and hop-scotching within and among *fractally recursive* (Irvine and Gal 2000) sociolinguistic scales. In this chapter, I argue that interactional scale-shifting between the general and particular is a crucial way in which ethnographers and their interlocutors establish a sense of inhabiting a common, morally saturated world and that this sense of *moral mutuality* (Gable 2014) constitutes much of what anthropologists reflexively call rapport.

2 Sociolinguistic Scale

Sociolinguistic scale as an analytic concept highlights the fact that language intrinsically indexes and enacts hierarchically ordered magnitudes of braided space, time, and sociality (Bakhtin 1981; Hymes 1996; Blommaert 2010; Goebel 2015; Carr and Lempert 2016). Sociolinguistic scale draws on concepts of scale first developed by cultural geographers (Wallerstein 1988; Marston 2000; Tsing 2000), however this genealogy is beyond the scope of the current chapter. For the sake of concision, I will focus specifically on *sociolinguistic* scale, which was introduced by Blommaert (2007), building on Bakhtin's (1981) seminal concept of the chronotope. Blommaert points out that to understand linguistic inequalities, we must become aware of how language varieties are construed in tropes of temporal, spatial, and social magnitude. This is especially true of the hierarchical ordering of registers and languages in highly mobile, intensely heterogeneous speech communities. For example, "standard" varieties of a language are often imagined to be translocal and temporally stable compared to so-called dialectal varieties that are construed as local and ephemeral. This has obvious consequences for the reproduction of social inequalities given that access to standard varieties is unevenly distributed.

In Blommaert's (2015) formulation, sociolinguistic scales operate both horizontally and vertically. The horizontal dimension of sociolinguistic scales is familiar from dialectology in terms like "distribution," "spread," "contact," and "community." These terms imagine languages either bounded in communities or seeping like liquids across a two-dimensional surface. To complement this horizontal image, Blommaert subsumes a great deal of recent sociolinguistic theorization by proposing an additional and intertwined vertical dimension figured in terms of "TimeSpace" values (Wallerstein 1988). Thus, interlocutors may "up-scale" by using forms that evoke timeless, translocal social orders relative to the momentary and local. This is what the Geertzes' impromptu host does when he references their status as privileged social types—"American scholars"—to the police officer. Over time, these scalar hierarchies inflect the social valuation of different registers and named language so that some ways of speaking come to be seen as uniquely suited to timeless universal truths (Kuipers 1990; Eco 1997; Haeri 2003). These scalar hierarchies, however, are open to revision when scales are enacted within richly detailed participant structures (Harr 2016).

On an interactional level, Blommaert (2007: 6) offers this small, elegant example of sociolinguistic scale at work:

Student: "I'll start my dissertation with a chapter reporting on my fieldwork."
Tutor: "We start our dissertations with a literature review chapter here."

In this exchange, the tutor exerts subtle power over the student through a scale-jump from the personal and idiosyncratic to the collective and general. The tutor does this by shifting from "I" to "we," by shifting from the possible future to the gnomic present tense, and by invoking a vague, encompassing "here." Space, time, and sociality are braided in an everyday exercise of institutionalized power. We might summarize the dynamics of scale through the following dichotomies, adapted from Blommaert (2007: 6).

Lower Scale	Higher Scale
Momentary	Timeless
Localized	Widespread
Individual	Collective
Subjective	Objective
Specific	General
Token	Type

Figure 1: Relative Scale.

Crucially, scaling is not absolute but relative. Susan Gal (2016: 91) reminds us that "scaling is a relational practice that relies on situated comparisons among events, persons, and activities. The results of comparison enable and justify action and institutional relationships." In other words, scale emerges interactionally through the discursive juxtaposition of grammaticalized magnitudes of space, time, and sociality. To analyze how this relational process is enacted in social interaction, Zane Goebel and others (2016) have introduced the concept of *scalar shifters*, which they define as "signs used to organize units and unitizations of scale in discourse to enable the identification of relevant participant frameworks with respect to time, space, and/or size" (11). These signs are both tools for constructing and clues for interpreting shifting sociolinguistic scales. In this vein, I argue that rapport emerges through scalar shifts, when interlocutors make cooperative scale jumps between the particular and the general. In the remainder of this chapter, I delineate the relationship between rapport and sociolinguistic scale by considering the effects of sociolinguistic scaling in my research in the highlands the island of Flores in eastern Indonesia. I begin by sketching a working model of rapport.

3 Rapport and Intersubjectivity

Despite its avowed centrality to ethnographic methods, rapport has remained "a largely underdeveloped concept" (Goebel 2016: 6). Like so much of language, rapport is often either taken for granted or pressed into folk metaphors (Reddy 1979) that construe rapport as the equivalent of a clear channel for the real business of communication, as in this definition from a classic textbook:

> Rapport is a harmonious relationship between ethnographer and informant. It means that a basic sense of trust has developed that allows for the free flow of information. Both the ethnographer and the informant have positive feelings about the interviews, perhaps even enjoy them. (Spradley 1979: 78)

Here rapport is posited as a "sense of trust" separate from the "free flow of information" itself. Goebel (2016) offers a more nuanced view of rapport as a mutual trust that is constructed part-and-parcel with the flow of information in an interview. As in Spradley's definition, however, rapport is most often reduced to a purely "phatic" function (Jakobson 1960; Coupland et al. 1992), thus contrasting rapport with referentiality, as in Tannen's (1990) popularized distinction between "rapport talk" and "report talk." As Agha (2007) has shown, however, reference, and rapport are most often intertwined.

I propose that rapport is one possible mode of the phenomenological state that has come to be called intersubjectivity (Tomasello 2007; Robbins and Rumsey 2008; Duranti 2010; Gable 2014). Anthropological discussions often reduce intersubjectivity to "mutual understanding" based on reciprocally presupposing the intentions or mental states of those we interact with (Tomasello et al. 2005); but Duranti (2010) has argued that Husserls' original concept is much broader in scope and provides much greater utility for theorizing human sociality. For instance, ethnographic evidence shows that theories of interpretation as intention-guessing are culture-bound and do not account for "societies in which people either refuse to engage in mind-reading or argue that one cannot really know what is in the mind of another human being" (Duranti 2010: 5). Basing a theory of rapport on a broader theory of intersubjectivity makes room for investigating how variable theories of mind and sociality might condition ethnographic and other kinds of rapport (Danziger 2006; Robbins and Rumsey 2008; Rumsey and Danziger 2013; Harr 2013). Given that rapport is evidently not a monolithic phenomenon, grounding rapport in intersubjectivity makes room for a theorization of rapport's variability.

According to Duranti, Husserl formulates intersubjectivity broadly as "the condition whereby I maintain the assumption that the world as it presents itself to me is the same world as it presents itself to you, not because you can 'read my mind' but because I assume that if you were in my place you would see it the way I see it" (2010: 6). Thus, where rapport is often theorized as a property of a dyadic relationship between interlocutors, theorizing rapport in terms of intersubjectivity allows us to see rapport emerging in a multiplex relationship between interlocutors and their separate but semiotically entwined senses of a more or less shared world. A rudimentary form of this triadic engagement is joint attention achieved through pointing behavior—a capacity that is available to infants, but which eludes our primate relatives (Tomasello et al. 2005; Tomasello 2006). According to Liszkowksi et al. (2004), when a 12-month-old infant engages in declarative pointing, i. e. pointing with the intention of directing an adult's attention, the infant will only be satisfied if the adult looks at both the target of pointing and back at the infant. This suggests that the infant's aim is not only to instrumentally direct the adult's attention, but to engage in joint attention for its own sake. I experienced this with my own infant daughter when a noisy gaggle of geese flew over: she pointed and vocalized emphatically until I looked up at the geese and then back down at her face, beaming with apparent joy that we were seeing the same thing together. I, too, felt the delight that is commonly called "seeing the world through the eyes of a child."

Of course, many of the things we jointly attend to are less tangible than geese in flight. Many of the entities in the world that we jointly attend to are cultural objects that are generated, reproduced, or made explicit in interaction as *common ground* (Enfield 2006). I suggest that this triadic relation between "self," "other," and a co-ratified "world" emerges in speaking in the context of scalar shifts, when we observe our interlocutors—and they observe us—making intelligible scale jumps between the particular and the general. If intersubjectivity is fundamentally the sense that one inhabits a common world with another person, then scale-shifting is a key way in which people construct their sense of a common world. Husserl's concept of intersubjectivity is of course much broader than rapport, and many forms of intersubjectivity so defined would not entail rapport. But rapport is clearly dependent on the achievement of this sort of triadic engagement, and viewing rapport through the lenses of intersubjectivity and scale-shifting can help us see how it is achieved and maintained through interaction.

4 Down-Scaling to Ethnographic Particulars

Having sketched a bird's eye view of rapport, I turn to a worm's eye view of my own experience with ethnographic rapport in central Flores. If indeed ethnographic rapport is conditioned by variable understandings (and combinations of understandings) of personhood and sociality, then it follows that ethnographic rapport must be described *in situ*. I'll begin by giving a demographic overview of this part of Flores before describing how I arrived there and how I was received over time.

Nearly all my time in the field was spent in a cluster of villages in the south-central highlands of Ende district, one of eight districts on Flores in East Nusa Tenggara province. Ende district has a population of around 230,000 divided into two self-identifying ethnolinguistic groupings: the Endenese and the Lionese. My own ethnographic perspective is very much rooted in extended participant-observation in the lives of people who identify themselves as *Ata Lio* 'Lio people'. This is a designation claimed by approximately 170,000 people—just under three-quarters of the district. As Aoki (2004) reminds us, however, Lio people participate in several intersecting transnational linkages, so that Lio is only one of several situational self-identifications an individual might claim. Lio people who move to Java or Sumatra for work, school, or marriage learn to identify themselves as *orang Timur* 'eastern people', an identity that includes people hailing from across Nusa Tenggara Timur. Within Lio territory, "Lio" is rarely claimed as an identity category and people tend to designate themselves as belonging to *nua pu'u* 'an ancestral source village'. Thus, ethnic self-identification is a matter of scalar alignment that is dependent on the speaker's location and relationship with the addressee. For present purposes, however, "Lio" serves as a useful simplification. Most Lio people speak Indonesian—the national language—in addition to a variety of Lionese, an Austronesian language in the Central Malayo-Polynesian subgroup (Blust 1993; Fox 1998). Many speak one or more other Indonesian languages.

Alongside coastal communities of Muslim Lio people, as well as a few scattered Lio Protestants, the overwhelming majority of Lio people participate to some degree both in Catholic sacraments and in ancestral rites. Ancestors are sometimes described as intercessors between the living and God. As one informant, a prominent member of the Catholic Church, expressed it: "Where is God? But I can show you the graves of my father and his father." Ancestral rites pay homage to the dead, who gave to the living an ordered, habitable world. As I describe below, ancestors, though invisible, continue to intervene in the everyday lives of their descendants.

In the villages where I carried out my research, people make their living primarily by cultivating rice, coffee, cloves, and candlenuts, which they sell to merchants in the weekly village market and in the district capital Ende. An increasing number of residents gain additional income operating homestay lodging for the steady and increasing flow of domestic and international tourists. Eking out a meager living in the steep highlands, my informants often lamented their marginalized political, religious, and economic status in Indonesia's vast bureaucratic archipelago. They express the view that, as a religious minority living far from the national center, Catholics in Flores have been bypassed in Indonesia's development. For the most part the people who talked to me used

Indonesian terms invoking a nationalist scale to describe their position as "isolated" (*terasing*) people living in a "backward" (*terbelakang*) corner of Indonesia.

5 Upscaling to Ethnographic Rapport

I have proposed that rapport is fundamentally dependent on the sense that one inhabits the same world as another person and that sociolinguistic scale-shifting is a key way in which people construct this sense. In the case of ethnographic rapport, the ethnographer carries primary responsibility for imagining and entering the world of her informants. This is so because the researcher is certain to be vastly outnumbered by her informants and, crucially, because rapport is likely to be of the most importance to the researcher. In my own case, I felt that establishing good rapport was vital to the success of my research, and my dissertation, as well as my ability to find a job, make my parents proud, and support a family. I was, to say the very least, highly motivated to establish good relations with the people who I hoped would inform my research.

Arriving in Flores to begin long-term fieldwork in 2006, my naïve approach to establishing ethnographic rapport was essentially the same as my habitual approach to establishing personal rapport in my native settings in America: I tried to be deferential, to show an interest in people, to share my personal history, and to smile a bit more than comes naturally. I tried to be, as Americans describe it, "friendly." This approach was not entirely unsuccessful. I was generally warmly received, especially after I told folks that I wanted to learn to speak the Lio language. Some individuals eyed me coldly, seemingly searching for a way to profit from me, but many more took evident delight in my habit of writing down Lio words in my little notebooks. Several seemed to genuinely enjoy thinking out loud about their own language and culture. Despite the warmth of my reception, however, I found that the hospitality I received initially served to reinforce my status as a guest and thus as an outsider. I did not have the Geertzes' baptismal moment. Rather, I gradually learned to inhabit the discursive worlds of the people I lived with and eventually found that I had good rapport across an extensive social network, as well as the ability to establish rapport relatively quickly with new acquaintances. To achieve anything like this *communicative competence* (Hymes 1966), I was dependent on a handful of people who had both a high degree of reflexive awareness about Lio social norms and were generous enough to teach me the rudiments of Lio social personhood. These people became my instructors in Lio ways of "doing" rapport.

A prime example of this is the gift exchanges that are woven into the fabric of everyday life in the Flores highlands (Howell 1989). I was instructed that the appropriate giving and occasional receiving of cloth, tobacco, livestock, cigarettes, betel, or money is crucial to establishing and maintaining relationships. Gift exchange is, of course, a perennial topic in anthropology (e. g. Mauss [1950] 1990; Weiner 1992; Keane 1994; Gregory 2015); here, I focus on how the naming of gifts and gifting relationships affected rapport in my own ethnographic setting.

5.1 Naming Gifts and Gifting Relationships

The people who informed my research chiefly described our relationship in idioms of exchange. In a trunk village where I conducted participant-observation in meetings of a *musyawara mosa laki* 'council of ritual leaders', I was somewhat jokingly addressed as *ture jadi*, which is a term of address for someone from a village with whom one's own village has an agreed upon exchange relationship, called *pore jadi*. *Pore jadi* relationships are typically codified in an oath that expresses in metaphorical language the nature of obligations entailed in the relationship. In general, the *pore jadi* relationship means that members of different villages may freely eat from each other's fields when traveling, though some *pore jadi* are more specific, e. g. stipulating that one village must supply materials for a ceremonial drum to another village. Individuals, too, may enact a *pore jadi* relationship regardless of their village affiliations. I was addressed as *ture jadi* after I donated a pig in a ceremonial manner—as I was instructed to do by my host—for use as a sacrifice in the performance of village ritual (Harr 2013). I was told that in making this donation I had acted as a *tuku du, kebe sani* 'crossbar that supports, earthwork that stops erosion'.

Members of a household in another village described our relationship as a different kind of exchange partnership: *aji ji'e, ka'e pawe* 'good younger same-sex sibling, kind older same-sex sibling'. This describes a quasi-familial bond between individuals who are not otherwise unrelated but who are mutually supporting. This household generously fed me, took care of me when I got sick, and gave me company and a place to sleep in addition to taking the time to inform my research. In return, I regularly brought them gifts of food, toys, books, and newspapers from my travels. I also gave occasional gifts of cash, which I proffered while saying *Aku mo'o pati gula sa lo'o* 'I humbly give a little sugar'. These words, which I had been instructed to use when giving such monetary gifts, framed my cash as a gift perpetuating our social relationship rather than a payment completing an obligation. As Keane (1994) points out, gifts do not speak for themselves. Rather, referential acts often accompany exchange objects and specify their social value. Cash, a semiotically volatile medium of exchange (Parry and Bloch 1989), is perhaps especially in need of referential specification. By counterintuitively referring to my envelopes of cash as "sugar," they were scaled up from a momentary token of payment to a relatively transcendent type of gift between members of a social category—*aji ji'e, ka'e pawe*. This mutual recognition of the gift, I suggest, made me less of an inscrutable stranger and more of a recognizable social type.

Similarly, when visiting respected elders, I was instructed to always take a gift of tobacco or *arak* 'local alcoholic beverage', depending on the person's preference. Regardless of which substance I brought, I was taught to proffer it while saying *Aku mo'o pati nata* 'I humbly give betel', referring to betel with the ritually enregistered term *nata* rather than the everyday term *mota keu*. As with calling an envelope of money "sugar," referring to tobacco or arak as "betel" upscaled the gift and indexed normative ideals of Lio etiquette when approaching an elder for help, advice, or knowledge. Referentially establishing the correct scalar connection between a particular instance of giving and transcendent categories of gift, giver, and receiver indexed my understanding of my proper moral relation to the receiver as mediated by the gift.

5.2 Diagnosing Calamity

Because of the centrality of gift exchange in Lio social life, I was given explicit instructions early in my field research on how to name and present gifts; but I had to gradually learn on my own to name other abstract moral and metaphysical entities. It was necessary, for example, that I learn to see and name certain accidents and ailments as tokens of a moral type. As I have described elsewhere (Harr 2013), calamities in Lio society are often understood to have moral origins. For example, a seventy-three-year-old man explained to me his older sister's lifelong childlessness by telling me how he had arrogantly refused a gifted sarong from his wife's family 50 years earlier. Elsewhere, a ceremonial leader's swollen belly and yellowed skin was attributed to a rival's poisonous envy. My own month-long gut affliction was narrated back to me as being the result of *wiwi riwu, lema ngesu* 'a thousand lips, a hundred tongues', meaning that too many people had been discussing me as I jogged promiscuously down the road on my evening run.

There are systematic correlations of various kinds of calamity with the assignment of different sources. For example, chronic ailments—those that persist or recur over a span of time—are generally seen as stemming from the displeasure of a "hungry ancestor" (*ata mata lowa*), who requires a graveside offering to be assuaged. On the other hand, house fires, acute ailments, and accidents like slipping on a rock and falling in a stream are more often judged to arise from the living, with the sufferer being the target of "witchcraft" (*ko'o polo*), the focus of intense jealousy (*ate lo'o*; literally "small liver"), or the subject of gossip (*wiwi riwu, lema ngesu*). Each of these diagnoses constitutes an upscaling from a momentary circumstance to a timeless moral cause. Kuipers (1990) argues exhaustively that for Weyewa people in West Sumba a form of ritualized upscaling is also the solution to these sorts of calamities because it restores an atemporal moral order.

The discussion and diagnosis of large and small calamities is a common topic of conversation for many Lio people. Indeed, over time I came to see these moral–causal mechanisms as being subjectively at work in my own aches, coughs, and slips. I took an intense interest in the diagnostic criteria and found that speculating with others on possible causes for calamities was a rapport-building way for me to take part in conversations. Engaging in this kind of diagnosis with my interlocutors affirmed a kind of *moral mutuality* (Gable 2014), or intersubjective sense that we inhabit a common world of moral causality. Together, we discursively "pointed" at moral forces at work in the world. Moreover, in these conversations, I aligned myself with a kind of reasoning that my interlocutors understood outsiders, particularly White Westerners, to view as "backwards" (*terbelakang*) and "primitive" (*primitif*).

Although I developed discursive habits that allowed me to develop a sense of rapport with new acquaintances, this rapport often felt fragile. The question that I feared most in my fieldwork was, *Berapa ongkos dari Amerika*? 'how much did your ticket from America cost?' This question, and any honest answer I might give, only highlighted the fact that my interlocutors and I did not inhabit quite the same world. This was underscored by a rhetorical question that often followed: *Kapan kami bisa ke Amerika*? 'When can we go to America?' For nearly everyone I talked to in the Flores highlands, the answer that was too obvious to be stated was "never." Never mind that my home country is not the paradise many imagined where no one has to work or ever gets sick; the questions showcased my mobility and access to scales of action denied to my interlocutors. In a mirror image of the Geertzes' baptismal moment at the cockfight, moments like this introduced a palpable rupture between me and the people around me. The discomfort of these moments was an additional incentive to seek the means of creating rapport.

6 Conclusion

Neither scale-shifting nor rapport is unique to ethnographic encounters. Scale alignment and shifting are, Blommaert (2015) argues, ever present conditions and outcomes of social interaction. But ethnographic rapport amplifies key issues of scale, like interactants' relative ability to access or be mobile across scales (Hymes 1996; Blommaert 2005), as well as the ethnographer's capacity to communicate at an appropriate scale. Furthermore, rapport forms the interactional ground against which much linguistic anthropological theory is figured and for that reason alone is worth closer analytical attention. Rooting the theorization of rapport in the human capacity for intersubjectivity and examining intersubjectivity in terms of scale-shifting offers avenues for investigating rapport as it is created in real-time in ethnographic encounters.

References

Agha, Asif. 2007. *Language and social relations*. New York: Cambridge University Press.
Aoki, Eriko. 2004. Austronesian cosmopolitanism and Indonesia as a politico-economic system. *Antropologi Indonesia* 74. 75–86.
Bakhtin, Mikhail. 1981. *The dialogic imagination: Four essays*. Austin: University of Texas Press.
Blommaert, Jan. 2005. *Discourse: A critical introduction*. New York: Cambridge University Press.
Blommaert, Jan. 2007. Sociolinguistic scales. *Intercultural Pragmatics* 4(1). 1–19.
Blommaert, Jan. 2010. *The sociolinguistics of globalization*. New York: Cambridge University Press.
Blommaert, Jan. 2015. Chronotopes, scales, and complexity in the study of language in society. *Annual Review of Anthropology* 44. 105–116.
Blust, Robert A. 1993. Central and central eastern Malayo-Polynesian. *Oceanic Linguistics* 32. 241–293.
Carr, E. Summerson & Michael Lempert. 2016. *Scale: Discourse and dimensions of social life*. Berkeley: University of California Press.
Coupland, Justine, Nikolas Coupland & Jeffrey D. Robinson. 1992. "How are you?": Negotiating phatic communion. *Language in Society* 21(2). 207–230.
Crapanzano, Vincent. 1986. Hermes dilemma: The masking of subversion in ethnographic description. In James Clifford & George Marcus (eds.), *Writing Culture: The poetics and politics of ethnography*, 51–76. Berkeley: University of California Press.
Danziger, Eve. 2006. The thought that counts: Interactional consequences of variation in cultural theories of meaning. In Nicholas Enfield & Steven Levenson (eds.), *Roots of human sociality: Culture, cognition, and interaction*. New York: Berg.
Duranti, Alessandro. 2010. Husserl, intersubjectivity, and anthropology. *Anthropological Theory* 10(1). 1–20.
Eco, Umberto. 1997. *The search for the perfect language (The making of Europe)*. Malden, MA: Wiley Blackwell.
Enfield, Nicholas. 2006. Social consequences of common ground. In Nicholas Enfield & Stephen Levinson (eds.), *Roots of human sociality: Culture, cognition, and interaction*, 399–430. New York: Berg.
Fox, James J. 1998. Foreword: The linguistic context of Florenese culture. *Antropologi Indonesia* 56. 1–11.

Gable, Eric. 2014. The anthropology of guilt and rapport: Moral mutuality in ethnographic fieldwork. *Hau: Journal of Ethnographic Theory* 4(1). 237–258.
Gal, Susan. 2016. Scale-making: Comparison and perspective as ideological projects. In E. Summerson Carr & Michael Lempert (eds.), *Scale: Discourse and dimensions of social life*, 91–111. Berkeley: University of California Press.
Geertz, Clifford. 1972. Deep play: Notes on a Balinese cockfight. *Daedalus* 101(1). 1–37.
Goebel, Zane. 2015. *Language and superdiversity: Indonesians knowledging at home and abroad*. New York: Oxford University Press.
Goebel, Zane. 2016. Rapport and believability in interviews. Working Paper. https://www.academia.edu/23643832/Rapport_and_believability_in_interviews. (Accessed 22 February 2019).
Goebel, Zane, Howard Manns & Deborah Cole. 2016. Theorizing semiotic complexity: Contact registers and scalar shifters. In Zane Goebel, Howard Manns & Deborah Cole (eds.), *Margins, Hubs, and Peripheries in a Decentralizing Indonesia* (Tilburg Papers in Culture Studies 162), 4–16.
Gregory, Christopher. 2015. *Gifts and commodities*. 2nd edn. Chicago: Hau Books.
Haeri, Niloofar. 2003. *Sacred language, ordinary people: dilemmas of culture and politics in Egypt*. New York: Palgrave Macmillan.
Harr, Adam. 2013. Suspicious minds: Problems of cooperation in a Lio ceremonial council. *Language and Communication* 33(3). 317–325.
Harr, Adam. 2016. Recentering the margins? The politics of language in a decentralizing Indonesia. In Zane Goebel, Howard Manns & Deborah Cole (eds.), *Margins, Hubs, and Peripheries in a Decentralizing Indonesia* (Tilburg Papers in Culture Studies 162). 70–76.
Hymes, Dell. 1966. Two types of linguistic relativity. In William Bright (ed.), *Sociolinguistics*, 114–158. The Hague: Mouton.
Hymes, Dell. 1996. *Ethnography, linguistics, narrative inequality: Toward an understanding of voice*. (*Critical perspectives on literacy and education*.) Bristol PA: Taylor and Francis.
Irvine, Judith & Susan Gal. 2000. Language ideology and linguistic differentiation. In Paul Kroskrity (ed.), *Regimes of language: Ideologies, polities, and identities*, 35–84. Santa Fe, New Mexico: School of American Research Press.
Jakobson, Roman. 1960. Linguistics and poetics. In Thomas Sebeok (ed.), *Style in Language*, 350–377. Cambridge: MIT Press.
Keane, Webb. 1994. The value of words and the meaning of things in eastern Indonesian exchange. *Man* 29(3). 605–629.
Kuipers, Joel. 1990. *Power in performance: The creation of ritual authority in Weyewa ritual speech*. Philadelphia: University of Pennsylvania Press.
Liszkowksi, Ulf, Malinda Carpenter, Anne Henning, Tricia Striana & Michael Tomasello. 2004. Twelve-month-olds point to share attention and interest. *Developmental Science* 7(3). 297–307.
Marcus, George E. 1997. The uses of complicity in the changing mise-en-scene of anthropological fieldwork. *Representations* 59. 85–108.
Marston, Sallie A. 2000. The social construction of scale. *Progress in Human Geography* 24(2). 219–242.
Mauss, Marcel. 1990. *The gift: The form and reason for exchange in archaic societies*. New York: Norton.
Parry, Jonathan & Maurice Bloch. 1989. *Money and the morality of exchange*. Cambridge: Cambridge University Press.

Reddy, Michael. 1979. The conduit metaphor: A case study of frame conflict in our language about language. In Anthony Ortony (ed.), *Metaphor and thought*, 284–310. Cambridge: Cambridge University Press.

Robbins, Joel & Alan Rumsey. 2008. Cultural and linguistic anthropology and the opacity of other minds. *Anthropological Quarterly* 81. 407–494.

Rumsey, Alan & Eve Danziger. 2013. Intersubjectivity: Cultural limits, extensions, construals. *Language and Communication* 33(3). 247–343.

Spradley, James. 1979: *The ethnographic interview*. New York: Harcourt, Brace, and Jovanovich.

Tannen, Deborah. 1990. *You just don't understand: Women and men in conversation*. New York: Harper Collins.

Tomasello, Michael. 2006. Why don't apes point? In Nicholas Enfield & Stephen Levinson (eds.), *Roots of human sociality: Culture, cognition, and interaction*, 506–524. New York: Berg.

Tomasello, Michael. 2007. Shared intentionality. *Developmental Science* 10. 121–125.

Tomasello, Michael, Malinda Carpenter, Josep Call, Tanya Behne & Henrike Moll. 2005. Understanding and sharing intentions: The origins of cultural cognition. *Behavioral and Brain Sciences* 28. 675–735.

Tsing, Anna. 2000. The global situation. *Cultural Anthropology* 15(3). 327–360.

Uitermark, Justus. 2002. Re-scaling, 'scale fragmentation,' and the regulation of antagonistic relationships. *Progress in Human Geography* 26(6). 743–765.

Wallerstein, Immanuel. 1988. The inventions of timespace realities: Towards an understanding of our historical systems. *Geography* 73(4). 289–297.

Weiner, Annette. 1992. *Inalienable possessions: The paradox of keeping while giving*. Berkeley: University of California Press.

Bernard Arps
8 The Ethnolinguistic Listener: Narrativity and Ideologies of Local Language in Urban Banyuwangi

1 Introduction

Models of language and communication abstract from the complexities of the sociolingual life they should enable understanding. That is fine; abstraction is what gives a model its explanatory power. Nonetheless, established academic models of language and communication are not the one truth. They come from a Euro-American scholarly tradition rooted in particular historically determined ideologies of language. Other models exist, with different cultural backgrounds and points of attention, which may enrich academic enquiry.

The most influential of established models freeze lingual life and zoom in on a moment of communication, producing a still picture of a speaker, something said, and in some models an addressee. This kind of model renders it difficult to consider and theorize the many aspects of language that are fundamentally changeable over the course of interaction, as well as the aspects grounded in events and considerations beyond the short moment of communication that is treated as focal.

Rapport is a dimension of interaction for which this limitation of mainstream models has critical consequences. Rapport is not simply a quality that does or does not pertain to a social relationship in various gradations and forms. Much is gained by not conceptualizing rapport as atemporal and unstructured, but as a quality that emerges. This quality is maintained (or not), changes, fades or is cut short. It has ends. It is subject to evaluation and may be challenged. It occurs in discursive and physical circumstances, as well as a wider social context. In other words, much is gained by viewing rapport as a phenomenon in a social life that is felt to comprise a *dramatis personae*, place, temporality, and plots—a phenomenon in a world that possesses *narrativity*. Here I consider the interaction in which rapport may come into being from this vantage point. The empirical case study is from the far east of Java, Indonesia.

Bernard Arps, Leiden University, Leiden, The Netherlands

2 The Town of Banyuwangi and Its Lingual Makeup

In the regency of Banyuwangi in East Java, a chain of Javanese dialects that used to be considered by speakers and outsiders alike as a rustic *patois* is being fashioned into an autonomous language, recognized by government and the public as Banyuwangi's unique and alluring Regional Language. The campaign for the recognition of this language, called Osing, as both modern and distinct from Javanese has been going on for almost 50 years, centred in the regency capital, also called Banyuwangi.[1] Meanwhile the originating village dialects continue to be spoken outside town. In several dozen communities to the west and south-west of the capital, they are the primary means of everyday interaction. Many of these villages are at least two centuries old.[2]

In the town of Banyuwangi, too, there are such communities, but the urban population as a whole (*c.* 100,000) is more diverse linguistically and culturally, as a consequence of immigration throughout the town's existence. The town is the administrative center for the entire regency, which has *c.* 1.5 million inhabitants, among whom, depending on who makes the estimate, one fifth to a half speak Osing.[3] It is a regional center of commerce and education. A concentration of media and cultural organizations are headquartered here. Outsiders come to conduct their business, and in the 2000s it became a tourist destination, primarily for Indonesian domestic tourists.

While the town's status as a meeting-ground is of long standing, Osing dialects have had a presence from the onset. When it was founded by the Dutch United East India Company in 1774 after a war that devastated the kingdom of Blambangan located in the south of the region,[4] the town was composed of several quarters, most with a specific ethnic make-up. To this day, wards like Temenggungan and Kepatihan, named after the indigenous officials who resided there—

---

[1] A bird's-eye view of the historical process is in Arps (2010). This article, in Indonesian, is to be incorporated into an English-language monograph (in progress) on media, performance, and Islam in the making of Osing. The language is part of a struggle over local world-making that reaches beyond language, but language is at its core.

[2] They and their heads are listed in the *Babad Bayu*, a historical narrative set in 1771 though written in 1827 (Winarsih 1995: 153–154, 183, and 185). Language is not mentioned, but the currently known toponyms in the lists refer to villages that are or were known to be Osing-speaking, while current villages missing from the list are populated by speakers of central and east Javanese varieties or Madurese. Immigration into the Banyuwangi region from Java further west and Madura took off in the 1870s (Kumar 1979: 192).

[3] The 2000 Indonesian census registered 297,372 "Using-Osing" people (Suryadinata et al. 2003: 21). Osing activists estimated the number at 500,000 to 750,000 (Arps 2009: 9).

[4] Sri Margana 2007: 164–168.

the regent who bore the noble title of *Raden Tumenggung* and his chancellor the *Raden Patih*[5]—are regarded as Osing communities. Other parts of the current administrative district of Banyuwangi town (*kecamatan kota* in Indonesian), like Welaran, Cungking, and Pakis, used to be separate villages[6] but have been incorporated into the town. They, too, are considered Osing. The varieties spoken in downtown neighborhoods have lost some of their local distinctiveness and are merging into a general Banyuwangi town variety of Osing.[7] More outlying areas like Cungking and Pakis retain local idiosyncrasies. The town also continues to have quarters dominated by other ethnicities—especially the Chinese area popularly known as the *pecinan* (a Chinatown of sorts) and the Arab neighbourhood called *kampung Arab* 'Arab compound'—while some quarters are officially named after immigrant groups that used to be clustered there, although these groups may have largely dissolved into the general urban mix. Examples are *Kampung Melayu* 'Malay Compound', *Kampung Mandar* 'Mandarese Compound', *Kampung Bali* 'Balinese Compound', and *Kebalénan* 'the Balinese place'.[8]

Not all neighbourhoods in Banyuwangi town, then, are ethnically and sociolinguistically like villages; they are more diverse. The town in its entirety is fundamentally *unlike* villages—save in one crucial cultural respect. It is just as homogeneous, like those villages, in that almost all Banyuwanginese, be they speakers of Osing or otherwise, are Muslims. Islam is paramount in social and public life.

---

5 Epp 1849: 252.
6 The first two are among the villages listed in the *Babad Bayu* (Winarsih 1995: 153, 185), which does not mention Banyuwangi itself.
7 Which does not have an established name but I have heard referred to as *cara Using kota* 'urban Osing', in which *kota* is Indonesian for 'town, city'. According to oral history, the dialectal distinctions between adjacent neighbourhoods are due to the fact that different village populations from throughout the region that had fled into the wilderness during the wars with the East India Company were relocated in separate settlements around the new capital after 1774 (p. c. from the late Hasan Ali, 4 August 2002).
8 In 1846, alongside the Javanese or "Blambangers" (named after the former kingdom of Blambangan) who made up 91% of the regency's population, Epp identified Madurese, Balinese, Mandarese, Chinese, Arabs or Moors, and Europeans (Epp 1849: 247; Arps 2009: 5). Epp indicated that nearly all immigrant groups lived in the then-district of Banyuwangi (the northern half of the regency, as opposed to the southern district of Ragajampi) (1849: 254). Most will in fact have resided in the capital. Epp explicitly mentions that "the Balinese inhabit a small, dirty kampong" where they are headed by a *gusti* (lord), interact little with the Javanese on account of their different religion and customs, and are building a temple, while "the Chinese inhabit, in the capital town, the most unwholesome kampong along the beach, surrounded by marshes" (1849: 249; my translations from Dutch). The former refers to the present-day ward (*kelurahan*) of Kebalenan or, more likely, the Kampung Bali neighbourhood in the ward of Penganjuran, and the latter to the Chinese quarter (still adjacent to marshland), all in Banyuwangi town.

It is striking, therefore, that Islam has been virtually absent from Osing language activism and promotion. This historically established, politically inspired avoidance of Islamic themes, genres, and arguments in the making of Osing plays a role in the urban language ideologies that envelop Osing and help to constitute it.[9]

In this chapter the focus is on rapport in this multicultural context. The data come from my own fieldwork experience. I address key language-ideological features underlying the emergence of rapport—sometimes quickly, sometimes gradual, possibly under a persistent shadow of reserve—between myself, a Dutch and non-Muslim researcher of Osing language and performance, and acquaintances in the town. I have been visiting since 1983 and lived there in 1989 and 1996–1997. Over the years, I developed friendly relations particularly with members of three urban families that differ markedly from each other in ethnoreligious background and repertoire of language varieties. While central members of each family have an interest in Osing, it is other varieties that serve as the household language. While I share this interest, my interactions with them have been in Indonesian. This externality, as one could call it, of Osing in all three households is in fact typical of Banyuwangi town; it, too, is key in local language ideologies.

3 Models of Language Use

The fact that Banyuwangi town is a meeting-ground for people with different backgrounds and competencies has significant consequences for the lingual dimension of interaction and representation—that is, for language. The models through which mainstream linguistic scholarship attempts to identify the essential properties—functional, formal, semantic, pragmatic—of language, as well as its more social and cultural dimensions, are poorly suited to such a situation. If ideologies about language or linguistic ideologies are, to quote an influential definition, "any sets of beliefs about language articulated by the users as a rationalization or justification of perceived language structure and use" (Silverstein 1979: 193), and linguists are among "the users", these scholarly models are themselves language ideologies. Influential Euro-American models identify *the speech event* or *the situation of utterance* (or a similar concept) as the material wellspring

---

9 Representing other religions in Osing is unimaginable (although in practice it happens). Elsewhere I hope to discuss Islam's historical absence from Osing language activism, as well as the seemingly paradoxical fact that Osing has had a presence in Islamic popular culture since the 1990s and increasingly since *c*. 2010, when the current regent (*bupati*), Azwar Anas, in many of whose policies Islam is a weighty factor, took power.

of language's general properties. In an alternative model (Chomsky's), an ideal speaker–listener or speaker–hearer applies his cognitive grasp of a language to his discourse in a completely homogeneous speech-community. In these pattern-seeking models, a single generic moment or situation is supposed to represent language as it should be conceived.

As an example, in Jakobson's model of "the constitutive factors in any speech event, in any act of verbal communication" (1960: 353), the six factors he recognized allow one to distinguish "the six basic functions of verbal communication" (1960: 357), of language (1960: 353). However, the *speaker* and *addressee* are tacitly assumed to share and be communicating in the same stable language (the "*code*"). While there is "a *context* referred to [...], seizable by the addressee, and either verbal or capable of being verbalized" (1960: 353), in terms of place, time, and sociolingual dynamics other properties of the setting are assumed to be constant, invariable, and irrelevant for the model. In her programmatic critique a quarter century later, Pratt (1987) argued that it is misleading to consider such a model emblematic of language, if the model is to reflect actual language use in contact zones.

As I examine co-present situations of language use characterized by contextual as well as lingual heterogeneity and fluidity, I follow Pratt's lead. In the discourse that happens in Banyuwangi town, language varieties may be contextually flexible, changing dynamically even in the course of a single conversation, and all interlocutors do not necessarily draw on the same language.[10] Settings, too, may shift spatially and sociolingually during conversation.

Clearly an interpretive model that helps to make sense of this situation should allow for change. It would be useful also if it took into account the conventions and considerations that give this change direction. I contend that analytical models of language use should extend beyond a still picture of interactants communicating, and be sensitive to temporalities of variable magnitude, direction, and form; temporalities whose cohesion may be animated by a plethora of factors. Such models should allow for concatenations of events linked causally. They should allow also for long events (processes) that are driven internally by various causalities. They should allow for courses from past to present, or other vectors depending on what overall form of temporal relationality is invoked: cyclical, parallel, metaphorical, and so on. They should allow for pathways into the future, in all sorts of ontological modalities: hoped for, imperative, potential, undesirable, and so on.

---

10 When I represent certain language varieties (languages, dialects, styles) as distinct, they are relatively stably enregistered (Agha 2005) or commonly identified as distinct. It is not implied that all languages are equally stable, widely spread, and shared.

The need for understandings that must, in the interest of transcultural analytical capacity, be abstract and schematic, but that range beyond the unitary moment is abundantly clear when one considers the central theme of this volume. *Rapport* tends to be conceived as a quality of interpersonal relationships. But rapport at first sight, so to speak, is rare. Rapport is emergent. It comes into being in a process of interaction that may extend over numerous encounters; it has its beginnings and is sparked and fueled by motivations. If it is not actively maintained, rapport is likely to dissolve and may even be destroyed. And, as we know from the textbooks, rapport has its yields in the long run: friendship at the very least, a rewarding fieldwork experience perhaps, and fruitful ethnographic research. In other words, rapport and the discursive interaction in which it emerges and to which it is ascribed possess not only a *dramatis personae* and a setting, but also temporality and indeed a plot. Rapport, in a word, has narrativity.

This is why in this chapter I advocate theoretical openness to the narrative dimension, to narrativity, of models of language use, communication, or lingual interaction. Let narrativity in language ideologies be studied. And let this study begin with lived, "folk" language ideologies. Despite the fact that other, emblematic kinds of ideology that have been thoroughly explored in scholarship are clearly primarily oriented towards change and consolidation (think of Marxism, nationalism, and many religions), academic studies of language ideology have given scanty analytical attention to the narrativity of ideas and feelings about language.[11] Javanese models suggest an interesting and enlightening enhancement. As models, they too are schematic. They too are focused on persons, perhaps even more strongly than Western academic ones.[12] But, Javanese models represent persons not so much under the aspect of interactants in a dyadic exchange

---

[11] Two important near-exceptions are Blommaert (1999) and Makihara and Schieffelin (2007). Blommaert's introduction reveals that he attached considerable importance to narrativity—although he did not identify it as such, but rather referred to the social nature of "time" (which is something of a misnomer). In Makihara and Schieffelin's (2007: 15) introduction process and change are recognized as important in connection with language ideology and it is pointed out that there is an "accumulation of many small choices", but the narrative structure of that process and of the way those choices mesh escapes notice. This kind of attempt to understand sociolingual change would benefit from an explanatory model that besides interparticipant relations attends to plot.

[12] Even Goffman (1979) dissects out participants, classifying them according to their roles with respect to an utterance. In his comparatively complex but nonetheless deliberately memorable model of the components of speech acts and speech events, Hymes (1974: 55–57) recognizes not only time, place, and physical circumstances (grouped together as "setting") and participants but also a factor "ends". It consists of the communally-conventionally recognized "purpose" of speech acts and the individual motives of participants ("goals"). However, Hymes limits his discussion of temporality and causality to this particular teleological aspect of language use (in

as under the aspect of *dramatis personae*, a conception that allows for a broader range of participants and that invokes other dimensions of narrativity as well: timing, placement, and plot. Such elements and qualities are projected upon the chaos of the lifeworld as a way of apprehending it, as if it is like a narrative. The same narrative elements and qualities serve as productive patterns for behaviour as well. Whether before or after the fact, or during it, narrativity is a modality of giving sense to worlds, of world-making.[13]

In this chapter, I distinguish four ideological models that are prevalent among Banyuwanginese in respect of Osing. Each model profiles a type of member of the *dramatis personae* involved in the day-to-day appearance of the language. These models also help to draw out my own perceived position as language user, which, I suggest, helps to understand the rapport I experienced. Rapport between locals and outsider participant–observers is a social phenomenon that is part of worldmaking. Linguistic models, insofar as they serve as reality-constructing ideologies for the users of the languages that are modelled, and especially those models that help to make sense of interaction between ethnolingual others, play a role in rapport. Such models may be about language in general but also vary by language; my focus here is on Osing.

These models are not always expressed; they may have to be discovered through careful observation of interaction and metadiscursive behaviour.[14] The analysis here takes the shape of a series of vignettes derived from fieldwork in 1996–1997 and 2002 (described largely in the ethnographic present tense), and incorporating insights developed during earlier and later visits as well. The sketches analyze encounters of varying duration and density, with participants with different lingual backgrounds and baggage. Like all in-the-flesh encounters, they are predicated upon mobility, and one among them typically takes place in a state of physical motion, which, as we shall see, is relevant for the ontology of Osing in the town.

---

fact, under the specific aspect of motivation). He represents it as orientations towards the future that are collapsed, like in the less socially sensitive linguistic models, into a singular and timeless speech event or speech act. Although he did not use the term plot, let alone narrativity, obviously Hymes's motivations are input for emplotment.

13 This idea of *world-making* is transdisciplinary and eclectic in origin. It has three main sources of inspiration: the French narratological concept of *diegesis*, embraced especially in film studies, the cultural anthropological idea of the discursive and especially performative creation of sociocultural reality, and Goodman's (1978) philosophical ideas, from which I took the name.

14 My general approach is that of philology, conceived as the artefact-focused study of worldmaking (Arps 2016b). The focal artefact in this case is the Osing language. A full philology would study its artefactuality, apprehensibility, compositionality, historicity, and contextuality.

I begin with three sketches of long-lasting encounters: family situations. The people in these examples adjust their language to each other and to their residential environment and social networks in various ways. After a theoretical interlude drawing a profile of the typical Osing user in the regency capital *vis-à-vis* other typical users of the language, next is a sketch of mode of public transport in the town, the minibus or *lin*, dedicated to facilitating movement and encounters. Speakers here create complex patterns of language choice. This helps to deepen my account of the typical Osing user, whose profile—characterized as it is by narrativity—is realized in events and strings of events. Issues of ethnicity and religion surface in the concluding two vignettes, which analyze single events belonging to types that are common in city life: a ritual meal and an impromptu get-together of friends and colleagues in a food stall. To round off, I connect the profile of the urban Osing user with my persona as a researcher, my acquaintances, and rapport.

4 The Home as an Urban Contact Zone

The neighbourhood popularly known as *Kampung Arab* lies about a kilometre north of the town center, between a market and minibus terminal and the coast. South and west of it lie neighbourhoods regarded as Osing, while the area to the north is partly industrial and to the extent that it is populated, this is mostly by Madurese.

It is called *Kampung Arab* because it used to be inhabited most prominently by people of Arab extraction. This remains true today. The houses along the two main streets cutting through the neighbourhood are single-storied (as are almost all houses in Banyuwangi), built of brick, plastered and white-washed. Some boast pillared porches that betray the homes' age (they were built in the late nineteenth century) and the wealth of their owners. Some double as shops or workshops. Three kinds of businesses are conspicuous: furniture makers, butchers that sell goat meat, and agencies sending women to Saudi Arabia as domestic workers. Some inhabitants are *sayyid*, descendants of the Prophet Muhammad, and Islam has an unmistakable presence in the area. There is a relatively large mosque (of the reformist Muslim organization *Muhammadiyah*) and a kindergarten of the Arab–Indonesian socio-religious organization al-Irsyad. The alleys off the main streets are inhabited by poorer people, many living in houses of wood and plaited bamboo. Most are Madurese who earn their livelihood with menial jobs like pedicab driving and domestic labor.

Many of the people in the streets appear physiologically different from other Banyuwanginese; their skins tend to be darker or on the contrary lighter, their hair is curly. Almost without exception, the women wear headscarves, often plain white or black. The language heard does not sound like average Indonesian either. To be sure, it is a variety of Malay, but not standard Indonesian or common Javanese Indonesian, as it is characterized by a number of words uncommon in those varieties, like *kau* for non-polite 'you' and *énté* for polite 'you'. Other typical vocabulary too, like *abah* for 'father' and *umi* for 'mother', are loans from Arabic and give the language an Arabic flavour, even if the great majority of inhabitants of Kampung Arab do not speak conversational Arabic. The main exception is the few very old people who were born in Hadramauth and moved here in their youth. Of a very different nature is the Qur'anic Arabic that everyone has learned to recite as children. The intonation of the Kampung Arab variety of Malay is also peculiar; it has the tuneful pathos of Osing. Influence from Osing is also evident via certain loanwords, such as *tembung* for 'ball', and calques such as the frequent use of *sudah* 'already', often reduced to *sedah*, to mark the end of declarative sentences. This corresponds to one of the uses of *wis* or *wih* in Osing.

When people move into the neighbourhood, marrying into an Arab family, they adopt this language. But many inhabitants also master other varieties, which they speak with outsiders. As traders, they have frequent contacts with Madurese Osing people in the region, and they tend to speak at least a smattering of both languages. Many are well-educated and have mastered standard Indonesian as well. From the mosque's loudspeakers and the pulpit they hear Islamic matters thematized in Indonesian and Islamic sensibilities invoked in Arabic. Wedding celebrations are usually enlivened by the music-and-dance genre called *gambus*, strongly associated with Arab–Indonesians of Yemeni descent; the songs amplified over the neighbourhood are in Arabic and Malay.

One of the families here is that of *Paq* Asan,[15] my friend, whom I got to know in 1989 when I researched literary rituals in the Banyuwangi countryside. At the time he worked at the local Department of Education and Culture as a school inspector. Considered both cosmopolitan and knowledgeable about local customs, he was assigned to help me (and probably to keep an eye on me). Our relationship soon turned into friendship. *Paq* Asan was born in this neighbourhood in the late 1930s and lived here most of his life, with some intervals when he felt forced to move elsewhere for political reasons. In his twenties he married an Arab woman; they have three sons. Two live in Kampung Arab and one, after marrying a woman also of Arabic descent, moved to a town in the south to trade there. The youngest son is unmarried and lives with his parents.

Paq Asan has never been wealthy. He became a primary schoolteacher and did other jobs to provide for his family when, as a staunch Sukarnoist, he was

---

15 A pseudonym, like the other names I will mention.

prevented from teaching under the New Order as considerable pressure was put on civil servants to become members of the government party, which he stubbornly refused to do.[16] *Paq* Asan commands respect, particularly among Osing and Madurese acquaintances, not only because of his age and his well-known determination in the face of political adversity, but also as a former teacher and because, as an Arab, he is automatically credited with more than average knowledge of Islam. As a teacher and political activist, and because he has lived in a Madurese village in the north, *Paq* Asan has many contacts throughout the area and besides the local Malay and standard Indonesian he speaks Madurese and Osing quite fluently, as well as some Javanese. He delights in displaying his knowledge of Osing sayings and proverbs. His wife, meanwhile, has never travelled outside the region and communicates in Malay, mainly the local variety, although she has a smattering of standard Indonesian as well.

Paq Asan's eldest son lives a stone's throw from *Paq* Asan, with his wife, an Arab from Bali. He finished secondary school but earns his living from driving. He drove a lorry for some time and in those years lived in Jakarta. After moving back to Banyuwangi he bought his present home, with financial help from his wife who hails from a prosperous family of furniture traders in Bali. For several years, he drove a pickup truck owned by a relative and, when taxis were introduced in Banyuwangi in 2001, he became a taxi driver. He speaks Indonesian well but in this neighbourhood and in family circles a Kampung Arab quality colors his speech. He is acquainted with Madurese, Osing, and Javanese but has no all-round mastery of any of them. His wife speaks Balinese and Arabic, the latter because she worked in Saudi Arabia for some years, and of course the local Malay variety as well as Indonesian, but not Javanese, Osing, or Madurese.

Gunadi was born in Banyuwangi in 1957 into the entrepreneurial class of Chinese origin. His uncle owned a downtown grocery store, and his father managed an expansive coffee plantation a dozen kilometres from town. Gunadi spent part of his youth among the Madurese plantation workers there and also got to know people from a nearby Osing village. Having finished university in central Java, he returned to Banyuwangi to take over most of his father's duties at the plantation. Gunadi married a woman from central Java, also Chinese, who went to university in the United States and used to be a teacher, but now that she lives in Banyuwangi earns a little money from selling quality clothes she purchases in Surabaya to other Chinese women around town. There is no financial need to do this; she has her own money, as her family is wealthy. They have two daughters

---

[16] Sukarnoism is associated with the tenure of Indonesia's first president, while the New Order period, 1966–1998, is associated with Indonesia's second president, Soeharto.

who go to what is reputedly the best primary school in Banyuwangi, a Catholic one. They are destined to attend secondary school in Surabaya (where Gunadi's mother lives) or perhaps Singapore (where there are also relatives).

As ethnic Chinese, the family are universally supposed to be not Muslims but Christians, Buddhists, or Confucianists. They do not display their (Christian) affinities in any way, but neither do they enter mosques or attend the Islamic sermons and lectures that have become a standard component of religious life among the Muslim populace of Indonesia. Of course, they do hear the call to prayer (in Arabic) and occasional sermons (in Indonesian or sometimes Javanese) amplified from the ubiquitous mosques, and because Gunadi's professional network includes many Muslims he, and occasionally the other members of the family, may attend *selametan* ritual meals and hear Javanese, Indonesian, and Arabic prayers there, but that will normally be it as far as Islam is concerned.

The family lives in a modern, fenced house on a road that runs from the town center outwards, from which the plantation is easily reached. The house lies within the town boundaries, but is part of ribbon development; behind the homes on either side of the road, alternating with a few government buildings, rice paddies stretch out. This is not an urban compound or neighbourhood (*kampung*), nor a village (*désa*). All the neighbors are wealthy; their houses are big, and by Banyuwangi standards there is little contact among them. The family values its privacy. They employ domestic staff who cook, clean, and when necessary drive, but rather unusually they do not live in. They live in nearby Osing-dominated neighbourhoods (formerly villages). All are ethnically Osing.

The language spoken in this household is the Javano–Malay that is typical of ethnic Indonesian–Chinese all over Java. It is basically Malay with Javanese loans, affixes, and pronunciation. The Javanese component in Gunadi's family is regionally coloured rather than strictly local; its base is not Osing but a variety I would characterize as common eastern Javanese.[17] All speak standard Indonesian well, and the mother has English and a little Javanese, but no Osing or Madurese, while her Chinese is limited to well-known words and phrases. The children have no Osing either, but of course they do master the common eastern Javanese current among pupils at their school, many of whom are also of Chinese descent (not surprising since this is a Catholic school in an area heavily dominated by Islam). Finally, Gunadi speaks a fair amount of Osing, Madurese, and even formal Javanese, as well as English. In these respects, he is exceptional among the Chinese population of his generation in Banyuwangi. In fact, people generally find it almost

---

17 Like the other local varieties of Chinese Javano–Malay described by Rafferty 1984, Oetomo 1987, and Oetomo 1991: 64–65.

impossible to imagine Chinese as speaking Osing.[18] Gunadi's ability in Osing is due to the fact that he spends many an evening in an Osing village roughly midway between Banyuwangi town and the plantation, chatting deep into the night with friends from that village and nearby places, many of whom are ethnic Osing. It was in this village that I first met Gunadi, but at the time I felt no inclination to get to know him better. We became friends years later, after he had briefly visited the Netherlands with a group of musicians and dancers from the village. Gunadi's wife and children are rarely seen in this village (although they do spend the occasional weekend at the plantation), and they lack the cultural affinity with Osing people that Gunadi evidently feels.

With their three daughters and one son, Marwati and her husband Hanafi live in a small partly brick house in an alley behind one of the streets of Kampung Arab. Like their neighbours, most of whom are Madurese, they are poor and have had no education beyond primary school. Hanafi is a pedicab driver and handyman and Marwati a domestic worker. This is how I got to know the family: When I lived in Banyuwangi, in Kampung Arab, in 1996–1997 she worked for us. Hanafi has also been a pop musician, playing the popular Islamically tinged genre *dangdut* (with Indonesian and occasionally Javanese lyrics) and Banyuwangi pop music (with lyrics in Osing), but the instruments had to be sold. Despite their dismal economic situation, they manage to send their children to school. The two eldest daughters, identical twins aged 15, go to a Senior High School for Business and Commerce, the third to primary school, while the son has not reached school age.

Marwati is Madurese like most inhabitants of Kampung Arab's alleys, her husband is Osing like most people in adjacent quarters. Despite this and the fact that the main streets of the neighbourhood are dominated by Arab-style Malay, in their home another language is spoken: common eastern Javanese. Both parents are proficient in this language; it was, so to speak, lingual middle ground. Indonesian, the national language, is not a realistic option for familial dialogue in this working class milieu. All master Indonesian, especially the father and the children (whose Indonesian is rather colloquial and, depending on the context, influenced by local languages in terms of intonation patterns, pronunciation, sometimes loanwords and expressions, and affective particles), but Indonesian feels formal and geographically and culturally distant. The household members en-

---

[18] I have heard a major Osing language activist, who was not averse to puristic sentiments, declare that a simple and incontrovertible sign that a particular village was more purely Osing-speaking than another was that no Chinese lived in the former. I have witnessed a discussion in another Osing village about Gunadi's ethnicity (in his absence). The interlocutors settled on the idea that he must be Korean.

counter Indonesian particularly in educational and religious contexts. Like everywhere, the Arabic they hear connotes Islamic ritual and affect. The two teenage daughters—one of whom I got to know much better than her twin sister and their younger siblings—understand Madurese, but speak only a little and definitely not the polite variety. This becomes problematic when their mother's older relatives, to whom they owe deference, come to visit. The daughters do speak Osing, for instance with relatives from Hanafi's side of the family. Asked to which ethnicity they feel they belong, they answer without hesitation: Osing. About the language they say: "Osing is pleasant, it's about spontaneously speaking your mind."[19]

The members of these three households live their daily lives in very different lingual environments and have differing competencies in Osing. Their practical-discursive and affective relationships *vis-à-vis* Osing vary. I will show next that they do share a profile in their capacity as users of Osing. Although this profile is an indistinct one that is not named and must be formulated abstractly, it is an ideological reality that helps to give social sense to their lives as language users in Banyuwangi.

On separate occasions, my key interlocutors in these three families—Gunadi, *Paq* Asan, and one of the twin teenagers—came (along with me or, in the case of Gunadi, on his own) to an all-Osing village. It was fascinating to observe their interactions with Osing speakers there. These interactions underscored two points. First, the status of an individual as a user of languages not only changes over time, but is situationally variable, and it emerges interactionally. Second, such a status can be thematized in discourse and thereby reified and modelled. While in town my friends in their capacity as users of languages were very unlike each other, for the villagers the differences in lingual competency and cultural baggage were of subordinate importance. (I am not claiming that no differences were observed.) In the village one is basically assigned to one of two groups, speakers of the local language (a variety of Osing, a term that is rarely used here) and people who do not. Gunadi was often seen in the village, *Paq* Asan had been there occasionally, and the teenage girl had never visited before, but in all cases, their command of Osing put them squarely into the first category. In multilingual Banyuwangi town on the other hand, where Osing speakers do not dominate but where government-related organizations, activists, and a local media industry work on Osing, the set of ambient ideologically recognized types of Osing language users is more complex.

---

19 In the original Indonesian: "Kalau bahasa Using itu énaq, langsung nyeplos gitu aja" (interview 22 February 1997).

5 The Typical Urban Osing User: A Profile

The Muslim family in the Arab quarter of Banyuwangi speak distinctly Arabic-flavored Malay in the home and neighbourhood, but they interact frequently with speakers of Osing. The Christian family of Chinese ancestry use the Javano–Malay typical of ethnic Chinese all over Java, and only few of them move in Osing circles. In the home of the working-class Muslim family of which the father is Osing and the mother Madurese the language is East Javanese, a compromise inspired by the wider region's dominant vernacular, although the children self-identify as Osing. For all their variation, these family situations reveal the contours of an ideology of Osing that is shared across the town. The adult and adolescent members of these families know that Osing is politically significant in Banyuwangi as an emblem of regional identity. They are familiar with its sounds and from time to time perceive it being spoken, although, remarkably, not in public on religious matters. Most, however, utter Osing rarely if ever. If some of them do, it is in certain circumstances only, on specific themes, perhaps in particular states of mind, and drawing on a small lexical and grammatical repertoire. One of the most prominent active spoken uses of Osing that my friends do regularly engage in (also with me, knowing that I am interested) is exchange of phatic formulas: greetings and kindred pleasantries, and occasionally in the case of *Paq* Asan proverbs and sayings.[20]

Language ideologies come in many shapes and sizes.[21] In Java, person-centred ones, images of typical, normal, ideal users or simply *the user* of language or *a* language, are very common. This particular focus is in harmony with the centrality of person in Javanese ideologies of world-making generally.[22] Besides helping to give meaning to language use, these models are powerful determinants of what is considered feasible modes and structures of interaction. On more than one occasion in Java, I have been unable to engage in interaction with people because they just could not hear my utterances as intelligible (they really were!).

---

[20] This is akin to the phatic use of Osing write-in (and call-in) radio music programmes analysed in Arps 2003. Even when I communicate long-distance via sms and Facebook, which I do with Gunadi, we tend to open with phatic formulas in Osing.

[21] And after Silverstein's (1979) influential essay critical attention has been paid to language ideologies in several important collections (e. g. Schieffelin et al. 1998; Blommaert 1999; Kroskrity 2000; Makihara and Schieffelin 2007).

[22] See the discussions of a famous Javanese incantatory prayer in Arps (1996: 96), of spatial affect in Arps (2016a), and of the orientation of shadow puppetry theory in Arps (2016b: 37, 41). With regard to Banyuwangi specifically, there is of course the figure of the "Osing Kid" (Arps 2009), further discussed subsequently.

The very idea of conversing with an evident alien in a local language was *a priori* inconceivable.

It would be short-sighted and totally not in line with these world-making ideologies widespread in Java to regard the language-using person in a spatial, temporal, and social vacuum and as unbound by procedure. Except in gross and short-hand references, the language-using person is imagined and categorized in Javanese lingual ideology as an actor performing against a background of place, history, and community, in more or less patterned courses of events. Let me focus here on these models' central component, the person, and refer to the other dimensions later. In respect of Osing, four main types of people are distinguished in town. The first is the *wong Using* (in Osing and Javanese), *orang Osing* (Indonesian), or Osinger (to anglicize a colonial-era Dutch term). He or she is an "all-round" Osing user, assumed always to be able to speak and understand Osing about everything discussable in a spectrum of ways. The Osinger is likely to come from a village or one of the Osing parts of town (like Temenggungan, Welaran, Cungking, or Pakis). They will be a Muslim.

The second profile, the opposite of the Osinger, is that of the ignoramus. Only never having resided in Banyuwangi makes it possible to be entirely ignorant of Osing, such is the idea. But it is recognized that many have never done so and will not either. This Osing-related profile corresponds largely with the more general sociocultural category of 'outsider' (*orang luar* in Indonesian, *wong luwar* in Osing and Javanese).

Thirdly there is the *Laré Using*, as he or she is called in Osing, the 'Osing Kid'. There is no Javanese or Indonesian equivalent, demonstrating the label's intended intrinsic Osingness. This model is more crystallized than the Osinger and the ignoramus. It is not just a profile, a featureless silhouette that can be coloured in many ways, but what I have called a *figure*, prominently thematized in Banyuwangi discourse, employed strategically in the campaign for recognition of Osing, commercially in marketing Banyuwangi to domestic tourists, and in the service of local identity in other ambient discourses such as football fandom (Arps 2009). In recent years, the Osing Kid has come to be assigned a distinctive dress, socially expected to be worn at official ceremonial occasions (though not at primarily Islamic ones): for men especially, a batik shirt displaying a particular motif and an intricately folded headband, for women a batik wraparound skirt with the same motif. Thus the figure of the Osing kid can be readily visualized.

The language modelled in dominant western linguistic models tends to be spontaneous and *ad hoc*, and spoken. This would in fact disqualify the Osing Kid as a model for language-userhood. But on the ground s/he very much is one. Indeed we know that people sing, that language as ideologically salient cultural performance often includes or even *is* song, and that song can play a major role in language acquisition (Faudree 2013). As a language-user model, then, the Osing Kid sings. What he or she utters is pre-fabricated language: pop song lyrics, invariably in Osing. This prefabricated language, which is played, sung, and heard by many across the region, is about Banyuwangi patriotism or love (Arps 2009), and not about Islam, even positively avoiding it.

The last profile is the typical urban Osing user. Like the Osing Kid, in mainstream linguistics it would be out of order as a model of language use. The socially established profile of the common urban Osing user involves, primarily, hearing the language being uttered by others, and listening to it with interest. This person does not hear Osing all the time, nor everywhere. Built into the model is the presumption of temporal structure and mobility. The typical urban user of Osing will normally hear Islamic matters discussed and Islamic feelings invoked in other language varieties. The typical urban Osing user may venture some Osing from time to time, but only in limited ways, especially in phatic formulas. S/he may on occasion project her- or himself as an Osing Kid. But by and large the language is only heard by them.

Unlike the speakers and addressees modelled in western academic linguistics, these profiles possess narrativity. They posit language users as actors. They obtain in a place, the regency of Banyuwangi and its capital especially. They obtain at certain times, from always to moments of leisure or ceremony. Perhaps most importantly, these profiles incorporate assumptions and desires regarding their roles in plots—sometimes rudimentary protoplots—that run, smoothly or event after event, from an antecedent past (here or elsewhere) to now (here, on a variety of occasions) and possibly into a desired future.

Next are three analyses of urban language use in domains other than the familial, which highlight other matters beside lingual competencies and repertoires. They show how the model of the typical urban Osing user has more intricacy and depth, and accommodates greater fluidity than the sketch just given necessarily suggests. These vignettes concern a type of public place and two types of frequent event. They will help to form an understanding of the narrative basis of the lingual world-making phenomenon that was my rapport with members of the three families and incidental interlocutors.[23]

---

[23] They can also help to explain the form that the campaign for Osing has been taking (e. g. Arps 2010).

6 Events in Public Space

While a language ideology may be regarded as something in its own league, it is also part of the larger category of world-making ideologies. Even if person-centred, these can be about *where* to make one's world as a language user (mostly with others: as language users), and *how* to build it there. The following description shows that the worlds made by language users have an aspect one could call eventness. This is a property of the narrativity of these worlds. The events thus created are emplotted in different and complex ways both internally and in relation to each other.

The only form of public transport in town that runs along fixed routes—fixed most of the time, because they can be chartered and when school is out and throngs of passengers present themselves all at once, they readily change their routes—are the yellow minibuses (passenger vans) called *lin* or *elin* (from Dutch *lijn* 'line'). *Lin* operate in the daytime, largely within the municipal borders, and can be hailed anywhere along the way; they let off passengers anywhere too. They are used by men, women, and children who want to move relatively quickly at low cost (a fixed fare) over a distance that is too long for walking in Banyuwangi's sultry heat. There is no room for baggage inside, but bulky items can be put on the roof. Wealthy people avoid *lin*. They are small, hot, grimy, possibly ramshackle, and often cramped, while these people own motorcycles and cars and can afford a pedicab or taxi. But for those who lack access to such means of transport and for those who want to continue on from one of the terminals by coach, train, or ferry, *lin* are handy. Gunadi and his wife, for instance, do not use them because they have cars, but their daughters may to go to school and back; *Paq* Asan, his wife, and their sons and daughters-in-law use them if they want to travel long-distance from a bus terminal, although they prefer *Paq* Asan's or one of his sons' motorcycles; while Marwati and Hanafi as well as their children, who do not own a motorcycle, use them often.

Lin are mobile meeting-grounds. Two passengers can sit next to the driver, and about twelve adults can sit on the two opposite low benches along the length of the vehicle or the short ones behind the front seats and along the back, plus the movable wooden stool on which, if he is there, the conductor (*kernét*) sits in the door opening, hailing potential passengers and receiving the fare when they get off. The stool can be moved inside when the vehicle is really full, in which case the conductor and perhaps an additional passenger hang in the doorway, partly outside. The continual entering and getting-off of passengers fills an unavoidably intimate space with an ever-changing mixture of potential speakers, often seated face-to-face. Many indeed talk.

The facilitators of these conversations are themselves by and large "all-round" Osing speakers. This sector of public transport is largely in the hands of men from Osing neighbourhoods around town. The drivers often own the vehicles, and they make these spaces not only their own, with stickers and pendants, but also render them lingually Osing. Some have car music systems that blare out Osing pop. The drivers and conductors often talk, or rather shout, to colleagues in other passing *lin* and to potential passengers along the street—though this is often limited to the destination, such as *Pérot Pérot Pérot!* for Sasak Pérot terminus or *ngalor!* (Osing and Javanese for 'northward'). Drivers and conductors converse among themselves in their shared language, Osing. They are also prone to talk to passengers. They treat Osing as the proper language of the space in which they work. That space may be public but it belongs to them. They feel no scruples against addressing their passengers in Osing.

Although some remain silent, many passengers, too, engage in conversation. Strangers may exchange phatic talk, the most usual initial subject of which is each other's origin or destination, while acquaintances of course talk about all manner of things. In a *lin* one hears conversations in Osing, but also eastern Javanese (not least among schoolchildren), Indonesian and other varieties of Malay, and Madurese. Most remarkable are those dialogues where the interlocutors do not speak each other's preferred language but understand enough of it to be able to communicate nonetheless. Such nonreciprocal bilingual dialogue, usually Madurese–Osing, Osing–Javanese, or Javanese–Madurese, is by no means uncommon here.

During my periods in Banyuwangi, I used *lin* frequently. Sometimes there was talk about me, to which I just listened. Once I was characterized in idiomatic Osing as *turis kepaling*, a 'Caucasian/tourist gone astray'. A certain transitory rapport would arise when drivers noticed I understood and spoke some Osing.[24] The rapport grew if it was noticed that I lived in an Osing part of town and was, as one driver exclaimed, one of his own neighbours. But this was the sort of brief connection one may feel with strangers who will remain strangers and whom one is likely to forget.

Lin, then, make an almost subaltern contribution to the languagescape of urban Banyuwangi, to lingually constructing the town. Through their own stubborn use of Osing while criss-crossing it, drivers and conductors help to render it Osing. Unlike the contributions made by media (especially radio and VCDs) to the language that is ambient in town (Arps 2009), the Osing they strew around is ver-

---

[24] In which I became rather fluent over the course my stay in 1996–97, especially from speaking it, and about it, with my teacher, the late Buhari, in a nearby all-Osing village.

nacular, "native", face-to-face speech. Yet this discourse is sporadic, transient, largely bound to working-class and youth interlocutors and listeners, and it flows only by day. Amidst a continual entering, leaving, and passing of participants, the passengers and crew engage in, depending on their lingual competencies, all-Osing or bilingual dialogue, or they just listen to a fleeting social world being made Osing in part, for them as well.

It is in public, but at the same time intimate environments like in a minibus, that as an average urban Banyuwanginese, one gets to hear Osing-tinged (and occasionally Osing-themed) world-making events from close by. One is also confronted there with the existence of the other profiles of "all-round" Osing language users, ignorami, and Osing Kids. In both contexts, I was initially assumed by many to be a *turis*, an ethnic category also grounded in place and time and assigned a (minimalist) backstory. *Turis* are strangers, they belong elsewhere, they come and go at once; their presence is temporary. Where Osing is concerned, they are assumed to be ignorami. Rapport is beside the point. But the same goes for many other users of public facilities. In this respect there my presence was ordinary.

7 Two Frequent Types of Gathering

Language ideology interfaces with other types of world-making ideologies. Religiosity and ethnicity are prime among them in Banyuwangi. In the preceding example, focused on a public service, ethnicity featured to some extent, religion hardly at all. Ethnic and religious facets of world-making do interact squarely with ideology of language in the events analyzed in the concluding examples. These events foreground the temporality of narrative world-making by language-using persons.

Throughout Indonesia, Saturday night is for going out on the town. Around 6 p.m. on Saturday 27 July 2002, the streets of Banyuwangi were busy as Dul and I drove from his all-Osing village of Kemirén to an event in town on his motorcycle. Our destination turned out to be a public telephone facility on the outside of the thick high walls of the Military District Command (*Kodim*), a fearful place for wrongdoers and dissidents that was once the Dutch fort. The place was in a back street that at daytime tends to be lively because the second-hand goods market is nearby. It was quiet now; those who were at home were watching television. In a small reception room behind an open door, I saw some men seated on the floor in front of a TV set, gazing at the screen, one of them grasping a mike and singing. Karaoke is popular.

That evening, the *keroncong* orchestra Gempita—a name that means 'Resounding' but that is also an acronym of <u>Gema</u> <u>P</u>esona <u>I</u>rama Nusan<u>ta</u>ra or 'Echoes of the Rhythmic Enchantment of the Archipelago'—finally held its inaugural *selametan*, a communal ritual meal. The orchestra had been founded a year earlier and performed thrice since, but there had been no opportunity to launch it with such a ceremonial sharing of food, always preceded by a dedicatory speech and Islamic Arabic prayers for well-being. That would happen tonight, also in the hope of invoking success for the next performance, to be given the following evening. Invitations had been sent out for the *selametan*, announcing that it would commence at 18:00, after the sunset prayer. In fact, the proceedings started around 6:30, and many participants came much later.

Keroncong is a genre of popular music thought to have ancient roots in Portuguese mestizo music making in Batavia, as Jakarta used to be called. It has spread throughout Indonesia, and in Java is considered a pastime for musically conservative people of middle age and above. Gempita was a Banyuwanginese orchestra, but its musicians were not Osing, Madurese, Arab, or Chinese, as these groups tend to have other ethnically specific musical preferences. Although there have been *keroncong* bands in Banyuwangi since at least the 1950s with part of their repertoire locally composed and sung in Osing,[25] the genre is generally considered to be Javanese here; that is, central or eastern Javanese. Gempita's musicians indeed belonged to this ethnic group. Most were military men from the Kodim. The military in Banyuwangi tend to come from elsewhere on the island, and they do Javanese things such as *keroncong*. One of the group's leaders was from the region of Solo in Central Java. Another was born and raised in Banyuwangi, but both his parents were immigrants; he claimed to be a poor speaker of Osing and, for that matter, of Javanese.[26]

Earlier incarnations of Gempita had had Osing evergreens in their repertoire,[27] but this had not resulted in the desired popularity. The instrumentation of *keroncong* was felt to be too boring. Hence, the leadership had decided that in the rhythm section they wanted a set of *kendhang* (hand-struck double-sided barrel drums) with vivacious Banyuwangi-style drumming.[28] They had realized that this was a must, if they wanted to be hired by locals. At first, they had asked

---

[25] P. c. with the late Husin Bamaisarah, 29 November 1996.
[26] He probably meant the polite vocabulary or the standard Central Javanese dialect.
[27] For instance an orchestra broadcast by the Special Radio of the Regional Government station on 26 October 1996.
[28] Accordingly, they called their music *keroncong campursari*. *Campursari* 'fusion-of-essences' is a common name or name-component for hybrid genres involving *gamelan* and *gamelan*-like instruments, tunings, and structures in Java (Sumarsam 2014: 103–106; Cooper 2015).

a Javanese *gamelan* musician from the neighbourhood to drum, but this did not work out. That is why Dul from Kemirén, a farmer and tailor who is also a talented musician specializing in the *kendhang*, had been invited to join three months earlier.

After our arrival Dul and I chatted with people outside, where the locals and I were concerned largely employing a formal, central Javanese style of language. While participants continued to trickle in we entered the room, sitting down on mats in a rectangle facing inwards. Talking continued whilst food was brought in and placed in the middle. The ritual commenced when the men were requested to put out their clove cigarettes, and a man spoke a word of welcome in Indonesian on behalf of the group's management. A Muslim prayer was recited in formal Javanese, another in Arabic, while a third, also in Arabic, was pronounced in unison by those who mastered it. The management representative then invited us to partake of the meal.

After the plates and remaining food had been cleared, the *selametan* became a serious rehearsal, with only a little time between songs, mostly used for retuning instruments. The overarching genre was *keroncong*, but the repertoire was diverse. The lyrics were in several languages as well. They were sung by men and women who were invited to contribute a song or just took their turn. Two or three songs were *keroncong* proper, in Indonesian. Dul did not play *kendhang* here; a cello was plucked percussively instead. Two songs resembled Sundanese music (from West Java) in terms of scale and melodic structure, although the lyrics were Indonesian. Two other songs belonged to the immensely popular national pop genre *dangdut*—a hybrid genre with Indian film music influence and a Muslim flavour (Weintraub 2010)—but they were sung in Javanese rather than the more mainstream Indonesian. At least four songs were from the Banyuwangi popular music repertoire, with lyrics in Osing. Some were golden oldies, others current hits. Here Dul could let himself go with his *kendhang*, and he was visibly enjoying himself. But in the two hours I attended, most compositions (about seven) belonged to the sub-genre of *keroncong* called *langgam Jawa* or 'Javanese variety', which incorporates structural elements from *gamelan* music and has certain *keroncong* instruments imitate *gamelan* instruments, with sentimental lyrics in Javanese (Cooper 2015: 63). Some of these songs were popular recent compositions. Finally, I also heard a song in Madurese, but with a *langgam Jawa* musical structure.

The eventness of this meeting unfolded on multiple levels. To the extent that it was an artistic performance, the songs were focal. But besides that and a *selametan*, it was also a social gathering. There was a lot of informal talk among people sitting next to each other inside the room, as well as the men seated outside, where a bench and plastic chairs had been placed under a small awning with a neon tube and some festive hangings. They, and I, conversed in central Javanese. It was clear that some owed each other respect: they employed the courteous style (*basa*), which is not widespread in Banyuwangi town. Dul adapted to this lingual atmosphere and spoke politely as well, but the base for his speech was Kemirénese. The polite vocabulary he employed was the one corresponding to Javanese *basa*, which in Kemirén is called *besiki* and which is used rarely, mainly to people of the age of one's grandparents whom one does not know well. Apart from song lyrics and Dul's dialect, no Osing was heard during the *selametan* and rehearsal.

Although on the one hand the *selametan* is rejected by Islamic reformists and puritans and on the other it has been embraced by other religious traditions as well, the default religious interpretation of the introductory ritual would be that it was Islamic, not least given the Arabic prayers. What other denominations were represented among the participants is not clear. Although a central theme of the event was Osing, the religious world-making that went on was Javanese, Arabic, Indonesian, and decidedly non-Osing, reinforcing the urban areligiosity of that language.

As regards ethnic world-making and its relation to language ideology and the models of language users in Banyuwangi: *keroncong*, which in Banyuwangi already comes with Javanese connotations, is expressly javanized further in *langgam Jawa*—a musical style coupled with a language variety—and can subsequently be made Osing instrumentally in the same *langgam Jawa* genre, and lingually and instrumentally in renditions of "classical" Osing songs. However, these layers of instrumentation, structure and style of composition, and language variety of the lyrics are not necessarily entirely congruent, revealing a disjunction between these ideologies.

Listening to and producing Osing popular music, the participants profiled themselves as Osing Kids. They did this because they were rehearsing for Banyuwangi audiences that wanted to be profiled as such. This profiling is of course temporary. On this particular occasion, participants could be typical urban Osing users as well, though only when listening to Dul's contribution to the dialogues and identifying it as Osing, rather than as dialectal polite Javanese, which, given the fluidity of these categories, would be another feasible interpretation.

My last sketch analyzes a social event that, though mostly gender-specific to men (or men with girlfriends), is extremely common: going with a group to a food stall in the evening to eat, talk, and (in this case) cast glances at a television set. This particular instance—on Sunday 4 August 2002, *c.* 10:00–11:15 pm—was ethnically circumscribed. Except me and my companion, Gunadi, the participants were Osingers, by ethnic heritage or achieved. This was no coincidence. The preceding event from which this one sprung was one in which ethnicity and race and (*almost* directly) religion had been thematized in conjunction with Osingness and Osing language. This was a rehearsal for a performance of Osing songs and music (in the local *angklung* genre that features bamboo xylophones) by ethnic Chinese from Banyuwangi. It was a government initiative and took place at a government venue, the municipal library. None of the Chinese singers and musicians came along to the food stall. The participants were about ten acquaintances who had been at this event, all Osingers, basically prominent artists (*seniman*) and civil servants. I tagged along with Gunadi in his car, although we had not attended the preceding rehearsal (despite the fact that Gunadi belonged to the target group). On the road, Gunadi was in contact with one of men about the choice of venue by mobile phone. Having arrived at the food stall, we sat on mats on the floor around low tables. Soon a lively, even boisterous atmosphere emerged. A TV set showed wrestling and boxing. The stall served simple pan-Indonesian fare: fried chicken, fried rice, fried noodles and the like. But it was conversation that we came for.

A philological perspective reveals that ethnicity was critical but unproblematic in this event. The participants included a well-known singer of Banyuwangi pop songs and a senior literary author who publishes in Indonesian and Osing, also directs Osing drama and acts, and is considered an expert on matters Osing. The former, however, is of Moluccan extraction (from eastern Indonesia), and the latter has a Javanese background. On several other occasions, I heard them being called "more Osing than an Osinger." While they were considered Osing for all relevant intents and purposes (even if the former had one thing that disqualified him for this in another sense: his presumably being a Christian), Ben and Gunadi (the tag-alongs) were known to be merely Osing-interested. Other participants were a prominent *angklung* musician, two famous senior composers of Osing popular music, the presenter of an Osing music program on the regency government's radio station who also writes the texts of this station's Osing newscasts and dabbles in Osing drama, and several heads of local government departments—all Osingers and "all-round" Osing speakers. The food stall was on the access road to Banyuwangi from the south, in Pakis, the southernmost ward of Banyuwangi town, which is an Osing area. This, too, helped to create an invisible but perceptible Osingophone ambience.

A little Indonesian was heard, some Javanese (linked to the personal repertoire of Gunadi), but overwhelmingly Osing, including a tiny bit of *besiki* spoken publicly to break up the event. This kind of nearly monolingual Osing-speaking event involving a relatively large group is rare in this white-collar social class. Several conversations went on simultaneously. I talked about Osing culture and its history and mediation with the senior cultural expert. Given the preceding event from which this one followed on and the professional expertise of most participants, presumably I was not the only person discussing Osing-related matters. It was my impression that networking was going on, that government affairs were being unofficially conducted or at least prepared, that deals were being struck.

This was a group of people sharing (except me and Gunadi) the profile of an active, proficient, all-round Osinger, by heritage or achieved; and indeed acknowledged as such by the wider community. These all-round Osing speakers were involved in, indeed *behind*, a course of events designed to make Chinese people in Banyuwangi, who were assumed and indeed *expected* (because it involves an interest in Osing) to fit the profile of the typical urban Osing user, into Osing Kids, by having them perform the language. The atmosphere was convivial but this occasion there was not much rapport between me and these people (except with Gunadi). The subjectivity assigned to me did not correspond to that of the core circle of participants, all-round Osing speakers. I experienced a lot of rapport in Banyuwangi, but not now; I sensed that I was viewed as an alien researcher wanting, as researchers do, to profit from collecting knowledge in Banyuwangi. I was regarded by most with suspicion or indifference.

The *selametan*/rehearsal and the gathering at the food stall were both occasions when, in different ways, ethnicity, encompassing religiosity, was thematized. Ethnicity and language-userhood may be modified strategically. At the rehearsal, for the duration of an Osing song, the singer and by proxy the listeners were Osing Kids concerned with love between the sexes or local patrotism, even if before and after they were ethnic Javanese and Muslims. The event from which the informal gathering at the *warung* ensued, and the campaign of which it was part, were precisely dedicated to effecting such temporal and indeed long-term change, making people from ordinary urban Osing language users—but Chinese, held to be deeply resistant to this kind of modification—into Osing Kids.

8 Conclusion: Ideologies of World-Making, a Researcher's Persona, and Rapport

On the basis of an Indonesia-wide census, Steinhauer (1994: 758) suggests that "inter-ethnic contacts", which facilitate the acquisition of Indonesian, and "domains and topics for which the use of Indonesian is more appropriate than a regional language, are a common feature of urban life, while they are rare phenomena in traditional rural communities." He notes that "Indonesian is closely connected with urban culture" (Steinhauer 1994: 761). My research in Banyuwangi does not contradict this observation, but it does demonstrate that urban culture was by no means exclusively created in Indonesian; although it is the language of state, I doubt even whether Indonesian could be said to dominate. Other vernaculars feature in the urban languagescape, and some of them—in Banyuwangi Osing above all—do so with robust institutional backing. Overall, urban culture—in Banyuwangi and probably elsewhere in Indonesia—is characterized by lingual diversity as much as by Indonesian.

To get an analytical handle on this diversity I have highlighted the model of the Osing-hearing person (who listens with attention) within an ideology of world-making in urban Banyuwangi. Alongside the more concrete profiles of Osinger, ignoramus, and Osing Kid, this profile, though ideologically not salient, is applicable to many Banyuwanginese. The sketches of families, a mobile public space, and events in this chapter show that this profile and the ones with which it interrelates—person-focused models in line with world-making ideologies in Java more generally—are *dramatis personae* in the social world of Banyuwangi. It is in events—which combine personal contours with temporal and spatial dimensions and communal aspects, and which are patterned internally and externally, yielding plot-like structures—where these profiles crystallize.

I have tried to conceptualize rapport with reference to language ideology and these profiles. Person-centred models are well-suited to a context of lingual difference, perhaps better than the models that are more common in academic studies of language. My interlocutors' models help to understand the rapport I, in some respects a very different kind of person, experienced in Banyuwangi. With "Osing" at the core, the vignettes pictured how people in urban Banyuwangi make their lifeworlds and how I was allowed to play a role in some of those lifeworlds. My perceived subjectivity corresponded to one of the socially established language-user profiles. In this profile, Osing is present but is comfortably treated as external; while not necessarily spoken or sung, it is heard and listened to. This audible externality of the language featured in the three urban households and it was seen in the other places and events analyzed as well. It belongs to the ideology of lingual world-making that rules in Banyuwangi. I could become part of my urban friends' worlds because we shared the same focal but distant interest in Osing, and they recognized in me the same kind of stance *vis-à-vis* Osing that they identified in themselves. This correspondence, underneath much difference, facilitated rapport.

Besides the lingual, at least two other domains of world-making figured in the rapport we felt: ethnic and religious. The first is straightforward. In respect of the language user listening to Osing, ethnicity is not so much irrelevant as concomitant with lingual competence. The listener-to-Osing profile is not just linguistic but ethnolinguistic. An ignoramus fails to be Osing in any way; one can be attributed Osingerhood by being well-versed in the language; one can become an Osing Kid by singing it. In town my perceived subjectivity was not that of an Osinger, ignoramus, or Osing Kid. Neither were most of those with whom I experienced sustained rapport.

Religion is a different matter. It is one of the properties of the urban listener to Osing that in this capacity they can be secular. If, whilst using Osing, Gunadi were recognized as Christian, Buddhist, or Confucianist, or the Moluccan singer and Ben Arps as Christian, they would be allo-religious. This would be problematic because, whereas Islam is taken for granted as a dimension of Osing worldmaking, the Osing language that the average Banyuwanginese gets to hear in town is a-religious.

On a theoretical level, I hope to have shown that for rapport in fieldwork and other ethnographic situations, studying narrativity is productive in two respects. Once communication is considered not as instantaneous interaction between individuals but as a continuing process with *dramatis personae*, a sociopolitical context, historical backgrounds, considerations beyond the here-and-now and a *de facto* or assumed or desired course of events, it becomes clear that a researcher perforce becomes a member of that *dramatis personae* and its plot, not a fly on the wall. S/he tends to be a peculiar member: an outsider who inserts themselves into this narrativity, both presupposing and creating plot disruption. Rapport is a way to manage the disruption of the narrativity that occurs as a stranger joins the cast. Secondly, researchers will do well to take into account—and if necessary investigate—the kind of narrativity that characterizes the relevant local models of language userhood. Besides being a fascinating field of enquiry in its own right, this narrativity will colour the understanding of the participating observer's subjectivity.

References

Agha, Asif. 2005. Voice, footing, enregisterment. *Journal of Linguistic Anthropology* 15(1). 38–59.

Arps, Bernard. 1996. The song guarding at night: Grounds for cogency in a Javanese incantation. In Stephen Headley (ed.), *Towards an anthropology of prayer: Javanese ethnolinguistic studies*, 47–113. Aix-en-Provence: Publications de l'Université de Provence.

Arps, Bernard. 2003. Letters on air in Banyuwangi (and beyond): Radio and phatic performance. *Indonesia and the Malay World* 31(91). 301–316.

Arps, Bernard. 2009. Osing kids and the banners of Blambangan: Ethnolinguistic identity and the regional past as ambient themes in an East Javanese town. *Wacana: Jurnal Ilmu Pengetahuan Budaya* 11(1). 1–38.

Arps, Bernard. 2010. Terwujudnya bahasa Using di Banyuwangi dan peranan media elektronik di dalamnya (selayang pandang, 1970–2009). In Mikihiro Moriyama & Manneke Budiman (eds.), *Geliat bahasa selaras zaman: Perubahan bahasa-bahasa di Indonesia pasca-Orde Baru*, 225–248. Jakarta: Kepustakaan Populer Gramedia.

Arps, Bernard. 2016a. Flat puppets on an empty screen, stories in the round: Imagining space in *wayang kulit* and the worlds beyond. *Wacana: Journal of the Humanities of Indonesia* 17(3). 438–472.

Arps, Bernard. 2016b. *Tall tree, nest of the wind: The Javanese shadow-play* Dewa Ruci *performed by Ki Anom Soeroto. A study in performance philology*. Singapore: NUS Press.

Blommaert, Jan (ed.). 1999. *Language ideological debates*. Berlin and New York: Mouton de Gruyter.

Cooper, Nancy I. 2015. Retuning Javanese identities: The ironies of a popular genre. *Asian Music* 46(2). 55–88.

Epp, F. 1849. Banjoewangi. *Tijdschrift voor Nederlandsch-Indië* 7–12. 241–261.

Faudree, Paja. 2013. *Singing for the dead: The politics of indigenous revival in Mexico*. Durham and London: Duke University Press.

Goffman, Irving. 1979. Footing. *Semiotica* 25. 1–29.

Goodman, Nelson. 1978. *Ways of worldmaking*. Hassocks: The Harvester Press.

Hymes, Dell. 1974. *Foundations in sociolinguistics: An ethnographic approach*. Philadelphia: University of Pennsylvania Press.

Jakobson, Roman. 1960. Closing statement: Linguistics and poetics. In Thomas Sebeok (ed.), *Style in language*, 350–377. Cambridge, Mass.: The M.I.T. Press.

Kroskrity, Paul (ed.). 2000. *Regimes of language: ideologies, polities, and identities*. Santa Fe: School of American Research Press.

Kumar, Ann. 1979. Javanese historiography in and of the 'colonial period': A case study. In Anthony Reid & David Marr (eds.), *Perceptions of the past in Southeast Asia*, 187–206. Singapore: Heinemann. Asian Studies Association of Australia.

Makihara, Miki & Bambi B. Schieffelin (eds.). 2007. *Consequences of contact: Language ideologies and sociocultural transformations in Pacific societies*. Oxford: Oxford University Press.

Oetomo, Dédé. 1987. *The Chinese of Pasuruan: Their language and identity*. Pacific Linguistics, D-63 (Materials in Languages of Indonesia 26). Canberra: Department of Linguistics, Research School of Pacific Studies, Australian National University.

Oetomo, Dédé. 1991. The Chinese of Indonesia and the development of the Indonesian language. *Indonesia* (unnumbered special issue, July). 53–66.

Pratt, Mary. 1987. Linguistic utopias. In Nigel Fabb, Derek Attridge, Alan Durant & Colin MacCabe (eds.), *The linguistics of writing: Arguments between language and literature*, 48–66. Manchester: Manchester University Press.

Rafferty, Ellen. 1984. Languages of the Chinese of Java: An historical review. *Journal of Asian Studies* 43. 247–272.

Schieffelin, Bambi, Kathryn A. Woolard & Paul Kroskrity (eds.). 1998. *Language ideologies: Practice and theory*. New York: Oxford University Press.

Silverstein, Michael. 1979. Language structure and linguistic ideology. In Paul Clyne, William Hanks & Carol Hofbauer (eds.), *The elements: A parasession on linguistic units and levels*, 193–247. Chicago: University Of Chicago.

Sri Margana. 2007. *Java's last frontier: The struggle for hegemony of Blambangan, c. 1763–1813*. Leiden University Doctoral dissertation.

Steinhauer, Hein. 1994. The Indonesian language situation and linguistics: Prospects and possibilities. *Bijdragen tot de Taal-, Land- en Volkenkunde* 150. 755–784.

Sumarsam. 2014. Past and present issues of Javanese–European musical hybridity: *Gendhing mares* and other hybrid genres. In Bart Barendregt & Els Bogaerts (eds.), *Recollecting resonances: Indonesian–Dutch musical encounters*, 87–107. Leiden and Boston: Brill.

Suryadinata, Leo, Evi Nurvidya Arifin & Aris Ananta. 2003. *Indonesia's population: Ethnicity and religion in a changing political landscape*. Singapore: Institute of Southeast Asian Studies.

Weintraub, Andrew. 2010. *Dangdut stories: A social and musical history of Indonesia's most popular music*. New York: Oxford University Press.

Winarsih, Partaningrat Arifin (ed.). 1995. *Babad Blambangan*. Yogyakarta: Ecole Française d'Extrême-Orient and Yayasan Bentang Budaya. Naskah dan Dokumen Nusantara 10.

Mikihiro Moriyama
9 The Discursive Co-Construction of Social Relations in Sundanese-Speaking Areas in West Java

1 Introduction

The language we use creates and reproduces relationship between people. The language we use is significant because it is used to establish common ground through discursive practices that include the pursuit of social sameness (Bucholtz and Hall 2004: 494–495). Social sameness can be achieved through a whole host of practices, but in this paper I will focus primarily on language choice. As researchers, we try to create good relationships with our consultants during our fieldwork, not only for our research purpose's sake, but also for friendship. These relationships are commonly referred to as "rapport" (Hume and Mulcock 2004: 5). In contrast to this literature, this paper argues that rapport is discursively created and recreated from one situation to another, rather than being an enduring relationship between researcher and researched during a period of fieldwork. In the papers in Hume and Mulcock (2004), we also hear that rapport has many dimensions including trust, empathy, disclosure, and so on. What we don't hear in these papers, or indeed in other collections on researcher–researched relations is what this looks like post-fieldwork. My aim in this paper is to point to how rapport is situation specific in fieldwork settings, while sketching a potential new area of investigation: one which investigates how social relations are discursively created between researcher and researched in post-fieldwork settings. I do this by first offering a reflexive account of the relationship between language choice and social relations during my 30 years of work in Sundanese speaking areas before then focusing attention on electronic exchanges after my initial contact with one family.

It seems appropriate to begin with a brief survey of the use of Sundanese. Sundanese is the regional language of West Java, whose speakers number around 30 million. The Sundanese people have for a long time regarded Sundanese as the most important representation of their culture since Dutch colonial time. Sundanese people consistently have thought that their first language firmly relates to

---

Acknowledgement: I thank Zane Goebel for his precious comments on this paper. This research was supported in part by a grant from Nanzan University Pache Research Subsidy I-A-2 for 2019 academic year.

Mikihiro Moriyama, Nanzan University, Nagoya, Japan

https://doi.org/10.1515/9781501507830-009

their identity. This can be attested with reference to a great number of Sundanese-language books that have been published since Dutch colonial times until the present day. Sundanese literature has survived throughout the last century and into the 21st century, with a considerable number of novels, poems and short stories produced every year (Purwanto 2003: 32–35). Sundanese traditional music and pop songs are still popular among the population of West Java and beyond.

Since the mid-19th century, the Sundanese have seen the city of Bandung as their cultural and political centre, but there are significant differences between the position of Sundanese in Bandung and its environs and in rural West Java as a whole. The Sundanese in Bandung has been constructed as more refined, while the rural variant has been constructed as less refined.[1]

In rural areas, such as the regional towns and villages of my fieldwork sites, Sundanese was still dominant in both the public and private sphere in the 1980s through the 21st century. Even older people did not understand Indonesian when I was there in 1983. In these areas, there is almost no Indonesian used at all in places like markets, bus terminals, and on board different forms of public transport. In the homes of Sundanese people, the only Indonesian likely to be heard is in the form of television broadcasts. It is only in more formal public situations, such as government offices and schools, that Indonesian is the dominant language. These circumstances show that Sundanese has been used in most social domains. However, people who use Sundanese in conversation with their friends very rarely use it as a written language nowadays. It can be said that Sundanese is primarily a spoken language. In sum, Sundanese can be said to be holding its own in regional West Java, while Indonesian is becoming more and more conspicuous in the city of Bandung and its environs.

Sundanese has a speech-level system to differentiate high (*lemes* words) and low (*kasar* words) registers in Sundanese, *undak usuk Basa Sunda*. This system was imported from the Central Javanese cultural tradition during the period in

---

[1] In recent years, the image of Bandung as the Sundanese cultural centre has been tarnished, perhaps because the city is increasingly considered to be more closely connected to Jakarta, the national capital, than its regional surroundings. Language use has reinforced this perception, because in common with urban centres all over Indonesia, the use of Indonesian in the public sphere has become increasingly dominant, supplanting the regional language as the main linguistic medium in contemporary urban life. This trend is also reflected in language use within the home in Bandung. Increasingly, Indonesian is the language of communication with, and between, children in household settings, even where both parents are Sundanese and use Sundanese to communicate with each other. Language use in schools encourages this trend, because Indonesian is the language of education from first grade in primary school, and parents are aware that a mastery of Indonesian is essential for their children's future (Moriyama 2012: 83).

which the Sundanese-speaking region was under the control of the *Mataram* kingdom in the 17th century. Sundanese developed in its own way, with different and simpler speech forms compared to the more elaborate Javanese system. The system works by inserting about 300 *lemes* words in the basic sentence to make your utterance polite and to show your respect to addressees.

The image a language has in the eyes of its speakers is also an important element, in some respects perhaps the most important element, in language choice.[2] In my fieldwork for the last 35 years, the image of Sundanese has been both negative and positive. Similar mixed sentiments could be found in online newspapers, as the following remarks indicate: "Sundanese tends to be seen as a second class language";[3] "there is a fear of making a mistake in particular in the speech level system, because language use varies depending on the status of the person being addressed in Sundanese, and people are afraid of being called impolite, or even marked out as uncivilized";[4] "reading material in Sundanese has always been seen as something for village-dwellers".[5] On the other hand, more positive views of Sundanese surface in remarks such as "Sundanese can express complex feelings that can't be expressed in Indonesian",[6] and "Sundanese has a richer vocabulary than Indonesian".[7] By contrast, Indonesian is seen as a language which is modern, progressive, official, urban, educated and trendy—as well as being business-like, distanced, and cold—in particular for Sundanese in the rural areas.

In the New Order period (roughly 1966–1998), the use of regional languages tended to be discouraged by the central government, in the interests of maintaining and strengthening national unity. Regional languages were assigned a cultural and non-political role, and as a result, Sundanese was rarely used in the public realm. For a period of 30 plus years, few official documents were written

---

[2] This discussion partly overlaps with Moriyama (2012: 84).
[3] "Bahasa Sunda cenderung dianggap sebagai bahasa kelas dua" (Faturohman cited in Anggadhitya 2005).
[4] "takut salah, karena dalam bahasa Sunda ada undak-usuk, takut dikatakan tidak sopan, takut dicap tidak beradab" (Purba 2005.)
[5] "selama ini ada anggapan bahwa bacaan bahasa Sunda itu bacaan orang kampung" (Rosidi 2006).
[6] "bahasa Sunda dapat mengekspresikan perasaan rumit yang tak mampu diekspresikan dalam bahasa Indonesia".
[7] "bahasa Sunda mempunyai kosakata yang lebih kaya daripada bahasa Indonesia". This and the previous comment were made by Iskandarwassid, a Sundanese writer and professor at the Indonesian University of Education (Universitas Pendidikan Indonesia) on 30 August 2007 in Bandung.

in Sundanese, and a clear demarcation was observed between the role of Indonesian in the public sphere and political space, and Sundanese in the private sphere and cultural space. However, this division of roles between the two languages has slightly changed amid the social and political transformations of the post-New Order years. The extension of regional autonomy and new laws and regulations governing regional affairs have exerted a certain impact on attitudes to language and language use in West Java.[8]

2 Language Shift from Indonesian to Sundanese

It seems appropriate to view perceptions of me as a person who has different cultural background than Sundanese. I am often recognized as a person from a country which had once occupied their land for three-and-a-half years during World War II, so sometimes I am addressed as '*saudara tua*' or elder brother. On the other hand, I was regarded as a guest from a highly developed country in terms of technology symbolised by the robot. Japan has recovered from the damage of defeat in war in a short period, and has developed its own niche within the car, electronics, and robot technology industries. The cars, motorcycles, and electronic products from Japan are dominantly visible in daily life in Indonesia, while recently comics and anime such as *Doraemon* are occupying the life of children. Alongside the development of technology, the country is regarded as one which is maintaining its tradition, such as traditional architecture and performing arts. In general, Japan is imagined positively by Indonesian people, despite the bad memory of military occupation during wartime.

My background as a researcher from Japan positively worked on most occasions when conducting research on culture and language, which I commenced in 1982 in the Sundanese-speaking area in West Java. It is fortunate that my background provided me with many topics to start conversation with the people in my fieldwork. In my early research, I had conversations on these topics in Indonesian, which allowed me to introduce myself in the city of Bandung, where most of the Sundanese people used both Indonesian and Sundanese. The people then tried to teach me about Sundanese culture and language when they realised that I came to the Sundanese-speaking area to study their literature and language. The language used between us was Indonesian because of my limited command of Sundanese.

---

[8] For more details, see Moriyama (2012: 84–87).

I came to be close with a Sundanese music composer, Mr. N, and his family in Bandung soon after I arrived. Mr. N was a music teacher at a public high school of traditional music and was a music composer and music player himself. His wife was a traditional music singer who used to join music and dance performances organised by her husband. Our conversations were conducted in Indonesian from the beginning, but I was immediately aware that the conversation in his house was always in Sundanese among their family members. I observed that both Mr. N and his wife spoke more casually and intimately even emotionally in Sundanese than in Indonesian when communicating with each other and with their children, as well as with guests who visit their house. He had a frank and humble nature and had close relationship with his neighbours in the south of Bandung where his house was located. He received a great number of guests on a daily base. They consisted of relatives, neighbours, musicians, music producers, journalists, students, colleagues, and researchers. It is telling that most of their conversations were conducted in Sundanese, except specific topics, such as business or politics.

Their conversation started in Sundanese when a guest greeted in Sundanese. However, it is usual that Mr. N started conversation in Indonesian if a guest was a stranger or the guest greeted in Indonesian. He shifted the conversational language to Sundanese immediately after he came to realise the guest was a Sundanese. No sooner had the language shift occurred than the atmosphere became friendlier.

I also experienced such a shifting language from Indonesian to Sundanese many times after I obtained a command of Sundanese. I usually started conversations in Indonesian at a government office, and then I shifted the language to Sundanese when the person I was talking to asked me the purpose of my stay in Indonesia, and wished to hear a Japanese speaking Sundanese. The atmosphere at the office changed dramatically from formal to informal and friendly, as if we were not in a public but a private space. My administrative business was handled faster, and officers warmly received me in ways similar to that covered subsequently. This language shift generated a different setting and social relationship from the initial one. In this case, the use of semiotic forms associated with close social relations helped evoke this type of relationship, especially warmth, sympathy, a pseudo-family feeling, and empathy.

The effect of shifting language was clearly felt when I joined Mr. N's family's conversation after I had attained a certain command of Sundanese. He had three children and seven grandchildren when he passed away some years ago. It was remarkable that our relationship had changed to be friendlier when I tried to speak in Sundanese with Mr. N and his family members. They have regarded me as a family member in the course of our relationship for more than 30 years. While gift-giving and visiting were also important in the construction and maintenance of social relations, as we will see in the later email texts, the pursuit of social sameness in language choice was also crucial for the discursive co-construction of social relations.

For instance, one of our recent correspondences via e-mail shows our close relationship. An email sent by his daughter was as follows:

(1)

1	Hatur nuhun pisan kana	Thank you so much for your
2	pangangken Akang sakulawargi	acknowledgement as a family member and
3	parantos ngulem rombongan ka	inviting our group to your house.
4	bumi.	
5	Rombongan anu janten mios	Our group with only six people including
6	mung 6 jalmi, Bu D, abdi, sareng	my mother and me and four female relatives
7	opatan deui wargi-wargi Ibu. O.	will leave. Mrs. O. and others will not go
8	sareng anu sanesna henteu janten	because they could not get furlough from their
9	mios margi henteu kenging cuti ti	offices.
10	kantorna.	
11	Panginten aya sababaraha hal anu	Perhaps I should tell you a couple of
12	kedah didugikeun ka Akang,	things, namely the members of this group
13	anggota rombongan teh seueur	wish a lot, want to go here and there. This
14	kahoyongna, hoyong ka ditu-	makes me perplexed … haha. Because only
15	kadieu anu ngajantenkeun abdi	I have once stayed in Japan, they believe in
16	lieur…hehe. Ku margi mung abdi	me to make a travel plan during our stay
17	kantos di Jepang, janten sadayana	in Japan.
18	teh mercantenkeun abdi kanggo	
19	nyusun jadwal perjalanan salami	
20	di Jepang.	
21	Rencana ping 22 teh bade mios	We are planning to leave early morning at
22	enjing-enjing tabuh 8 ti Tokyo,	8 on 22th from Tokyo because they want to
23	maksadna, aya kahoyong ti	have a walk and shopping at Shinsaibashi,
24	rombongan wengina hoyong	Osaka in the evening. It is the reason why on
25	jalan-jalan balanja di Shinsaibashi	the following day they want to visit Kyoto,
26	Osaka. Margi enjingna aya	Kinkakuji, Ginkakuji and Kiyomizu temples.
27	rencana bd ka Kyoto hoyong ka	I do not know they are strong enough to walk
28	Kinkakuji, Ginkakuji, sareng	in so many places because of walking a lot,
29	Kiyomizu. Duka tah bakal	especially at Kiyomizu with the uphill
30	kariateun moal, seueur jalan-jalan	slopes. On the following day 24th we are
31	komo ka Kiyomizu mah jalanna	going back to Tokyo in the afternoon
32	nanjak… Enjingna ping 24	because they should do packing their
33	wangsul deui ka Tokyo pasisiang,	suitcases with a lot of shopping items. But,
34	supados tiasa packing koper,	I will not do shopping much because
35	margi tangtosna nu sanes mah	I do not have money.
36	seueur balanjaanana…hahaha.	

37	Abdi mah moal seueur balanja,	
38	teu gaduh artosna.	
39	Tah kitu panginten Kang rencana	This is perhaps the travel plan of our group
40	abdi sareng rombongan teh...	for the time being. I hope you will
41	Mugi tiasa dimaklum, paling oge	understand that we will not able to accept
42	tiasa ka Nagoya teh pasisiang	you and your family's invitation for dinner
43	henteu tiasa nedunan pangangken	in your house. At most we will call by at
44	Akang sareng kulawargi kanggo	Nagoya in the afternoon. My apology for
45	neda wengi di bumi Akang.	that.
46	Hapunten pisan.	
47	Kanggo komunikasi, rencana abdi	For the communication purpose I am
48	bade nyewa wifi ti Indonesia anu	planning to rent a Wi-Fi kit, which can be
49	tiasa dianggo salami aya di	used during my stay in Japan from
50	Jepang. Manawi kagungan	Indonesia. Perhaps do you have WhatsApp
51	WhatsApp atanapi Line? tapi tiasa	or Line? Or we can use FB messenger.
52	oge nganggo FB messenger.	
53	Samentawis sakitu heula, salam	So much for today, my best regards to your
54	baktos kanggo kulawargi.	family.
55	Salam ti Bandung,	Regards from Bandung,
56	R.	R.

This message projects what R sees as common ground or common knowledge between us. In this case, it highlights that visiting the house of a family member is of a great relational importance. While this letter is in Sundanese, it is not enough to simply continue to use Sundanese to maintain social relations in post-fieldwork settings, but it is also important to engage in visiting practices. In a sense, social relations appear to continue to be remade through these discursive moves. In this case, while my role as researcher is not fronted, my role as family member is. This is done through comments meant to maintain familial relations. Something that continued when R arrived in Japan. She sent another message from her mobile phone during her stay in Japan as follows:

(2)

1	Akang, oleh-oleh parantos	I gave presents for you to M-san. I am
2	dititipkeun ka M-san. Hapunten	sorry they are few only. At the same time I
3	mung sakedik. Sakantenan pamit	will send my farewell greeting to you from
4	oge, ieu abdi nuju dina shinkansen	Shinkansen bound for Tokyo and we will
5	ka Tokyo-keun, enjing wangsul	leave to Indonesia tomorrow. Best regards
6	ka Indonesia. Baktos bae ka	to all of your family.
7	kulawargi sadayana.	

My reply was as follows:

(3)

1	R. anu bageur, sababaraha dinten	Dearest R, M-san sent the presents from R
2	kamari M-san ngintun oleh-oleh ti	and your mother a couple of days ago. I
3	R sareng Ibu. Katampi pisan	appreciated your kind attention very much.
4	perhatosannana. Pun bojo tadi	My wife was wearing the T-shirt this morning.
5	enjing tos nganggo kaosna. Salam	My warm regards to your mother
6	sono ka Ibu D. sareng sadayana.	D and all of you.

Again her reply:

(4)

1	Sawangsulna Kang Miki. Hatur	My pleasure. Thank you very much if it
2	nuhun pisan upami tiasa kaanggo	is used. My apology because not coming to
3	mah. Hapunten pisan salami di	see you in Nagoya during my stay in Japan.
4	Jepang abdi henteu tiasa nganjang	Best regards to your family.
5	ka Nagoya. Salam baktos ka	
6	kulawargi.	

It is interesting that she made her apologies again for not visiting my house (*nganjang*) during her short stay in Japan. It shows that she was afraid she broke our familial relations on the basis of the norms she recreated in her first email.

These exchange of messages show our mutual empathy, trust, and emotional attachment as if we were real family members. Such a relationship is referred to with the word *panganken* (acknowledgement). Another example, the address term *Akang* in the previous message shows our close relationship in the family.[9] Her texts used words associated with *lemes* (refined) Sundanese. This represents her respect to me along with intimate feeling and shows her educated quality at the same time. In the next section we will examine another discursive co-construction with the *lemes* words in Sundanese speech level (*undak usuk*).

3 Sundanese Speech Level and the Discursive Co-Construction of Social Relations

Over the last 30 years I have lived with four Sundanese families for various periods of time. I will give an example from the first Sundanese family who lived in a sub-district of Wanayasa, Regency of Purwakarta, to show how I built rapport with

---

[9] The word *akang* is used in the daily communication to address an elder male person without any family relationship. But, the usage seen in the quoted message appears different from one of the common usage as observed from the whole context of message, that is, of my dearest brother.

them through language use.[10] The language I used was Sundanese. I tried to add new Sundanese words to my vocabulary by asking for equivalents in Indonesian in my fieldwork. It is worthwhile to explore facets of my identity before describing how language use figures in the development of researcher–researched relations, because informants usually asked me of my identity before I was accepted into their house as a researcher.

One precondition of rapport that seemed important was religion. I used to introduce myself as follows: I am non-Muslim and a Buddhist and hold belief in *Shintoism* by birth. I was born in a small city situated in the north of Kyoto where most of the land is still used for agriculture, such as rice and vegetables, but woods cover most of the rural area of the city. My house is in a small valley of the woods with a small stream in front of the house, and our family has maintained agricultural fields for generations. My father was a local-government civil servant of the city, grew rice and vegetables, and maintained our ancestor's land with my mother after my grandparents passed away. Such a rural family has a close tie with the gods of the land (this belief constitutes a root of Shintoism), especially the rice field. Of note, my belief in god, related to rice farming, Shintoism's *Amaterasu*, was understood by my consultants through analogy with Sundanese beliefs about the goddess of rice, *Nyi Pohaci Sanghyiang Sri*. In short, these discursive moves were all about pursuing social sameness and working out what things we had in common, i. e. common ground.

The second question they often asked was about my family. I am married and have three children. My wife is also Japanese and does not speak either Indonesian or Sundanese, but can speak English. My family has not stayed in Indonesia, but my wife once visited a couple of places as a tourist. Another question usually asked was what was the staple food for Japanese: bread or rice or other food for every meal. The Japanese eat rice, as the Sundanese do, was my answer. All of the above discussions helped to grow trust and common ground between myself and my consultants and represent a type of precondition of rapport.

As I mentioned earlier, the Sundanese spoken in the rural area was regarded as a less refined variant compared with the 'proper' and 'superior' Sundanese used in the Priangan area, the core area of Sundanese culture consisting of Bandung and surrounding regencies since the mid-19th century. The Regency of Pur-

---

10 The second family with which I stayed was in a subdistrict of Cikalong Kulon, Cianjur Regency in 1984 for four months. The third was in a house located in a village of Cipasung, subdistrict of Singaparna, Regency of Tasikmalaya, in 2006 for a month and several times for a couple of days thereafter. A well-known Islamic institution, Pesantren Cipasung, and students' dormitory occupy the village in the subdistrict of Singaparna. The fourth was in a village of subdistrict of Banyuresmi in Garut Regency in 2009 for one month.

wakarta and a subdistrict Wanayasa are outside of the Priangan regencies. The Sundanese in Wanayasa is regarded as having a rural accent and to be less sophisticated. The people in the village often expressed this themselves: our Sundanese is not as good as that found in Bandung and in urban Sundanese-speaking areas. Interestingly, it was not the case when I stayed at the second site of fieldwork, Cikalong Kulon in Regency of Cianjur. The language in Cianjur has been considered to have a melodious intonation (*lentongna sae*: good in intonation) and as a refined variant of Sundanese.[11] In contrast to Purwarta, I did not notice feelings of linguistic inferiority from the people I worked with in Cianjur. This points to the variability in Sundanese which visiting researchers, such as I, need to understand in order to pursue social sameness in other settings. The main point is that there are limits to how far speaking any particular language will get you in pursuing common ground.

The first family I stayed with for four months in 1983 was located in a small village behind the Mount Tangkuban Perahu on the other side of city of Bandung. The main road connecting *kecamatan* "sub-district" Subang and sub-district Wanayasa goes through the village. Most of the villagers were farmers who cultivated rice, vegetables, and clove as a profitable commercial crop. All of the inhabitants of the village were Muslim. The head of the household Mr. A was working at the local government office of the Department of Religion as a civil servant. He proudly used an aristocratic title *Raden* before his name. He had learned Islam at a religious school and was teaching the Arabic language and reading of the Quran in the evening at his house. On his days off, he would farm the fields around his house and care for his poultry. He had a Sundanese wife and five children, one of whom was living in Bandung for study. At that time, his wife's elderly mother stayed at the same house. His wife was operating a kindergarten at home in the morning. Their life was modest because they did not have large enough rice fields or any extra income other than his salary, and educating their children was expensive.

The language used in the village was Sundanese. Indonesian was rarely heard in daily life. Even older people did not understand Indonesian when I was there in 1983. The conversation between my host family and me started in a mixture of Indonesian and Sundanese. I was trying to learn Sundanese by finding Sundanese equivalent words for Indonesian. My main language for communication gradually shifted from Indonesian to Sundanese. The Sundanese I tried to learn was *lemes* (refined) words in the speech-level system, which differentiates high and low registers in Sundanese.

---

11 For further details see Moriyama (Moriyama 2005: 17).

Since the beginning of my stay Mr. A and his wife were pleased to know that a foreigner was trying to learn Sundanese, and they helped to train me by having our conversation in Sundanese as much as possible. They helped me by paraphrasing in Indonesian when I did not understand their Sundanese. Mr. A's vocabulary had a certain tendency to mix in Arabic words or sentences in his speech due to his vocational background. He sometimes paraphrased a Sundanese word or an Arabic sentence in Indonesian. The couple and their children began to show empathy toward me through their use of Sundanese. Moreover, the *lemes* words that I was learning and using evoked their sympathy and respect, because they thought that differentiating refined words from low words was difficult even for them.

This attitude is not limited to the family members whom I intensively had contact during my stay but also holds true with most Sundanese I encountered and had conversation with. Usually they seemed to admire my command of Sundanese and showed empathy and respect as they found my Sundanese wording polite and correct in terms of standard usage of the speech level system. In other words, the ability to use *lemes* words correctly was perceived as of great significance for building good relationships between myself and consultants in the field. My experiences and observations of interactions between Mr. A and his family suggested that using *kasar* "unrefined" varieties with them would not have helped pursue social sameness in terms of linguistic exchange patterns.[12] This experience enabled opportunities to continue research that may not have been possible had I simply continued to pursue common ground in the Indonesian language. One example of my experiences in the immigration office will suffice.

In July 2005 I went to Indonesia to research how Sundanese has changed after regional autonomy was extended during the post-New Order years. I did not realize that the validity of my passport was shorter than my three-month planned stay. This was pointed out to me by an immigration official when I arrived at the Jakarta International airport. I had to go to a separate office, and another higher officer explained that I could not enter the country in a formal and official manner. I was so embarrassed and did not know what to do. But, I noticed that he was a Sundanese from the name plate on his uniform. He asked the purpose of my visit to Indonesia. I answered my purpose was to visit Sundanese friends in a remote village in West Java. Then, he asked whether I could speak Sundanese.

---

12 The term for Sundanese speech-level system is formally called *undak usuk Basa Sunda* as mentioned above, however another term *lemes-kasar* is usually used to denote the system. The term *kasar* means literally rough and coarse, but it represents words of normal and daily use and shows intimacy. And also *kasar* varieties are used for writing such as articles in newspapers and magazines and literary works.

I answered in the *lemes* speech, *Muhun, Pa. Abdi kantos diajar basa Sunda sareng sastra Sunda di Unpad* "Yes, Sir. I have studied Sundanese language and literature in Padjadjaran University." All of a sudden, the atmosphere in the office changed from official and formal to friendly. He shifted his conversation from Indonesian to Sundanese immediately and enthusiastically asked me of my experiences in the Sundanese-speaking area and then talked about his home town in West Java. He treated me as if we were friends and served a cup of tea. All our topics were about Sundanese culture, and we talked for some time. The language we used were in *lemes* speech which was not too formal but respectful and friendly. At the end of our conversation, and while putting a stamp on my passport, he advised me that I had to be careful of the expiration date on my passport when I visited Indonesia next time. This episode shows that my long-term pursuit of social sameness with Sundanese-speaking people became a productive resource for pursuing social sameness in another setting. Even so, it is a resource that doesn't enable this everywhere.

Here a couple of points can be made concerning Sundanese speech levels. The first point is that *lemes* speech is not monolithic. Ideologically, *lemes* words are part of a formal utterance in general, while at the same time express respect to others and have an aesthetic sonic quality. In practice, you cannot speak only with *lemes* words because there are only around 300 *lemes* words. You have to put *lemes* words in a basic sentence that consists mostly of basic or *kasar* words. The speaker can adjust the degree of formality and intimacy by selecting *lemes* words. So, you can express your respect, intimacy, and friendliness at the same time in one utterance, as we have seen in the message exchange with a daughter of Mr. N.

The second point is that not all Sundanese welcome someone from outside their culture speaking Sundanese with them, no matter what registers and speech level he or she used. Sundanese speech levels are part of a feudal history, and their use evinces hierarchy between speakers. Their use defines relationship as soon as a speaker uses a certain speech level. The person in a higher position or of older age may use basic/kasar words to someone of young age or in a lower social class, but it sounds less refined and aesthetic, and even arrogant. In fact, there arises a certain relationship although he or she does not intend to establish it. For instance, a senior Sundanese scholar does not want to use Sundanese with me perhaps because he does not want me to enter his cultural domain or perhaps because he does not know how to place me in his Sundanese cultural context. He seemed to feel uneasy using both *lemes* speech to a younger person and *kasar* speech to someone who is not yet intimate. However, when one of my supervisors used *kasar* words to me, it indexed empathy without indexing arrogance. In this case, he treated me as if I were his young friend of Sundanese origin because he believed that I understood how to use Sundanese speech levels. In other words, he establishes our relationship in Sundanese cultural context, though it can be said to be a rare case.

The third point is the case of a kind of academic conversation. Most of my friends who are of the same age or younger use *lemes* words when speaking with me. It does not embarrass them to use a *lemes* register. I basically use *lemes* varieties even though Sundanese norm allows me to use *kasar* words to them. I try to keep showing respect to them, but sometimes I mix some words of non-*lemes* words to show my intimacy with them. Our conversation is a mixture of *lemes* and *kasar* words. However, other conversations do not continue in Sundanese. We switch Sundanese to Indonesian when our topic changes to academic or non-Sundanese cultural topics. *Lemes* speech between us can disturb our discussion. For instance, a Sundanese poet shifted from Sundanese to Indonesian when our conversation is of non-family and daily topic. It is possible that he uses Sundanese for that topic to his fellow Sundanese in a *kasar* register. He does not dare to do so to me because I am from outside his cultural domain and our relationship is neither lengthy nor intimate, as in the just-mentioned case of my supervisor. He chooses Indonesian instead to avoid embarrassment and uneasiness in our conversation.

4 Conclusion

I have argued that much of what makes up the idea of rapport are a series of interactions where social sameness is discursively pursued. In my case, this was done through pursuing common ground about religious beliefs and family status, but more importantly through linguistic exchanges of what is locally known as *lemes* speech. I reflected on my 30 plus years of research in Sundanese-speaking areas of Indonesia to point out how my learning of different types of Sundanese helped me to pursue social sameness and establish common ground with multiple research participants. I was especially concerned with examining what rapport might look like and whether this was an appropriate descriptor for the social relations that I maintained with an Indonesian family some 30 years after my initial fieldwork in 1982.

The image of Sundanese is not always positive even among Sundanese themselves. Some think it rural, backward, uneducated, and unpractical. However, some are proud of their own language. Even so, in my experience most really appreciated and respected my efforts to try and speak Sundanese, especially *lemes* registers. Typically, using such a register enabled me to build and nurture important and long-lasting productive relationships with my consultants. This was something that using Indonesian alone could not achieve. While Harr (this volume, Chapter 7) points to some similar experiences in Eastern Indonesia, we know little about other areas in Indonesia, and this could be a fruitful field for future research.

References

Anggadhitya, Riffa. 2005. Ki Sunda dalam kongres bahasa Sunda. *Republika Online*, http://www.republika.co.id/koran_detail.asp?id=205949&kat_id=306. (Accessed December 8, 2005).

Bucholtz, Mary & Kira Hall. 2004. Theorizing identity in language and sexuality research. *Language in Society* 33(4). 469–515.

Hume, Lynne & Jane Mulcock. 2004. Introduction: Awkward spaces, productive places. In Lynne Hume & Jane Mulcock (eds.), *Anthropologists in the field: Cases in participant observation*, xi–xxvii. New York: Colombia University Press.

Moriyama, Mikihiro. 2005. *Sundanese print culture and modernity in nineteenth-century West Java*. Singapore: NUS Press.

Moriyama, Mikihiro. 2012. Regional languages and decentralization in post-new order indonesia: The case of Sundanese. In Keith Foulcher, Mikihiro Moriyama & Manneke Budiman (eds.), *Words in motion: Language and discourse in post-New Order Indonesia*, 82–100. Singapore: National University of Singapore Press.

Purba, Dhipa Galuh. 2005. Menjelang kematian bahasa dan sastra Sunda. *Penulislepas.com: kiprah & komunitas penulis lepas di internet*, httpl://www.penulislepas.com/print.php?id=875_0_1. (Accessed April 19, 2005).

Purwanto. 2003. Buku-buku sunda 2003. *Cupumanik* 5. 32–36.

Rosidi, Ajip. (2006). Mendunia berkat sastra Sunda. *Republika Online*, http://www.republika.co.id/kolom_detail.asp?id=24198&kat_id=85. (Accessed May 29, 2007).

Izak Morin
10 Rapport, Affinity, and Kin Terms

1 Introduction

Language use, including terms of address, is an understudied aspect of rapport between researcher and consultant. This paper focuses on how social relations are built through the use of terms of address. In looking at the use of kinship terms of address, I will explore how this discursive work relates to Sahlins' (2013) idea of affinity. My focus will be on the use of terms of address amongst strangers in Jayapura, the capital city of Papua Province. Tanah Papua (consisting of Papua Province and West Papua Province) has about 275 languages but its people use Papuan Malay (PM) as their daily language of wider communication. PM kinship terms of address have become an integral part of daily conversations among Papuans. Many of these terms help identify the addressee as somewhere on the social continuum between *komin* 'Papuan/insider' and *amber* 'non-Papuan/foreigner/outsider'. In the cases presented here, I show how these ideologies about the relationship between kin terms used for address can metaphorically transform me from an *amber* relationship to a *komin* one with those I worked with in the field. My empirical focus will be data from my 2015 fieldwork in Jayapura, Tanah Papua, Indonesia.

2 Rapport and Kinship

Rapport has attracted sustained attention in the anthropological literature. Hume and Mulcock (2004a) introduce a collection of papers that show that rapport can include mutual trust, dependency, empathy, vulnerability, emotional attachment, reciprocity, and responsibility. Sahlins' (2013: 2) work tends to subsume these categories into one, namely a "mutuality of belonging" where interlocutors are "people who are intrinsic to one another's existence". This suggests that the use of language, including kin terms used for address, in communicative events can be a manifestation of this mutuality of belonging. He notes that kinship is not solely based on procreation, but can also be social constructed where kin terms can be used with others than kin, which he describes as "affinal" (Sahlins 2013: 2) interpersonal kinship relations or "metaphorical kinships" in Agha's (2007: 370) sense.

Izak Morin, Cenderawasih University, Jayapura, Indonesia

https://doi.org/10.1515/9781501507830-010

Drawing on Stasch's (2009) idea of *intersubjective belonging*, Sahlin points out that when speakers meet for the first time they recognize each other as kin through their talk, although like the papers in Hume and Mulcock (2004b), he does not provide any examples of such talk. In contrast, Agha (2007) provides an example drawn from Suzuki (1984) on how a younger stranger is addressed with kin terms such as *Onechan* [Big Sister] or *Onichan* [Big Brother] by an adult. The choice of such address terms may invoke kinship relations and the social norms associated with these kinship terms (Agha 2007: 370). Other examples of this can be found in the work of Angeli (2008), Goebel (2010), and Gold et al. (2014).

Angeli (2008), explains a shift from being greeted as *misis* [Mrs. in English] to *sista* [sister in English] while doing fieldwork in Honiara, Solomon Island. Similarly, Gold et al. (2014) points to her evolving relationship with Bhoju Ram Gujar and his extended family while working in Rajasthan. In this case, they began as employer/employee but over time she was finally addressed as *buaji* [Aunt in Hindi] by the family members. Looking at inter-ethnic interactions in two Indonesian neighbourhoods, Goebel (2010) shows how non-Javanese migrants learn and use fragments of Javanese to index affinal-type relationships with their neighbours. In all cases, the shift to kinship terms of address indexed a warm relationship between researcher and consultant and between new migrants and locals. In short, through the use of language, people were able to shift their identity from outsider to insider, and researchers and consultants became intimately tied to another's existence.

3 Tanah Papua and Terms of Address

Tanah Papua has about 275 languages. Of these 218 are non-Austronesian (Papuan) and 57 languages are Austronesian (Lewis et al. 2013). Despite such diverse languages, PM became authorized in Protestant and Catholic schools in 1857 and 1920 respectively. Then, under the Dutch school language policy from 1948 to 1961, its use expanded together with Malay. But when Indonesia annexed Papua in 1969, they not unexpectedly chose to use Indonesian as the language of wider communication, rather than the already established PM. In addition, standard Indonesian (SI) is also used as an official and national language. In some of the literature (e. g. Morin, 2016a, 2016b) it is reported that, in everyday communicative exchanges, Papuans use forms of address that are predominantly influenced by Papuan-Melanesian cultures. Specifically, some kinship forms of address such as *bapa* [father], *mama* or *ibu* [mother], *kaka* [big brother or sister], and *ade* [small brother or sister] are now used in many everyday social practices outside of family contexts (Morin, 2016a, 2016b).

The terms *bapa, mama* and *ibu* are used by a younger person to address anyone above his or her age (Morin, 2016b). In addition, they are also used by adults with the same age and/or with the same profession. Such terms of address stand in for PM second-person pronouns *ko/ koi* [you] (singular) and *kam/kamorang* [you] (plural). An adult speaker may also use them to refer to himself or herself, rather than the PM first person singular *sa* [I] when talking to the younger person or persons. The use of these alternative pronouns always stresses some aspect of interpersonal relationship whether familiarity or respect, or may be used for emphasis. While the use of the PM alternative pronominal term *bapa* is consistent across a wide range of social domains in Tanah Papua, including domains where the almost indistinguishable standard Indonesian (SI) form *bapak* is used, this is not the case for the term *mama* (Morin 2016b).

In some formal or service domains, such as education, the respectful kinship term *mama* is replaced with the SI term *ibu* to use in otherwise PM utterances to refer to professional/working females (Morin 2016b). The use of *ibu* in these contexts carries a meaning of respect and affection. In some cases, the terms *bapa* and *mama* or *ibu* are used before the family name or children's name to avoid using the first name (Morin 2016b). Apart from these terms, there are terms that indicate sibling relationships in Tanah Papua (Morin 2016a). These terms include *kaka* and *ade* which can be extended to refer to all sibling-like relationships. As with the case of *bapa, mama,* and *ibu*, in many contexts *kaka* and *ade* are used to replace the second personal pronoun *ko* or *koi* [you] (singular). Younger speakers use *kaka* to address older ones, and *ade* is used for younger addressees. Interchangeably, they can be used to address any close friends or acquaintances depending on the age of interlocutors (Morin 2016a).

4 Fieldwork and the Amber–Komin Continuum

In mid-December 2014, I returned to my home in Jayapura with a plan to conduct my research on language ideologies about Papuan Malay (PM). I began by collecting a variety of texts from bible translations, newspaper reports about language use, and published short stories about life in Papua. In February 2015, I started recording radio broadcasts and sermons from my local church, especially those that were in Papuan Malay (PM). At that time, I also gathered television broadcasts that were found on the internet, and I surveyed the linguistic landscape of Jayapura by regularly taking pictures of banners, billboards, announcement boards, and other signage that had fragments of PM. In addition, and the focus for this paper, was my participation and audio recording of the activities of two groups.

The first was the teaching staff of the English and Indonesian Program at the Department of Languages and Arts, Faculty of Teacher Training and Education, Cenderawasih University on its Abepura Campus. The second was the community of Pokhouw Village, were I normally live.

Establishing rapport was not straightforward, even though I was an academic from the English Program, and I had been living in Pokhouw village since 1996. What I report in the next section are my attempts at establishing rapport with relative strangers. Before turning to my analysis of the building of affinal interpersonal kinship relations, however, I want to outline how insider–outsider relations are ideologized in this area. In these contexts the choice of appropriate kinship terms of address gradually evolve with reference to what is locally known as the *amber–komin* continuum. *Amber* [we are not part of him/her] and *komin* [we are part of him/her] are words from Biak language that are now widely used in Tanah Papua to distinguish migrants or foreigners (non-Papuans) from Papuans. The former is used to refer to somebody who does not belong to a Papuan ethnic group, while the latter is used to include a person who is a Papuan.

The idea of *amber* 'exclusive' versus *komin* 'inclusive' strongly impacts the choice of forms of address a Papuan uses. In the case of inter-ethnic marriage, there are many possibilities in terms of the *amber–komin* continuum, as well as many possibilities for the use of terms of address. Ideologically, such a marriage might be referred to with the following sentence: *John de amber tapi de pu maitua itu komin* 'John is a non-Papuan but his wife is a Papuan'. Even so, the terms of address used can change over time. For example, in interactions outside his immediate family, John may have initially been addressed as *ko, koi, kamu* or *anda* 'you' in a conversation—e. g. *Ko/kamu/anda dari mana?* 'Where are *you* from?' or *Kalo ko/kamu/anda mo tinggal di kampung ini ko/kamu/anda harus lapor kapala kampung.* 'If *you* want to live in this village, *you* must report to the head of the village.'

But, after a period living in the village, he would be greeted as *bapa* 'father', *kaka* 'big brother', *ade* 'small brother', or *om* 'uncle' depending on how John's wife is greeted by her siblings and relatives. If the siblings call her *kaka*, then they call her husband *kaka*. If the relatives call her *mama/ibu*, then they also call her husband *bapa*. Similarly, the same forms are employed if John is a Papuan and his wife is a non-Papuan. The siblings and relatives greet John's wife depending on how they greet John. So, these kinship terms of address are based on the Papuan's cultural perspective rather than non-Papuan. Although John is a non-Papuan, he deserves the mutuality of belonging (intersubjective belonging) of Papuans by marriage. From this position, he has the right to address his in-laws in the similar way they address him. In sum, extended social contact has enabled the use of kinship terms in metaphorical ways.

5 Establishing and Showing Mutual Rapport at the Department of Languages and Arts

I found that rapport between myself and my participants fitted the concept of the *amber–komin* continuum. What I want to do in this section is to show how kinship terms were used and discuss how they related to this *amber–komin* continuum. Since I was scheduled to teach one subject in each semester in the English Program in the morning periods, I came to the department on a regular basis from January to October 2015. On these occasions I met both groups of teaching staff in their offices during lunchtime, seminars, and outside the office. I made use of such events to observe what languages were used among this group, between them and their students, and between students.

The examples below are extracted from an interview I conducted with two female teaching staff, Aleida Mawene and Adolina Lefaan, of the Indonesian Program in December 2015. I have used their real names because they insisted that I use them in the informed consent forms that they filled out. Two days earlier I had arranged this interview to be conducted with Aleida in her office, but when I arrived Adolina was present. This interview was about how they defined Papuan Malay and was not explicitly about kinship terms of address or the *amber–komin* continuum. Even so, we can learn much about kinship terms of address and their relationship to the *amber–komin* continuum because the interview involves two people who sit at different parts of the *amber–komin* continuum in relation to me.

I have known Aleida for over 20 years, first as a fellow student and then as a colleague. In contrast, Adolina, who was 20 years my junior, was a new colleague who had only started at my university just before I left for Australia to do my PhD. There were three parts to this interaction (represented later and in the rest of the paper as Event 1–3), but because I was focused on a different topic, I only recorded the second event. The first event was a common social encounter where exchanging greetings took place, followed by the completion of letters of consent, and preparation for recording, while the third event was my departure. Terms of address are in bold italics.

Excerpt 1: Interacting with a stranger at work

EVENT 1   PRE-INTERVIEW (NOT RECORDED)
Izak
01   Selamat siang ***bu*** Aleida dan ***bu*** Ina   Good afternoon, Aleida and Ina
Aleida
02   Selamat siang ***Pa*** Izak   Good afternoon, Izak
Adolina (Ina)
03   Selamat siang ***bapa***   Good afternoon, Izak

EVENT 2   THE INTERVIEW (RECORDED)
Izak

04	Dimana saja kitong lia orang pake Melayu	Where do we see people use Papuan
05	Papua ini?	Malay?
06	Mengapa sampe kitong pake	Why do we want to use
07	Melayu Papua?	Papuan Malay?
08	Melayu Papua akan tetap ada atau	Will Papuan Malay remain existing or
09	satu saat de akan off?	vanish one day?

Adolina (Ina)

10	**Bapa**, kalo saya Bahasa Melayu Papua	**Izak**, for me Papuan Malay Language
11	masuk dalam kelas orang muda. Jadi,	[already] enters into the life of youths. So,
12	de masuk dalam standar tetap eksis.	it stays on the surviving level.
13	Sampai kapan pun sulit untuk hilang.	It is hard to disappear.
14	**Bapa** betul. Eksistensi	**You** (Izak) are right. The existence of
15	Melayu Papua jauh mempengaruhi kita ...	Papuan Malay deeply affects us...

Aleida

16	**Pa** Izak kalo boleh sa tamba. Saya justru	**Izak,** may I add something. I even
17	pernah menulis tentang penggunaan	wrote about the use of
18	mob Melayu Papua sebagai ilustrasi	Papuan Malay jokes as an illustration
19	dalam pembelajaran Matematika dan	in teaching Mathematics and
20	Bahasa.	Language.
21	Ketika saya percaya pada **pa** Izak, **pa** Izak	I trust **you** (Izak) when **you** (Izak)
22	menggunakan bahasa ini. Saya percaya	use this language. I believe [that when]
23	saya sama dengan **pa** Izak	I [use] the same [language]with **you** (Izak)
24	saya akan lebih terbuka...	I will be more open...

EVENT 3   POST-INTERVIEW (NOT RECORDED)
Izak

25	Trima kasih **bu** Aleida	Thank **you** (Aleida)
26	Trima kasih **bu** Ina	Thank **you** (Ina)

Aleida

27	Trima kasih **Pa** Izak	Thank **yo**u (Izak)

Adolina (Ina)

28	Trima kasih **bapa**	Thank **yo**u (Izak)

In the first event I addressed both Aleida and Adolina (Ina) as *bu* followed by their first names (line 01). In response they addressed me as *pa* Izak and *bapa* respectively on lines 02 and 03. After a brief chat, we then began our interview, as represented in the second event. Even though both consultants demonstrated their truly warm relationship with me through the choice of kinship terms of address, they actually articulated them in different ways due to my age and our senior–junior relationship. For example, Adolina used *bapa* four times in her utterances (lines 03, 10, 14 and 28). The first was used to replace my name, and the second was to replace the second personal pronoun singular *ko* or *koi* (you). But, Aleida addressed me as *pa* Izak four times in this event (lines 21, 23, and 27), which avoided the need to use the second-personal pronoun singular.

Aleida is almost the same age as me, while Adolina is younger, and she is our junior teaching staff at the Department. Aleida used *pa* the short form of *bapa* and followed by my first name whereas Adolina used *bapa* without using my first name (lines 03, 10, 14, and 28). They also used similar forms of address when I expressed my gratitude after the interview. In interpreting this usage, we can say that, in the case of Aleida, the terms of address used between us were part of our daily conversational repertoire that we had been using for some 20 years and thus typically appeared in our talk. We avoided using *ko* or *koi* (the second-personal pronoun singular) because it would indicate an *amber* relationship that was different to our actual *komin* one. This contrasted with the unfamiliar relationship I had with Adolina, and this seems to explain the different use of kin terms of address.

6 Establishing and Showing Mutual Rapport in Pokhouw Village

I was involved in various activities of family, community, and church at Pokhouw Village from January to December 2015. This village is a multi-lingual community inhabited by Papuans from across many areas within Papua's two provinces. The multi-ethnic and multi-lingual nature of Pokhouw engendered PM in conversations among the residents. The members of the church congregation located in Pokhouw were mostly members of this village. My long term residence there (since 1996) and my regular involvement in the church community provided me with many opportunities to engage with various groups within this village, including religious school activities on Sundays for children including my youngest son (age 13), visits to the houses of children of the congregation each Monday, bible discussion sessions with youth, typically university students, on Tuesdays, bible interpretation gatherings for men on Wednesdays and for women on Thursdays, and families on Fridays.

In addition, I often attended and engaged in various conversations with the members of the congregation and visitors of the annual religious celebrations such as the Event of Gospel Arriving in Papua on February 5, Easter in March, Anniversary of the Eden Church on August 5, Anniversary of the Papuan GKI Church on October 26, Christmas Parties, and New Year Celebration. Over the course of these activities and celebrations, I noted that the terms *bapa, mama, ibu, ana/anak, ade* and *kaka* were commonly used as forms of address. Which form was used with whom, and for what purposes and effects, depended on participants' social status within the church and in the community (e. g. church elder, educated person, bureaucrat).

As with the previous section, here I will focus on my interactions with strangers. In this case I focus on Papuans coming from nearby churches. In such cases we might ideologically expect an *amber* relation, but we often addressed each other using the PM kinship terms of address that signalled a *komin* relationship. In this case, we engaged in a metaphorical practice of projecting a mutuality of belonging. Below are extracts from an interview conducted with Reverend Nelly Wanma in early October 2015. Like Aleida and Adolina, she preferred I use her real name in my research papers. This interaction consists of three parts, but, because I was focused on a different topic, I only recorded the second event. The first event was a common social encounter where exchanging greetings took place, followed by a brief explanation on my research, the completion of letter of consent, and preparation for recording, while the third event was my departure.

Excerpt 2: Indexing membership in the church community

EVENT 1   PRE-INTERVIEW (NOT RECORDED)

Izak
01   Selamat sore **ade**   Good afternoon, [my] *younger **sister*** (you)

Nelly
02   Selamat sore **kaka**   Good afternoon, [my] ***big brother*** (you)
03   Mari masuk **kaka**   Please come in, [my] ***big brother*** (you)

EVENT 2   THE INTERVIEW (RECORDED)

Izak
04   **Ade** punya beberapa kali khotbah   [My] ***younger sister*** (you) had some
05   [yang bikin] orang rasa bagian dari   sermons that made people feel [like]
06   apa yang disampaikan.   becoming part of what was preached.
07   Pola...cara [Rev Ormuserai]   The way Rev. Ormuserai
08   menyampaikan [khotbah] hampir sama   preached was was almost the same
09   dengan **ade** juga to.   as [my] ***younger sister*** (you) as well.

Nelly
10   Sa pikir kalo itu orang Papua smua,   I think if all Papuans,
11   misalnya, sperti   for example, [people] like
12   **kaka** dorang suda   [my] ***big brother*** (you) [who] has pursued
13   skolah sampe di tempat yang jauh tapi   education in a far place but
14   ketika kembali dengan bahasa ini.   when [you] return with this language.
15   Itu benar mengantar kita kepada siapa   That indeed brings us to know who
16   saya, jati diri itu, karena bahasa itu   we are, the identity, because the language
17   menunjuk diri kita   indexes us

Izak
18   **Ade** trima kasih.   Thank [my] ***younger sister*** (you)

Nelly
19   **Kaka** trima kasih juga.   Thank [my] ***big brother*** (you)

EVENT 3   POST-INTERVIEW (NOT RECORDED)
Isak
20   ***Ade, kaka*** permisi dulu.   [My] **younger sister**, [your] **big brother** (I)
21   Slamat malam   want to go. Good evening.
Nelly
27   Iyo, ***kaka***. Slamat malam.   Alright, [my] **big brother**. Good evening.

Reverend Nelly Wanma led a church in a nearby neighbourhood. I met her early February 2015 when she was scheduled to preach in my church. Since she preached in PM, I enlisted her as one of my potential consultants. So, after the church I met her and addressed her as *ade*, but she preferred using *bapa* to greet me instead of *kaka* in our first encounter. This suggests that our social status (i. e. age) impacted her choice of terms of address even though I made effort to establish a sibling-like relation. But, she begun to address me as *kaka* after four further visits to my church to preach and after we frequently met because of our involvement in a committee for the 'children story telling competition' in which my son was involved. In a late afternoon of early October 2015, I went to her house to record an interview (Event 2 above). In three events we used the kinship terms of address *kaka* (lines 02, 03, 12, 19, and 27) and *ade* (lines 01, 04, 09, 18, and 20) to greet each other. This provides linguistic evidence that an affinal interpersonal kinship relation had developed in the period since our first meeting. In short, we had moved from an *amber* to *komin* relationship, and this affinity was indexed through our use of kin terms of address.

7 Conclusion

In this chapter, I have contrasted accounts of my early interaction with strangers with subsequent interviews with them, as well as my interactions with strangers to demonstrate how kin terms of address are part of the discursive construction of social relations between myself (the researcher) and my consultants. Focusing on the use of Papuan Malay (PM) kinship forms of address in interviews conducted while doing fieldwork in my hometown of Jayapura, Tanah Papua, I pointed to how this usage can be interpreted in terms of affinal relationships that fit on the *amber* (stranger/non-Papuan)–*komin* (familiar/Papuan) continuum. I showed how these terms could be used to metaphorically display kinship in interactions among relative strangers and how over the course of series of interactions the indexical load of terms formally used metaphorically moved towards more literal means of kinship relations.

In relating this usage to ideas of rapport in general and Marshall Sahlin's (2013) ideas of the "mutuality of belonging" in particular, I showed how kin terms of address were used both metaphorically to bring about a *komin* relationship and to reflect a complex web of historical interactions. In using interactional data to look at these phenomena, we can say that attention to these discursive practices provides insights into what rapport looks like in an interactional sense. Of note, and in line with many of the papers in this collection, is the observation that rapport is not a relational endpoint but one that develops and changes from one interaction to the next.

References

Agha, Asif. 2007. *Language and social relations*. Cambridge: Cambridge University Press.
Angeli, Johanne. 2008. *"Mino whiteman, I mean": Language ideologies and attitudes toward English and Pijin among Solomon students, between social mobility and national consciousness*. Montreal: Concordia University Montreal PhD thesis.
Goebel, Zane. 2010. *Language, migration and identity: Neighborhood talk in Indonesia*. Cambridge: Cambridge University Press.
Gold, Ann, Bhoju Gujar, Madhu Gujar & Chinu Gujar. 2014. Ethnography shared knowledges: Family, fusion, fabric. *Ethnography* 15(3). 331–354.
Hume, Lynne & Jane Mulcock. 2004a. Introduction: Awkward spaces, productive places. In Lynne Hume & Jane Mulcock (eds.), *Anthropologists in the field: Cases in participant observation*, xi–xxvii. New York: Colombia University Press.
Hume, Lynne & Jane Mulcock (eds.). 2004b. *Anthropologists in the field: Cases in participant observation*. New York: Colombia University Press.
Lewis, M. Paul, Gary Simons & Charles Fennig (eds.). 2013. *Ethnologue: Languages of the world, nineteenth edn*. Dallas: SIL International. http://www.ethnologue.com/. (Accessed 26 April 2016).
Morin, Izak. 2016a. Ade deng kaka: Sapaan keakraban di Tanah Papua. *Komunitas Sastra Papua (KOSAPA)*. Online: http://www.sastrapapua.com/. http://www.sastrapapua.com/2016/05/ade-deng-kaka-sapaan-keakraban-di-tanah.html. (Accessed 16 June 2016).
Morin, Izak. 2016b. Bapa, mama deng ana/anak: Sapaan keakraban di Tanah Papua. *Komunitas Sastra Papua (KOSAPA)*. Online: http://www.sastrapapua.com/. http://www.sastrapapua.com/2016/06/bapa-mama-deng-anaanak-sapaan-keakraban.html. (Accessed 01 July 2016).
Sahlins, Marshal. 2013. *What kinship is—and is not*. Chicago: University of Chicago Press.
Stasch, Rupert. 2009. *Society of others. Kinship and mourning in a West Papuan place*. Berkeley: University of California Press.
Suzuki, Takao. 1984. *Words in context: A Japanese perspective on language and culture*. Tokyo: Kodansha International.

Dwi Noverini Djenar
11 Recognitional Reference and Rapport Building in the Author Interview

1 Introduction

Interviews are widely used in academic research as a method for eliciting data. In sociolinguistics, they are often used in conjunction with direct language elicitation to examine various speech phenomena. While direct elicitation focuses on language forms and features, interviews have been found to be particularly useful for eliciting "lots of talk" on topics of interest to participants (Schilling 2013: 93). Sociolinguistic interviews, as this kind of interviews have come to be known, are able to provide the kind of data direct elicitation could not, namely, more naturalistic language approximating conversation. Critics of this method have argued that, although interviewees may produce much talk, sociolinguistic interviews cannot genuinely represent the range of speech styles people use in casual conversation. Moreover, the asymmetrical power relation between researcher and interviewee can potentially put the latter at a social disadvantage (Schilling 2013: 106). As Briggs (1986: 5) points out, in interviews involving participants from different linguistic communities, the researcher may be unknowingly imposing their communicative norms on a community with very different norms, often causing puzzlement and even offense.

To address these kinds of problems, scholars propose that researchers rethink the over-emphasis on content (i. e. language) and approach research interviews as interactional events in which contextual elements such as material objects and the participants' bodily configurations contribute in important ways to the construction of social meaning (De Fina and Perrino 2011: 2; Koven 2014; Norrick 2010; Slembrouck 2011; Wortham et al. 2011; Yanovshevsky 2016). Wooffitt and Widdicombe (2006: 48) describe this kind of interviews as "interactional occasions conducted through language". When these interviews are successful, according to Schiffrin (2006: 116), they acquire a "blended or mixed quality, reflecting the goals, practices, form and content not only of research interviews, but also of conversation". In such interviews participant roles are dynamic; the researcher is not always the person posing questions to the interviewee, and similarly the interviewee's role is not limited to that of information supplier. Moreover, although the researcher may expect to maintain some degree of control over the interview process, as indeed any researcher collecting data would, the interactional model

---
Dwi Noverini Djenar, The University of Sydney, Sydney, Australia

https://doi.org/10.1515/9781501507830-011

allows the researcher to participate as less of an institutional authority and more of an interlocutor in a dialogic context.

Generally speaking, it is not unusual to find interviewees having difficulty responding to questions and interviewers assisting them by proffering wording (e. g. Norrick 2010). The opposite situation, where the interviewer is having difficulty in formulating questions, is perhaps less common. One might ask how the interviewee responds to this kind of situation. How does an interviewer's disfluency affect interactional dynamics? In addition, assuming the interviewer has prepared well for the interview, what could be the reasons for their disfluency? This paper explores these questions through an examination of the interviews I conducted with authors of Indonesian Teenlit novels. Approaching the interviews as interactional events, I show how the authors respond to my disfluency by treating it as an opportunity to initiate questions, offer additional information, and engage in mutual claim-making about persons and institutions. I argue that these actions constitute enactments of "positive face" (Brown and Levinson 1987) that contribute to rapport building.

Rapport, understood broadly as "harmony between people" (Spencer-Oatey 2005: 335), is considered here as a moment-by-moment process of trust building. It is a delicate process in the sense that trust that may be signaled through one sequence of talk could dissipate in another as a result of face threatening acts (Spencer-Oatey 2000). Making references to mutually known persons and institutions, particularly using forms that maximize recognizability—forms Sacks and Schegloff (2007 [1979]) call "recognitionals", namely, expressions linked to persons whom the addressee is assumed to know—is an example of action participants perform to establish common ground (in the sense of Clark 1996; Clark and Gerrig 1990) and build rapport at the beginning of interview. By mentioning the names of known persons, both researcher and interviewee co-establish a shared object of attention they can return to in the subsequent talk.

Nevertheless, in mentioning a name, one is not always guaranteed recognition. Achieving recognizability often requires negotiation of knowledge and acts of "convergent alignment" (Du Bois and Kärkkäinen 2012: 447). Du Bois and Kärkkäinen (2012) define "alignment" both in structural terms and in terms of social positioning and evaluation. Structurally, alignment is a "lining up" of elements from one utterance onto parallel elements in another utterance. In terms of positioning and evaluation, alignment refers to the lining up of differential affective stances, in relation to the shared object of affective orientation (2012: 440). As will be shown, alignment can be signalled through use of linguistic and non-linguistic resources including person reference, discourse markers, minimal responses, repetition, and shared laughter.

Interviews differ greatly not only in terms of the kinds of information the researcher is looking for, but also who is being interviewed and the personal and professional history they bring to the event. In the next section, I provide an overview of the fictional genre within which the authors I interviewed situate their writing practices and around which the interviews revolve. Following this, a description on the use of recognitional reference as a resource for establishing rapport is provided in section 3. From there the study proceeds with an analysis of beginning sequences of the interviews in section 4, showing the interviewer experiencing disfluency in formulating questions and the interviewee turning this into an opportunity to establish credibility by claiming shared knowledge of persons and institutions in the wider social world. Section 5 focuses on the analysis of the interviews beyond beginning sequences to demonstrate how rapport emerges as participants engage in the sharing of personal experience and mutual claims to knowledge.

2 Interview with Teenlit Authors

The interviews on which this study is based were conducted with the purpose of learning about how authors writing in a relatively new genre position themselves with respect to publishers who were keen to promote the genre and the wider public whose opinions were divided. Teenlit is a genre of teen romance introduced to the Indonesian audience initially through translation.

English language novels from the US—and primarily the series written by Meg Cabot—provided a model for the development of local novels in the late 1990s and early 2000s. Although the Indonesian audience was familiar with different romance genres, the arrival of Teenlit invited hostile reactions from educators and language gatekeepers, not unlike the situation in the 1970s when popular fiction (*sastra pop* 'pop literature') emerged in Indonesia (Maier 2004: 431–437). Teenlit differs from other sub-genres of popular romance in its focus on girl characters, and mainly urban high-school girls from middle-class families. The authors are also predominantly female, with some beginning their writing career in their mid-teens, which is also the age of the characters in the novels.

The emergence of Teenlit as a new genre in Indonesia broadly coincided with major changes in the sociopolitical life of the country that saw the government's tight grip on various aspects of people's lives (including the use of language) gradually loosening, affording greater scope for freedom of expression. By the year 2000, the state's campaign on language use, which had long focused on instructing citizens to use standard Indonesian in daily life, was beginning to lose its momentum. This situation, coupled with the popularity of Teenlit-in-translation, provided an opening for publishers to reinvigorate the local adolescent fiction market, which had suffered from a vacuum during the previous two decades. Publishers promoted the Teenlit genre by encouraging local writers to produce novels modelled loosely on the American teen romance. Authors were encouraged to use as much colloquial Indonesian as possible to make the dialogue appear authentic in order to attract adolescent readership (Djenar 2012).

While this strategy paid off and Teenlit experienced a 'boom' around the years 2004–2005, the novels received sharp criticisms from language gatekeepers and those with a bent for religious didacticism, who considered the use of colloquial language in fiction a threat to the integrity of Indonesian literature. They were also worried that stories focusing on the lifestyle of the middle class, replete with signs of excesses, would corrupt the minds of young readers. Concerns about language use were thus bound up with issues of morality—a situation not too dissimilar to that in other parts of the world where use of colloquial language by youth is often negatively evaluated (see e. g. Williams and Thurlow 2005; Thurlow and Bell 2009). Despite the criticisms, there was a general consensus among literary figures and the wider public that Teenlit also brought a positive influence on Indonesian adolescents in terms of encouraging them to read. Numerous articles in popular media published in 2004–2005 reported young Indonesians flocking to bookstores in large numbers to read the latest Teenlit publications, claiming that this indicated a level of interest in reading not seen in Indonesia's recent history.

While some members of the public were heartened by the increased interest in reading among adolescents, what adolescents were reading and who produced it remained under scrutiny. One of the methods used by educators and literary figures to perform a gatekeeping role was to subject Teenlit authors to public "interrogation". Authors were invited to panel discussions in which they were seated next to established literary figures only to be questioned about their writing practices.[1] In effect, these authors were asked to justify their choice of profession in a context where power imbalance was the condition created at the outset. This humiliating treatment fortunately did not last. As Teenlit became more established as a genre, "persecution" gave way to indifference.

Nevertheless, the panel events were widely reported both by the wider media and by the authors themselves through social media. Some authors defended their position openly while others chose not to engage with the debate. This history of being positioned at the periphery was something I wanted to know more about

---

[1] Interview with author Esti Kinasih, 7 January 2011.

through the interviews but was concerned not to probe lest it was a sensitive issue for the authors. When I conducted the interviews, it had been approximately six to seven years since Teenlit had reached its peak of popularity. By this time, public controversy had largely subsided, and I was hoping that this lapse of time would enable authors to speak about it with some degree of distance.

In preparing the interviews, I was conscious of the fact that, although the authors were publicly known, their position in the Indonesian literary world was marginal. I was also conscious of my position as an Australian academic who, albeit of Indonesian origin, was about to ask them to talk about the unpleasant treatment they received only a few years earlier. With this in mind, I was concerned to ensure that the interviews would be informal and minimally structured. Four interviews were conducted with both established and less known authors in three major Indonesian cities—Jakarta, Yogyakarta, and Surabaya—between December 2010 and January 2011.[2] The analysis presented here is based on the first 2–5 minutes of the audio recording. My decision to focus on this part of the interviews is motivated by the consideration that the beginning of interview is the point at which both interviewer and interviewee are generally keen to establish rapport and would therefore provide a useful source of data for examining how participants begin to negotiate their relationship. Needless to say, rapport building requires mutual and continuous effort throughout interaction, so, when I suggest that rapport is achieved, I limit the scope of my claim to the sequence of talk under discussion and not the entire interview.

3 Recognitional Reference and Rapport Building

Referring to person is a "fundamental phenomenon at the intersection between language and social structure" (Stivers, Enfield, and Levinson 2007: 2), a way of distinguishing individuals by identifying them relative to social categories. Persons may be distinguished by name, profession, kin relationship, or any combination of these (Stivers, Enfield, and Levinson 2007: 2). According to Schegloff (2007: 129), when speakers use referring expressions they either do "just referring" ("referring *simpliciter*" in his term) or something else in addition to referring. Sacks and Schegloff (2007 [1979]) identify two principles operative in references to person in English conversation: "minimization" and "recipient design". The principle of "minimization" specifies that, despite the availability of multiple

---

[2] Authors' names in the examples are all pseudonyms.

expressions for referring to person, the preference in English is overwhelmingly for a single form. The principle of "recipient design" points to the general preference for "recognitionals" to be used whenever possible to achieve recognition. By "recognitionals", they mean "such reference forms as invite and allow a recipient to find, from some 'this-referrer-use-of-a-reference-form' on some 'this-occasion-of-use', who, that recipient knows, is being referred to" (2007 [1979]: 24). In other words, recognitionals are expressions a speaker uses to maximize the possibility of the addressee recognizing the referent.

According to Sacks and Schegloff, names are used not only when they are known but are also introduced as a resource for participants to come back to later (2007 [1979]: 25). In the interviews examined, name—either the bare form (i. e. name only) or in combination with a kin term—is the preferred recognitional form. This is shown, for example, in the interview with author Kirana in (1). In lines 3–4 I mention the full name 'Ani Kencanasari', the name of Kirana's fellow Teenlit writer, in order to maximize recognizability. My attempt is successful and Kirana repeats the first name 'Ani' to indicate her recognition. Mentioning the name of a person, a speaker assumes the addressee knows is also a way of creating common ground and establishing interpersonal connection at the beginning of interview. Kirana's lengthened *oh* and her repetition of the first name 'Ani' in lines 5 and 7 are indication that a new common ground is established (now we know that we both know Ani). As Heritage (1984) points out, *oh* regularly occurs in response to informing, indicating receipt of hearing. In the example here, *oh* in conjunction with the first name 'Ani' indicates both hearing and referent recognition. Kirana repeats the name in line 7 to convey that she now knows that I know Ani. (Bold italics indicates points of analysis.)

(1) Kirana interview: Oh Ani

Novi
1 *Jadi... e= Mbak Kirana³.. saya tuh*   So, er *Mbak* Kirana I actually was
2 *sebetulnya.. dikenalkan karya-karyanya*   introduced to your works by er Ani
3 *Mbak Kirana tuh oleh.. e **Ani***   Kencanasari.
4 ***Kencanasari**.*
Kirana
5 *O=h **Ani***.   Oh Ani.
Novi
6 *[I=ya]*.   Yes.
Kirana
7 *[Ternyata] masih kenal dengan [**Ani** ya]*. So you know Ani do you.

---

3 *Mbak* is a kin term used to address or refer to an older sister or an adult female.

Novi
8   *[Iya]*.   Yes.
Kirana
9   *[Lha kok kebetulan sekali=]*.   Well what a great coincidence.
Novi
10   *[I=ya.. kenal]*.   Yes I know (her).

When the mention of a name fails to achieve recognition, a speaker may use a non-recognitional expression to maximize recognizability (Sacks and Schegloff 2007 [1979]: 25). In excerpt (2) from an interview with author Sinta, I mention 'Gramedia', the name of a large publishing house based in Jakarta, as a way of finding common ground. In the previous discourse, Sinta mentioned that she published with Gramedia. As I happen to know three editors from this publishing house, I ask her which editor she works with. In mentioning the publisher's name, I follow the principle of *recipient design* (Sacks and Schegloff 2007 [1979]). That is, by mentioning the name of a place the addressee previously referred to, my question is designed to maximize the possibility of getting the preferred response (namely, the editor's name).

However, in this instance, the name 'Gramedia' fails to accomplish what it is intended to do, for it is not specific enough to be interpreted as a metonym for 'editors working at Gramedia'. In line 2 Sinta is asking me to supply a more specific term to help her understand my question, using *apanya*, a question form dedicated to this from *apa* 'what' and clitic—*nya* '3SG', meaning 'what is the thing that you are treating as common ground, but that I cannot yet figure out?' (Djenar, Ewing and Manns 2018: 127). It is only when I respond with an alternative, more explicit formulation (*editornya* 'the editor' in line 3) that Sinta supplies the preferred response (i. e. that she works with *mbak* Ike, line 4). However, this response (see line 5) in turn fails to establish recognition. *Mbak* Ike is a name not known to me.

But instead of providing an alternative formulation to help me achieve recognition, Sinta draws on my non-recognition to ask me in return which editors I know at Gramedia, using a similar syntactic frame I employed earlier in line 1, only more specific (line 6), thereby structurally aligning her response with my previous utterance. By doing this, she effectively shifts her role from the person being asked questions (the putative role of interviewee) to one asking the question (the putative role of interviewer).

(2)   Sinta Interview: *Sama siapa?*
Novi
1   ***Sama siapa** kalo di.. Gramedia?*   Who are you with at Gramedia?
Sinta
2   *Apanya?*   What (do you mean)?

Novi
3   *E= editornya.*   Er the editor.
Sinta
4   ***Mbak Ike.***   *Mbak* Ike.
Novi
5   *Oh **Ike** saya belum pernah ketemu.*   Oh I haven't met Ike.
Sinta
6   *Kenalnya.. **ama mbak siapa**?*   Which *mbak* do you know then?
Novi
7   *Saya pernah ketemu.. **Mbak Vera***   I've met *Mbak* Vera.
Sinta
8   *Oh **Mbak Vera**, sekarang saya ama **Mbak***   Oh *Mbak* Vera, I'm with *Mbak* Vera now.
9   ***Vera.***
Novi
10 *Oh.*   Oh.

Of interest in these sequences is the use of the kin term *mbak*, a term prototypically employed for addressing or referring to a female person older than the speaker. However, age is not a necessary condition of its use. For instance, Ike is older than Sinta, but Vera is of similar age to her. Sinta uses *mbak* to refer to both of them. Similarly, in (1) I addressed Kirana with *mbak* even though she is younger than me, as a way of extending a polite gesture toward my interviewee. In addition, although *mbak* is often used for known persons (e. g. *mbak* Ike is known to Sinta, and *mbak* Vera is known to both Sinta and me), known persons who are not co-present may be referred to without it (e. g. Ani Kencanasari in (1)).

This variation suggests the contingent nature of social meaning. While *mbak* necessarily indexes gender, its other social functions, such as indexing convergent or divergent alignment, only emerge through interaction. For example, in (2) I employed *mbak* to refer to Vera, aligning with Sinta's use of the term in her question *Kenalnya ama **mbak** siapa?* 'Which *mbak* do you know?', even though I do not use it when referring to Vera in other contexts. Extending a polite gesture and showing alignment through use (and repetition of another person's use) of a kin term constitute social acts favourable to rapport building.

4 Disfluency and Rapport Building

A vague question, such as the one I posed to Sinta in (2), is among interactional phenomena I group together under the broad umbrella of *disfluency*, a term commonly used to refer to false starts, hesitation, and repair, but which I adopt here to refer to the style of interviewing that involves vagueness of expression, supply of incorrect information and failure to justify claims. Within the author interview, interviewer's disfluency could be interpreted as a desire not to be perceived as overcontrolling or as an inability to deliver questions in a fluent manner. Whether it is one way or the other is not an issue being pursued in this study. Instead disfluency is treated here as a usual part of interaction that could contribute to rapport building. For example, disfluency manifest in the supply of incorrect information could invite further talk from interviewee. Similarly, vague questions could lead to requests for clarification, and failure to support a claim could encourage role shifts where interviewee becomes the one holding interviewer to account. Disfluency therefore can be considered as functioning similarly to "negative face" (Brown and Levinson 1987) and could encourage the show of "positive face" from the co-participant.

4.1 Non-Recognition and Interviewee's Offer of Additional Information

In what follows, it is shown that an initial unsuccessful attempt at establishing recognizability can lead to an offer of additional information, and this is a strategy used by participants for ensuring that common ground is established. In example (3), which directly follows from (2), Sinta initiates further talk even though in the previous turn I already signalled closure with a freestanding *oh*. Sinta repeats the name '*Mbak* Ike' on line 11 to reinstate this recognitional form after its last mention in line 4 of example (2), which failed to establish recognition. I subsequently make several attempts to indicate, through minimal responses with falling intonation, that the information about Ike is not important. However, despite these attempts, Sinta continues describing the referent by mentioning Ike's age relative to mine and her current professional status. It is only when I utter another freestanding *oh*, this time lengthened, that she ends her talk. The lengthening is interactionally significant as it indicates receipt of hearing and a stronger attempt at closure.

(3) Sinta Interview: *Mbak* Ike resign

Sinta
11   Saya **Mbak Ike**, **Mbak Ike** *itu umurannya*   I (work with) *Mbak* Ike, *Mbak* Ike is quite
12   *lebih tua.. dari Mbak Novi.*   a bit older than (you) *Mbak* Novi.
Novi
13   *He-eh.*   Uh-huh.
Sinta
14   **Dia** *uda=h resign. Baru resign per*   She has resigned. Just resigned this
15   *Januari ini.*   January.
Novi
16   *Oya.*   Really.

Sinta
17   *Udah senior sekali.*   (She was) very senior.
Novi
18   O=h.   Oh.

Though the additional information supplied by Sinta about *Mbak* Ike is not requested, it is interactionally important in several respects. In terms of information accuracy, it qualifies Sinta's earlier statement (lines 4 and 11) that she works with *Mbak* Ike, which could be misinterpreted as referring to a current work arrangement. By informing me that Ike no longer works at Gramedia, Sinta makes it explicit that she no longer has Ike as her editor. In terms of Sinta's self-presentation, mentioning the name of a senior editor adds credibility to her standing as a Teenlit author because to work with someone senior from a reputable publishing house implies that one's work is of a quality worthy of the editor's attention. Sinta's offer of information about *Mbak* Ike can thus be considered as an enactment of "positive face", an "approach-based" response designed to address the problem of my non-recognition of the referent when the name was initially mentioned.

Using name in this case is also a way of claiming knowledge about the referent, a moral act that complements my disfluency and contributes toward building rapport. Rapport thus requires not only mutual empathy but also crucially, negotiation of moral positioning, of oneself vis à vis others (Harré and Davies 1990). Positioning is a local act; it may be "momentary and ephemeral" and could be deliberate or inadvertent (Harré et al. 2009: 10). Though positioning can be enacted at any point in an interview, the beginning is a crucial point where acts of positioning can affect the dynamics of the following interaction, hence it is the point where participants are keen to negotiate their relationship to maximize the chance of having a smooth interaction.

4.2 Non-Recognition and Interviewee's Claim to Knowledge

In the following, we will see how, in the face of a repeated instance of non-recognition, the interviewee's action is not limited to offering descriptive information about a referent but also extends to claiming professional knowledge and authority. Previously, I mentioned the name '*Mbak* Vera', an editor I know at Gramedia. In line (4), I mention 'Donna', the name of another editor I met there. Sinta wants to ascertain if it is the same person as Primadonna Angela, the Teenlit author she knows. My quick 'yes' answer to her request for confirmation of identity soon leads to a revelation that we are talking about two different persons. Proper name (short and full forms but without a kin term) and third person pronoun *dia* '3SG' are the preferred forms for establishing recognizability in this sequence.

(4) Sinta interview: Primadonna

Novi
1   ... *Satu lagi,.. **Donna**... **Donna** juga*   One more, Donna. I've also met Donna.
2   *[pernah] ketemu.*
Sinta
3   *[**Primadonna**]?*   Primadonna?
Novi
4   *Iya.*   Yes.
Sinta
5   ***Primadonna** kan juga penulis.. Teenlit.*   Primadonna is also a Teenlit author, you know.
Novi
6   *Oh **dia** [nulis juga?]*   Oh, **she** also writes?
Sinta
7   *[**Primadonna** kan?]*   Primadonna isn't it?
Novi
8   *Dia ngomongnya namanya **Donna** gitu.*   **She** just said her name was Donna. But
9   *Tapi **Donna** siapa saya nggak tau.*   which Donna I don't know.
Sinta
10 ***Primadonna Angela** [bukan]?*   Is it Primadonna Angela?
Novi
11   *[Mungkin ya]?*   Well maybe. Maybe it is **her**. (I'm) not
12 *Mungkin **dia** ya. [Nggak tau ya].*   sure really.
Sinta
13   *[Setahu saya] kalo --*   As far as I know,
14 *Tinggal di Bandung?*   Does (she) live in Bandung?
Novi
15 *Oh enggak. Kalo **dia** di sini. Lain kalo*   Oh no (I don't think so). **She** (lives) here
16 *gitu.*   actually. It's a different (person) then.
Sinta
17 *Mungkin rada-rada -- Ini ada*   Maybe a bit, there's a Primadonna
18 ***Primadonna Angela Dia** penulis.. GPU*   Angela, **she's** also a GPU author. But
19 *juga.*[4] *Tapi **dia** e= ini juga.. apa.. editor*   **she's** er also what-is-it, a freelance editor.
20 *lepas.*
Novi
21 *E=hm. O gitu.*   Hm. Is that so.
Sinta
22 *Iya.*   Yes.
Novi
23 *Mungkin ya. Nggak tau juga saya.*   Well maybe. I don't really know.

The sequence opens with me mentioning the name 'Donna' (line 1), which prompts Sinta to ask if the referent is the same person as Primadonna. In haste

---

4 GPU is an abbreviation for Gramedia Pustaka Utama.

I responded with *iya* 'yes' (line 4); however, this fails to establish mutual recognition and instead invites further requests for confirmation from Sinta. Using the discourse particle *kan* and repeating the name 'Primadonna' (line 5), Sinta draws my attention to her knowledge of the referent by informing me that Primadonna is an author, thereby pointing out the potential mismatch between my knowledge of the referent and her own. I respond to Sinta's informing with an *oh*-prefacing question to indicate non-recognition. This leads to further moves by Sinta in which she once again asks me to confirm recognizability by repeating the name 'Primadonna' (line 7). I subsequently admit to lack of knowledge about Primadonna, and this further prompts Sinta to use a different formulation, this time using the full name 'Primadonna Angela' (line 10) to establish recognition. In lines 15–16, I finally conclude that we have been talking about two different persons.

At different points in this interaction, I indicate the unimportance of pinning down the identity of 'Donna', for example, by saying *mungkin ya* 'maybe' and *nggak tahu* '(I) don't know'. However, it seems that for Sinta it is important to ascertain if knowledge of the referent is shared or not. When I confirm that we were talking about two different persons, Sinta takes the opportunity to provide a further description of the referent (lines 17–20) as a way of convincing me that the editor I know is not the same person as the Teenlit writer she knows. Sinta affirms her knowledge by using *iya* 'yes' (line 22). I close the sequence by once again indicating that determining the referent's identity is not important.

We can see from this example how my disfluency—in this case, the hasty 'yes' response which produces incorrect information—leads Sinta to hold me to account and to claim knowledge about a person known in the Teenlit publishing world of whom I do not hold knowledge. Like Sinta's mention of *Mbak* Ike in line (2), the name, Primadonna Angela, which refers to a person not known to the addressee, and whom the addressee has explicitly claimed no knowledge of, is a resource that enables Sinta to display professional knowledge. However, this claim does not need to be understood narrowly as an assertion of self-importance. Sinta's insistence on securing the identity of a referent known to her but unknown to me can be considered as a genuine attempt at filling in information where she could see lacking, thereby taking on the role of a helpful co-participant in the construction of knowledge. To this end, her talk can be considered as a contribution to rapport building.

4.3 Vague Question and Collaborative Talk

Authors differ in the way they respond to imprecise questions. Sinta tends to respond by explicitly asking for the question to be made more specific. Others, such as Agnes in (5), tend to repeat the question before providing an answer, and she does this in overlapping turns (as indicated by square brackets), making the talk highly collaborative. Such talk can be taken as evidence that rapport building is in process. An example of this is given in excerpt (5).

Agnes has authored a number of Teenlit and Chicklit novels and biographies.[5] I was keen to hear her views on public criticisms of Teenlit, and specifically the view that Teenlit themes are too narrowly focused on the lifestyle of the middle class. I open the sequence by framing my question with *kalo* 'if, whereas' to mark a shift from a previous topic to a new one. Without giving Agnes any background to my question (e. g. why I am asking about theme), I ask *temanya gimana*, 'what about the themes', which is ambiguous between asking what kinds of themes she knows are common in Teenlit novels and what her view is on the criticisms about Teenlit themes. Recognizing this ambiguity, Agnes seeks clarification by repeating the word *tema* 'theme' (line 2), to which I respond by providing historical information. Agnes of course knows this history, and she subsequently displays this knowledge by repeating my words (see lines 10 and 12), before giving her opinion in line 17.

(5) Agnes interview: Teenlit themes

Novi
1   *Kalo.. **temanya gimana**.*   Whereas what do you think of the themes.
Agnes
2   ***Tema**.*   Theme.
Novi
3   *Jadi, waktu pertengahan dua ribu=*   So around mid-2000s, around the year
4   *.. tahun dua ribuan ya karna ada kritik* 2000, because there were criticisms against
5   *[ni] terhadap **tema**.*   the themes
Agnes
6   *[Ha-ah].*   Uh-huh.
Novi
7   *novel remaja*   in teen novels
Agnes
8   *Iya.*   Yeah.
Novi
9   *dan e= Teenlit dan.. [Chicklit]*   and er Teenlit and Chicklit
Agnes
10   *[Teenlit] ya?*   Teenlit right?
Novi
11 *[[Ha-ah]]*   Uh-huh
Agnes
12 *[[dan]].. Chicklit?*   and Chicklit

---

5 Chicklit novels are aimed at an older audience (i. e. readers in their early to late 30s).

Novi
13   Ha-ah.. [[[ha-ah]]].   Uh-huh uh-huh
Agnes
14   [[[Ha-ah]]].   Uh-huh
Novi
15   Katanya kehidupannya.. [terlalu   They said the life portrayed in there is too
16   urba=n].   urban.
Agnes
17   [Hhh sebenernya sih] nggak pa-pa.   Hhh actually it's not a problem.

Immediate repetition of another's words, according to Schegloff (1997), serves various functions such as "registering receipt" and "targeting a next action". In line 3, Agnes repeats the word *tema* 'theme' to register receipt of hearing, which I also interpret as a request for further information. However, her subsequent repeats (lines 13, 15, and 17) are not receipt of hearing, but rather are "a kind of preliminary to the answer" (Schegloff 1997: 534). We also see here that the repetitions occur in overlapping turns, indicating heightened interpersonal involvement (Tannen 2007). Moreover, it is not only Agnes who repeats what I said, but I also repeat my own words/phrases. For example, Agnes repeats my use of *Teenlit* (line 13) and *Chicklit* (line 15), and I repeat my own *ha-ah* from line 14 by doubling it in line 16. Agnes subsequently repeats my *ha-ah* in line 17. Thus what begins as disfluency on my part ends up being a lively interaction with me supplying background information to my own question and Agnes repeating my words in overlapping turns before giving her answer. This collaborative talk provides an example of how rapport can emerge through a talk on a potentially sensitive topic.

5 Beyond Introductory Sequences

In this section, I consider interaction beyond initial/introductory sequences to show how interviewee and interviewer enhance rapport by participating in the sharing of personal experiences of mutually known persons. Whereas the discussion in the previous section underlines the authors' responses to my disfluency, the examples in this section highlight greater interpersonal involvement between the authors and me, as indicated by shared laughter, repetition, and mutual use of the discourse marker *kan*.

5.1 Laughter, Repetition, and Shared Knowledge

As illustrated in the previous examples, reference to person at the beginning of interview is a way of building interpersonal connection that could facilitate the interaction that follows. At the beginning of the interview with Kirana in (1), I mentioned the name of Ani Kencanasari, her fellow Teenlit author, which Kirana found pleasing. In the subsequent talk, Kirana and I found another point of convergence when we learned that we graduated from the same university and completed the same major (English literature). Kirana is now telling me that the supervisor for her thesis was *Pak* Tommy, whom I know from my undergraduate cohort.[6] Both Kirana and I subsequently claim knowledge of Tommy though our claims have different experiential bases. For example, we use the same evaluation expression to describe the referent (adjective *pinter* 'smart'), but this expression is given different meanings by virtue of the difference in the nature of our relationship with Tommy. Laughter is shared as the name '*Pak* Tommy' is mentioned, suggesting both Kirana and I find this second coincidence amusing (lines 1–4).

(6) Kirana Interview: Pak Tommy

Kirana
1	*Pembimbing saya ya Pak Tommy*	My supervisor was none other than Pak
2	*[itu@@].*	Tommy.

Novi
3	*[Iyah@]? @@@Teman seangkatan saya.*	Really? He's my friend from the same cohort (at University.)

Kirana
4	*@@Ho-oh@@.*	Yeah.

Novi
5	*Tapi dia dulu salah satu.. apa ya..*	But he was one of what-do-you-call-it the
6	*yang **paling pinter** di @angkatan kita.*	smartest in our cohort.

Kirana
7	***Masih paling pinter** .. dosen. Aduh*	(He) still is the smartest among the
8	*bingung saya.*	lecturers. I was always lost (when he talked to me about my thesis).

Novi
9	***Oya** .. **oya**? **Masih** ya?*	Oh really oh really? (He's) still (the smartest)?

Kirana
10	*@**Pinter**@**sekali** kan Pak Tommy@@*	He's so smart isn't he Pak Tommy

Novi
11	***Iya iya**. Dari dulu emang dia begitu.*	Yes yes. He's always been like that.

Kirana
12	*Hm-mh.*	Uh-huh.

In addition to laughter, repetition of one's own word(s) and that of another can be taken as evidence of the sense of connection participants feel toward each

---

[6] *Pak* (from *bapak* 'father') is a term used to address or refer to one's father or (older) adult males. Kirana uses this kin term to refer to Tommy, reflecting Tommy's role as her teacher/supervisor.

other and toward the person being referred to. The evaluative phrase *paling pinter* 'the smartest' I use in line 6 to describe Tommy is repeated by Kirana in the immediately following intonation unit (line 7). As mentioned, although both she and I claim to know Tommy, our epistemic knowledge is based on different experiences with the person. Whereas the shared knowledge is reflected in the repetition of *paling pinter*, the temporal difference in our experiences is indicated in Kirana's use of *masih* 'still' in line 7.

The different-speaker repetition (e. g. *masih* 'still' used by Kirana in line 7, which I repeat in line 9) and also same-speaker repetition (e. g. my doubling of the minimal response *oya* 'really' in line 9, and *iya* 'yes' in line 11) all indicate heightened involvement in and convergent stances toward what is being talked about. Towards the end, both Kirana and I affirm our shared knowledge and evaluation of Tommy. Convergent alignment is indicated through Kirana's repetition of her own evaluation (line 10)—which itself is a repetition of my evaluation in line 6—and my agreement with her evaluation (line 11), and finally Kirana's agreement with my final evaluation (line 12). We can see here how rapport is gradually built through mutual claims to knowledge, drawing on resources such as shared laughter and repetition indexical of converging stances.

5.2 Mutual Claims, Mutual Use of *Kan*

In addition to repetition and laughter, discourse markers are employed in the interviews as a resource for indexing mutual knowledge. In the interview with Rita, *kan* is the main discourse marker used for this. Rita is an author of Islamic Teenlit who knows Helvy Tiana Rosa (henceforth HTR), a respected author of Islamic fiction and founder of *Lingkar Pena* 'Circle of Pens', a national network of Islamic writers of which Rita is a member. I mentioned HTR's name in the preceding discourse as a way of establishing common ground. In the subsequent conversation, shown in (7), both Rita and I engage in the display of knowledge of this well-known figure.

Wouk (1998) posits the basic meaning of *kan* as "shared presupposition", arguing that the frequent use of *kan* reflects the value Indonesians place on social harmony. Wouk's study shows that presupposition is shared between speaker and addressee in the majority of cases, but in 22 % of the instances of *kan* that she examined, only the speaker has privileged knowledge while the addressee does not. Wouk argues that in these cases, *kan* indicates the speaker is trying to influence the addressee's perspective by treating them as if the addressee too holds knowledge. Building on Wouk's study and drawing on the notion of common ground, Djenar, Ewing and Manns (2018: 74) specify the basic relational meaning of *kan* as follows: "*Kan* is used by speaker to confirm that speaker and addressee share common ground; responsibility for this confirmation is shared by speaker and addressee". They argue that variation of this basic meaning emerges as *kan* is deployed in different interactional contexts. In the interview with Rita, *kan* is used both to confirm common ground and to persuade the addressee to treat the content of what one says as common ground. Like repetition and overlapping speech in the Agnes interview discussed earlier, the use of *kan* in (7), coupled with the evaluation of HTR and Rita's offer to help search for reference material on HTR all contribute to and also evince rapport building.

(7) Rita Interview: Helvy Tiana Rosa

Novi
1   ... *Tapi kalo dikontak lewat imel ini [ya*   But if (I) contact (her) by email is it
2   *bisa ya]*   possible
Rita
3   *[Lho*   But of course as you **know**, she's a nice
4   ***kan** orangnya baik].*   person.
Novi
5   *O=h [gitu] ya.*   Oh is that so.
Rita
6   *[Iya]. Nggak pa-pa. Kalo butuh..*   Yes. It's ok (if you want to contact her
7   *[referensi] lebih banyak lagi*   by email.) If you need more information (I
                                                              can find some for you)
Novi
8   *[He-eh [[iya ya itulah]].*   Uh-huh yes yes that's true.
Rita
9   *[[**Kan** .. **kan** ini]].. **beliau** yang*   **As you know as you know** this **she** is
10 *jadi gerbong [[[pelopor novel Islam].*   the leader pioneer of Islamic novels.
Novi
11   *[[[iya he-eh iya **ya kan** saya*   yes of course yes **well you know** I read
12 *mbaca]]] ininya dia, terus apa.. e=*   her thing and what-is-it er I read her blog.
13 *blognya= saya baca.*
Rita
14 *Karyanya segala itu.. ih ba=nyak sekali*   All her works so many of them have been
15 *sudah diterjemahkan ke berbagai*   translated into various languages.
16 *[bahasa].*
Novi
17 *[Gitu ya]?*   Is that so?
Rita
18 *Iya. Helvy Tiana Rosa.*   Yes. (That's) Helvy Tiana Rosa.

The excerpt begins with me asking Rita if HTR can be contacted by email. Rita responds affirmatively, using *lho*, a discourse marker used to assert the truth of what is said, followed by *kan*. The combination of the two discourse markers gives her utterance a strong tone, persuading me to treat her evaluation about HTR as presumed knowledge. However, we can see from my response (line 5) that this knowledge is not jointly held. It is only after Rita's reassurance that HTR is happy to be contacted by email that I signal a *change of state* through use of lengthened *oh* followed by *gitu ya* 'like that' (line 5). Rita and I now share the knowledge about HTR being a 'nice person'. We can compare this response to another response I gave following Rita's use of *kan* in line 9. In that turn unit, Rita uses *kan* twice to remind me that HTR is a pioneer of Islamic fiction. She refers to HTR using the honorific form *beliau* '3SG', indicating her respect for the person. I already know about HTR's standing and indicate this knowledge by saying *iya he-eh iya* 'yes of course yes', which also signals convergent alignment. I follow this with *ya kan* 'well you know' to indicate conjoint knowledge before proceeding to qualify it by saying that I read HTR's work as well as her blog.

However, despite my demonstration of conjoint knowledge, Rita expands her epistemic claim (lines 14–16) by saying HTR's work has been widely translated, and when I respond with *gitu ya* 'is that so?', she strengthens her claim with an emphatic *iya* 'yes'. Rita then ends her talk by uttering HTR's full name as a free-standing element in the final turn unit (line 18). In this case, the name is deployed not to fix a reference, but rather as a reassertion of knowledge and a summation of the attributes Rita assigns to the referent (i. e. nice person, pioneer of Islamic fiction, has works translated into various languages).

At a glance, the participants in this example seem to be asserting individual knowledge rather than seeking convergences. However, that impression could be supported only if one understands rapport to be a harmonious state of mutual agreement rather than a continuous process of negotiation to establish and maintain common ground. Rita's access to HTR is something I as the interviewer do not have, but which she willingly shares. This gesture coupled with the use of linguistic elements such as the discourse markers *lho, kan, iya,* and *gitu ya* surely need to be taken into account in determining whether rapport is in evidence or not.

6 Conclusion

The beginning of interview is an important part of the interview event. It is the part in which both the interviewer and interviewee are concerned to build common ground to facilitate the continuation of talk. For both interviewer and interviewee, referring to publicly known persons and institutions, more than simply name-dropping, is a social act designed to establish a shared object of attention and show credibility through claims to knowledge. Name (with or without kin term) is the preferred form of recognitional in the four interviews for establishing and affirming recognition. Attending to a mutually recognized object of attention contributes to and also evinces rapport. In this study, I treat rapport as moment-based; this means rapport is not something participants work towards and which, once achieved, remains stable throughout the interaction. Rather, it is a relation requiring constant working in the form of negotiation of knowledge and acts of alignment.

In the first part of my analysis, I focus on the interaction between my disfluency as interviewer and the interviewees' responses to it, showing how the interviewees treat disfluency as an opportunity to enact positive face. They request information by posing questions and offering information without being probed. The examples discussed here underline a key point in the author interview conceptualized as interactional events, namely that disfluency could provide a comfortable space for the display of shared knowledge, which can in turn contribute to rapport building. In the second part of the analysis, I showed that references to person continue to be an important resource for building rapport beyond initial sequences, and that ensuring recognizability is important for fostering interpersonal connection and indexing one's position in the social world beyond the immediate interaction.

Participants in the interviews analyzed here make use of a range of interactional resources including name, repetition of one's own and another's words, discourse particles, the doubling of minimal expressions, shared laughter and speech overlaps. But rapport can be discerned not only through use of these resources. Crucially, the authors' offers of additional information and their willingness to assist the interviewer with information gathering can be considered as social acts that contribute to the building of as well as serve as evidence of rapport.

Finally, one might argue that the authors' willingness to offer information is driven by a desire to present themselves in a positive light, given the history of public "persecution" they were subjected to and their marginal position in the literary world. However, to adopt this line would, in my view, be too generalist. The authors whose discourse is presented here vary greatly in their experiences with the public, the level of success in publishing, and the way they engage with media. That they were all keen participants in the interactional events described here can be attributed to a number of factors, of which interest in their own work and in talking about it is surely a significant one.

Appendix. Transcription Conventions

.	Final intonation contour
,	Continuing intonation contour
?	Appeal intonation contour
--	Truncated intonation unit
-	Truncated word
@	One pulse of laughter
=	Prosodic lengthening
..	Short pause
...	Long pause
[uh-huh]	Overlapping speech

References

Briggs, Charles. 1986. *Learning how to ask: A sociolinguistic appraisal of the role of the interview in social science research*. Cambridge: Cambridge University Press.
Brown, Penelope & Stephen Levinson. 1987. *Politeness: Some universals in language usage*. Cambridge: Cambridge University Press.
Clark, Herbert. 1996. *Using language*. Cambridge: Cambridge University Press.
Clark, Herbert & Richard Gerrig. 1990. Quotations as demonstrations. *Language* 66. 704–805.
De Fina, Anna & Sabina Perrino. 2011. Introduction: Interviews vs. 'natural' contexts: A false dilemma. *Language in Society* 40. 1–11.
Djenar, Dwi Noverini. 2012. Almost unbridled: Indonesian youth language and its critics. *South East Asia Research* 20(1). 35–51.
Djenar, Dwi Noverini, Michael C. Ewing & Howard Manns. 2018. *Style and intersubjectivity in youth interaction*. Berlin: De Gruyter Mouton.
Du Bois, John & Elise Kärkkäinen. 2012. Taking a stance on emotion: Affect, sequence, and intersubjectivity in dialogic interaction. *Text & Talk* 32(4). 433–451.
Harré, Rom & Bronwyn Davies. 1990. Positioning: The discursive production of selves. *Journal for the Theory of Social Behaviour* 20(1). 43–63.
Harré, Rom, Fathali Moghaddam, Tracey Cairnie, Daniel Rothbart & Steven Sabat. 2009. Recent advances in positioning theory. *Theory & Psychology* 19(1). 5–31.
Heritage, John. 1984. A change-of-state token and aspects of its sequential placement. In J. Maxwell Atkinson & John Heritage (eds.), *Structures of social action: Studies in conversation analysis*, 299–345. Cambridge, UK: Cambridge University Press.
Koven, Michèle. 2014. Interviewing: Practice, ideology, genre, and intertextuality. *Annual Review of Anthropology* 43. 499–520.
Maier, Henk. 2004. *We are playing relatives: A survey of Malay writing*. Leiden: KITLV Press.
Norrick, Neal. 2010. Listening practices in television celebrity interviews. *Journal of Pragmatics* 42: 525–543.
Sacks, Harvey and Emmanuel Schegloff. 2007 [1979]. Two preferences in the organization of reference to persons in conversation and their interaction. In Nick Enfield and Tanya

Stivers (eds.), *Person reference in interaction: Linguistic, cultural, and social perspectives*, 23–28. Cambridge: Cambridge University Press.
Schegloff, Emmanuel. 1997. Practices and actions: Boundary cases of other-initiated repair. *Discourse Processes* 23(3). 499–545.
Schegloff, Emmanuel. 2007. Conveying who you are: The presentation of self, strictly speaking. In Nick Enfield and Tanya Stivers (eds.), *Person reference in interaction: Linguistic, cultural, and social perspectives*, 123–148. Cambridge: Cambridge University Press.
Schilling, Natalie. 2013. *Sociolinguistic fieldwork*. New York: Cambridge University Press.
Schiffrin, Deborah. 2006. From linguistic reference to social reality. In Anna de Fina, Deborah Schiffrin, & Michael Bamberg (eds.), *Discourse and identity*, 103–131. Cambridge: Cambridge University Press.
Slembrouck, Stef. 2011. The research interview as a test: Alignment to boundary, topic, and interactional leeway in parental accounts of a child protection procedure. *Language in Society* 40. 51–61.
Spencer-Oatey, Helen. 2000. Rapport management: A framework for analysis. In Helen Spencer-Oatey (ed.), *Culturally speaking: Managing rapport through talk across cultures*, 11–46. London: Continuum.
Spencer-Oatey, Helen. 2005. Rapport management theory and culture. *Intercultural Pragmatics* 2–3. 335–346.
Stivers, Tanya, Nick Enfield & Stephen Levinson. 2007. Person reference in interaction. In Nick Enfield & Tanya Stivers (eds.), *Person reference in interaction: Linguistic, cultural, and social perspectives*, 1–20. Cambridge: Cambridge University Press.
Tannen, Deborah. 2007. *Talking voices: Repetition, dialogue, and imagery in conversational discourse*, 2nd edn. New York: Cambridge University Press.
Thurlow, Crispin & Katherine Bell. 2009. Against technologization: Young people's new media discourse as creative cultural practice. *Journal of Computer-Mediated Communication* 14(4). 1038–1049.
Williams, Angela & Crispin Thurlow (eds.). 2005. *Talking adolescence: Perspectives on communication in the teenage years*. New York: Peter Lang.
Wooffitt, Robin & Sue Widdicombe. 2006. Interaction in interviews. In Paul Drew, Geoffrey Raymond & Darin Weinberg (eds.), *Talk and interaction in social research methods*, 28–49. London: Sage.
Wortham, Stanton, Katherine Mortimer, Kathy Lee, Elaine Allard & Kimberly Daniel White. 2011. Interviews as interactional data. *Language in Society* 40. 39–50.
Wouk, Fay. 1998. Solidarity in Indonesian conversation: The discourse marker kan. *Multilingua* 17. 379–406.
Yanovshevsky, Galia. 2016. On the literariness of the author interview. *Poetics Today* 37(1). 181–213.

Joe Errington
12 Making Connections

Scenes of encounter described in these papers differ enough to raise broad questions about "rapport" as the rubric that brings them together. Some involve episodes of experiential sharedness that emerged in chance encounters, and others over years of acquaintance; some between persons with heavily overlapping biographies and backgrounds, and others between persons who knew each other barely at all. The ways "rapport" serves these authors as a term of metapragmatic art that aligns only partly with others—affinity, co-being, intimacy, "withness," etc.—raise broader comparative questions. I frame them here with two recurring themes or concerns in these accounts of interaction animated by some kind of affective surplus.

The first involves topical aspects of interaction that figure in what Bucholtz and Hall call *adequation*, which refers more broadly to ways people modify themselves, both topically and performatively, so as to be "sufficiently similar for current interactional purposes." (Bucholtz and Hall 2005: 599). In many different ways, persons are described as introducing, developing, and framing conversational topics to this end. In this way they make conditions of difference between interactional partners objects or topics of joint attention; in this way too, their talk about difference serves to mediate their interactional differences. Framed in broad semiotic terms, along the lines suggested by Harr, the first author, this mode of mutual recognition of social differences—backgrounds, biographies, competences, etc.—allows topics to figure as Peircian (1865: 293) Thirds in what DuBois (2007) calls a "stance triangle". The acts with which persons frame and evaluate difference, as DuBois points out, also situate them vis-à-vis interactional others: pragmatic presuppositions and entailments accompanying their speech acts in this way figure into ongoing dynamics of adequation.

The topical scale-jumping Harr describes, provides one notable way of enacting this connectedness both topically and intersubjectively. The shifts between conversational *topoi* he reports were jointly accomplished by interactional others, and so required shifts in perspectival continuity accomplished by both as topics shift. In this way topicality figures in their work of adequation as they jointly figure conditions of extrinsic difference in the mutuality of "here and now."

The second recurring concern shared by all these authors is rhetorical: finding ways to portray past verbal events as traces of intersubjective states they engendered, "there and then." Harr discusses this issue relative to research in the "classic" anthropological mode, and so can be aligned with James Clifford's (1983)

Joe Errington, Yale University, New Haven, USA

older comments on the concept of culture. Clifford pointed out that authorial appeals to "culture" legitimize ethnographic writing by helping to anonymize voices of those authors encountered in "the field," and to assimilate those voices to their own discursive projects.

As a theme, "rapport" serves a partly analogous role in these papers, but does so by licensing the ways authors choose to represent the voices of others, along with their own during interaction in "the field." They can only portray those relations of mutuality by portraying words addressed to them, so, independently of their own. In this way they are obliged to adopt the double guise familiar to work in the participant/observer mode: to describe themselves as participants in events "there and then", they must figure themselves as observers whose wider range of experience and knowledge enables them to select and frame these small parts of that participatory experience.

Arps' response to this challenge is instructive. Figuring himself as an "ethnolinguistic foreigner" enables an account of linguistic plurality in Banyuwangi, and in this in ways that can be usefully compared with Mikhail Bakhtin's (1981) discussion of heteroglossia in conditions of urban modernity. Bakhtin was concerned with distinctive qualities of novelistic discourse, in which the authorial voice assimilates and refracts a plurality of voices. Arps frames the linguistic diversity of Banyuwangi, on the other hand, from a position of overt exteriority, and in this way makes it possible for accounts of social engagements to inform a survey of the linguistic *registers* (Agha 2007) he could observe but could not voice himself.

So, his work develops an alternation between narrow and wide perspectives. The first brings into view his dealings with persons who became his familiars by dint of recurring encounters. This cumulative interactional experience brought his biography into alignment with theirs, creating the kind of mutuality described by the phenomenologist (Schutz 1967: 103) as existing between consociates: persons who share direct, immediate experience of each other, and so "grow older together." Schutz distinguishes these consociates from persons who count as contemporaries, those persons who one knows in ways that are anonymous, known of (but not known directly) as possessors of various traits and occupants of social categories. From this latter perspective, Arps describes social figures and associated linguistic registers that are widely recognized in Banyuwangi.

This alternating narration of dealings with consociates and types of contemporaries provides an autobiographical ground for his sociological perspective. It might be most striking in his account of a chance encounter with a previously unknown mini-bus driver. Their topical work of adequation produced the unexpected result of mutual awareness of their relation as neighbours, and this recognition of biographical proximity grounded a transient a sense of consociateship and a sense of "breakthrough" to rapport.

Moriyama, the second author, who narrates his experiences as an 'outsider', attends similarly to talk about social difference that effaced interactional difference with various Sundanese he encountered. But his expository strategy incorporates two other aspects of his experiences there. One is the depth of some of his biographical relations with some Sundanese. Those sustained over many years of engagements engendered senses of consociateship that became durable as they were shaped and renewed in encounters dispersed across space and time. This symmetric sharedness could be activated by the presence of members of his Sundanese "family" in Japan, and not just by his own presence in Indonesia.

Moriyama's status as an outsider was also interactionally mediated by another given of social life: the system of Sundanese linguistic politesse. Whenever spoken, by him as well as native speakers, polite Sundanese minimally marks a certain refinedness of self and regard for interactional others. But its import depends also on patterns of exchange of styles that persons create with each other. In symmetric exchange, polite Sundanese between two persons presupposes their mutual sense of regard or lack of intimacy; asymmetric exchange of polite for ordinary Sundanese presupposes the "giver" of polite Sundanese to be junior or subordinate to whoever "returns" unpolished styles. But in the mouth of an outsider like Moriyama, use of polite Sundanese has a different kind of meaning and effect because it flouts broader expectations about linguistic competences and social biographies.

In this way Moriyama's use of Sundanese was usually evaluated in tacit contrast to use of Indonesian as the language of outgroup communication. Speaking Sundanese then invited but did not require persons he addressed to reciprocate that manner of speaking, and in so doing adopt a stance of mutuality: polite but also presupposing a kind of quasi-ethnic solidarity. He shows how the interactional dynamic giving rise to this sense of "withness" can conform with Sundanese expectations about the proper ways of dealing with unfamiliar others; so too he shows how the availability of *lemes* Sundanese enables his performative as well as topical acts of adequation.

The states of rapport described in these two papers, by non-Indonesians, can be seen to differ as did the interactional strategies that give rise to them but also the discursive strategies used to frame events in which they came about. Morin and Novi,[1] as Indonesians, recount engagements with persons whose biographies and linguistic competences align much more closely with their own. Not coinci-

---

[1] As is appropriate between those who have not grown old together, in what follows I refer to these two authors using the kin terms Pak and Bu, which turn them into respected metaphorical kin of father and mother respectively.

dentally their accounts are also more descriptively specific and narratively granular.

Pak Morin describes interactional episodes with persons whose cultural, linguistic, and biographical commonalities with him are deeper than any others recounted in this collection. These conditions enable him, in turn, to raise the important issue of cross-cultural use of metapragmatic terms like "rapport." He frames this as a comparative issue when he counterposes this borrowing from French into English vocabulary with a distinction encoded in his native language between *amber* and *komin*.

Rightly emphasizing the breadth of this latter distinction, he shows how it applies to many more social relations than those suitably described as involving "rapport." They extend beyond consociates to connections between persons made salient by locale, status, kinship, and so on. This is one reason the term "affinity" is more congenial for his purposes: it helps to identify relations of mutuality without necessarily distinguishing between interactional partners and "third persons", including those who count, through kin relations, as "affines." By identifying third persons "shared" by speech partners, he shows how social identification is integral to their work of adequation. Such work enables senses of "withness" that he prefers to describe as states of affinity between *komin*, rather than as potentially transient senses of rapport between interactional partners.

Because Bu Novi presents the most fine-grained account of interactional dynamics, she also demonstrates most clearly how senses of "rapport" develop from aspects of interaction extending well beyond the exchange of words-and-ideas. Using techniques of conversation analysis, she demonstrates how it emerges from the coordination of bodily comportment, that is, the ways words are embodied.

Bu Novi attends in the first place, like Pak Morin, to techniques she and her interlocutors used to identify absent persons, with recognitionals, in their work of topical adequation. She shows how use of those recognitionals presuppose certain kinds of relations between speakers and third persons, shaping their "stance triangles" with speech partners. Beyond this, she foregrounds more intimate and less writable dynamics: the co-constructed mutuality of turn-taking. This is most striking in her account of transient interludes of nonverbal interaction, like the laughter she shared with Kirana. The laughter that punctuated conversation was in fact meaningful interactionally rather than referentially. This state of entrainment emerged as their bodily behavior became unconsciously and spontaneously synchronous. She also shows how conversational latchings and overlaps were integral to the continuance of this jointly improvised sense of rapport. Here her description recalls Tannen's (1987) concept of "high involvement styles" in American culture, but demonstrates that it has different meanings and effects. So while demonstrating how rapport is, as she points out, a kind of interactional "harmony," she also shows that it arises from the interactional counterpoint and rhythms of other-oriented comportment.

Each of these papers provides a revealing window on conditions and possibilities of interactional mutuality, and so as a group they provide an argument by example that "rapport" is a term with considerable heuristic and descriptive value. Broadly construed, it provides a rubric for a range of research methods and descriptive goals centered on the work of interactional adequation; it guides authors' selection of strategies for representing and transcribing social life at a distance from originary events. Beyond this, a broader awareness of the possibility of such mutuality presupposes an attunement to modes of co-being across obvious, fundamental lines of human difference. The prospect of such experientially immediate mutuality is both a goal and topic of this work because it can arise from unforeseen convergences of different habits of speech, thought, and feeling.

References

Agha, Asif. 2007. *Language and social relations*. Cambridge: Cambridge University Press.
Bakhtin, Mikhail. 1981. *The dialogic imagination: Four essays*. Translated by Caryl Emerson & Michael Holquist. Edited by Michael Holquist. Austin: University of Texas Press.
Bucholtz, Mary & Kira Hall. 2005. Identity and interaction: A sociocultural linguistic approach. *Discourse Studies* 7(4–5). 584–614.
Clifford, James. 1983. On ethnographic authority. *Representations* 2. 118–146.
DuBois, John. 2007. The stance triangle. In Robert Englebretson (ed.), *Stancetaking in discourse: Subjectivity, evaluation, interaction*, 139–182. Amsterdam: John Benjamins Publishing Company.
Peirce, C. S. 1865. On a new list of categories. *Proceedings of the American Academy of Arts and Sciences, Five Hundred and Eighty-Second Meeting. May 14, 1867. Monthly Meeting 7*. 287–298.
Schutz, Alfred. 1967. *The phenomenology of the social world*. Translated by F. Lehnert. Evanston: Northwestern University Press.
Tannen, Deborah. 1987. Conversational style. In Hans-Wilhelm Dechert & Manfred Raupach (eds.), *Psycholinguistic models of production*. Norwood, NJ: Ablex.

Index

adequation 30, 185
– and consociateship 186
– and intersubjectivity 185
– and rapport 185
– and social identification 188
– and stance 185
– definition of 185
affiliation
– and belonging 5
– definition of 5
alignment 89, 90
– coeval 91
– convergent 164, 170, 178, 180
– definition of 5, 164
– signaling of 164

Banyuwangi 112–136
believability 89, 94
– and represented speech 64, 67, 68
– definition of 67
belonging
– acts of 5, 7, 9–11
– intersubjective 154, 156, 160

chronotope
– and interdiscursivity 7
– definition of 5
– of Javanese speakerhood 59
common ground 3, 6, 89, 90, 139, 142, 145, 147–149, 151
– and acts of belonging 12
– and belonging 9
– and connection 19
– and contextualization 19
– and discourse markers 178–180
– and interdiscursivity 19
– and non-referentiality 19
– and precondition of rapport 6
– and pursuit of social sameness 5, 151
– and rapport 89
– and recognitionals 164, 168, 169, 171
– and referentiality 23
– and repetition 5–7, 18, 26, 90, 170, 175, 176, 178

– and role alignment 9, 12
– and rupture 8
– and world making 4
– building across speech events 90
– definition of 4
– emergence of 18
– establishing 74
– semiotic resources for establishing 10, 18, 89, 91, 139, 151, 176, 181
communicative competence 104
consociates
– and rapport 186
– definition of 186
context
– and data 87
– understandings of 87
conversation analysis 37
– and transcription 37
cross-chronotope alignment 55
– and believability 55, 62, 64
– and represented speech 64, 66
– definition of 55

disfluency
– and face 171
dramatis personae 111, 116, 117, 135, 136

emplotment 117, 127
enregisterment 36, 37
– definition of 36
ethnographic authority 1, 185
– and communicative practices 73, 186
event 111–136
eventness 127, 131

figures of personhood 37, 39, 91
– and play 36
– performing 21, 36
– voicing of 36
focus group 35
– benefits of 35
frame 35, 37, 38, 42
– and humour 43
– and play 37–39, 41, 47

– changes in 41, 43, 47

Geertz, Clifford 97, 98
genre
– regimentation of 166

honorification
– and linguistic debt 80
– and rapport 80
honorifics
– and hierarchy 75
humour
– and play 36
– and rapport 36, 37, 89, 91

ideologies of language 111–136
impression management 53
indexicality 25, 150
– of performance 25, 27
– of voice 25, 27
interdiscursivity 3, 10, 11, 36, 39, 41, 46, 47, 66, 82, 92
– and chronotope 7
– and frame 7
– and normativity 146
– and rapport 30, 73, 74
intersubjectivity 101, 102
intertextuality 3, 36, 47, 92
interviews 6–8, 87
– and common ground 180
– and connection 21, 165
– and humour 10
– and interdiscursivity 9, 165
– and narratives 54
– and reflexivity 9, 54, 167
– as interactional events 93, 163
– as performance 54
– critiques of 9
Islam 113, 114, 118–123, 125, 126, 130, 132, 136

kin terms
– and connotation 78
– and denotation 78
– and intimacy 78
– and Javanese 75
– and metaphorical kinship 154

– and reference 170
– and unfamiliarity 78
kinship
– construction of 156, 161
– ideologies about 156
– metaphorical 156, 160

language ideology 111–136
– and enregisterment 54
– and Indonesian 141
– and Javanese 6
– and Lio 6
– and Osing 6
– and Papuan Malay 7, 155
– and social relations 149
– and Sundanese 6, 139–142, 148, 150
– and unitary language 11
– and unitary models of language 9
– formation of 54
linguistic ideologies 111–136

medium
– regimentation of 166
metacommunication 18, 23
– and contextualization 25
– and data analysis 29
– and interviews 17, 28
– and intimacy 23
– and rapport 26, 30, 90, 91
– and repertoires 30
– and repetition 27, 30
models of language and communication 111, 114–117, 125, 126, 132, 135

narrativity 111, 116–118, 126, 127, 129, 136
native speakership 3
normativity 3
– in contact settings 77

objectivity 1, 22
– as professional ideology 22
observer's paradox 87, 93
Osing 112–136

participation framework 3, 7, 35
– and ratified overhearer 40
philology 117, 133

Index — **193**

place 111, 115–117, 125, 126, 129
plot 111, 116, 117, 126, 135, 136
polylinguistic
– definition of 33
presentation of self 53
profile
– language user 117, 118, 123–126, 129, 132, 134–136

rapport
– and anxiety 3, 82
– and common ground 89
– and face 164, 172
– and heteroglossia 186
– and interdiscursivity 88
– and pitch matching 18
– and positioning 172
– and positive social relations 3, 5
– and preconditions for 88, 147
– and problem of objectivity 11
– and professional ideology 74, 82, 93, 94
– and reflexivity 27, 73, 81, 147
– and scale 11, 82, 92, 93, 145, 187
– and terms of address and self reference 73, 77, 181
– and trajectories of socialization 92, 187
– and trust 164
– as connotation 2
– as emergent 18, 89, 92, 139, 149, 154, 162, 165, 167, 181
– as enduring 6
– as fieldwork goal 2
– as measure 2, 83
– as prerequisite 2, 83
– as product of discursive work 88, 90
– as situational 73
– definitions of 88, 89
– embodied 188
– mediation of 1, 187
– mediums of 75, 139, 143, 146, 148–151
rapport and anxiety 104, 107
rapport and gift exchange 105, 106
rapport and intersubjectivity 104
rapport and referentiality 105–107
recognitionals
– definition of 164

reference 17, 23, 28
– and evaluation 177, 178
– and kin terms 170
– and metacommunication 23, 29
– and minimization 167
– and rapport 27
– and recipient design 167, 169
reflexivity 10, 11, 17, 94, 139, 142, 143, 147, 149
– and connection 55, 81
– and ethnography 74, 87
– and intersubjectivity 87
– and language 54, 87
– and positionality 87, 88
– and rapport 87, 88
– and represented speech 53
– scalar 53
registers 139
– and rapport 139
– and social relations 143, 145
– and world making 143
– of Arabic 148, 149
– of English 47
– of Indonesian 35, 38, 40, 47, 140, 141, 148, 149, 151
– of Javanese 35, 38, 47
– of public and private 143
– of Sundanese 139–143, 146–151
represented speech 54
– and authority 57
– and believability 64, 67, 68
– and deictics 57
– and imitation 57
– and performance 64, 91
– and scalar reflexivity 59
role alignment 7, 9, 10, 24, 25, 30, 39, 41, 80, 169
– and interviews 93
– definition of 5
– resources for 77
rupture 90, 91
– and frame 48
– and interdiscursivity 3
– and rapport 75, 80
– definition of 8

scalar reflexivity
– and bureaucratic chronotopes 55
– and ethnic chronotopes 61
– and interpretation 59, 64, 92, 93
– and represented speech 59
– definition of 53, 55, 67
scalar shifters 100
scale alignment 98
scale-jump 98
scale-shifting 98, 102
social sameness 12, 90, 139
– pursuit of 144, 147–149, 151
sociolinguistic scale 99, 100

teacher-researcher 34, 35
teenlit
– and language ideology 165, 166
– definition of 165

– Indonesian 165
temporality 111, 115–117, 125, 126, 129, 134, 135
terms of address and self-reference
– and Jakarta 39
– and Javanese 77
– and metapragmatics 78, 79
– for negotiating pluralism 79

uptake 4, 5

world-making 10–12, 90, 117, 124–127, 129, 132, 135, 136
– and rapport 74, 143, 150, 151
– and rupture 8
– definition of 8
– out of the field 81

www.ingramcontent.com/pod-product-compliance
Lightning Source LLC
Chambersburg PA
CBHW052214240426
43670CB00037B/613